F L O R I D A
I N
P O E T R Y

FLORIDA IN POETRY

A History of the Imagination

Edited by

JANE ANDERSON JONES

&

MAURICE J. O'SULLIVAN

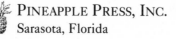

PINEAPPLE PRESS, INC.
Sarasota, Florida

Inquiries should be addressed to :
PINEAPPLE PRESS, INC.
P.O. Drawer 16008
Southside Station
Sarasota, Florida 34239

LIBRARY OF CONGRESS
CATALOGING IN PUBLICATION DATA

Jones, Jane Anderson and O'Sullivan, Maurice J.
    Florida in Poetry: a history of the imagination / edited by Jane Anderson Jones and Maurice O'Sullivan,
        p. cm.
    Includes glossary, index.
    ISBN 1-56164-083-2 (HB : alk. paper)
    1. American poetry—Florida. 2. Florida—Poetry. I.Jones, Jane Anderson, 1948- . II. O'Sullivan, Maurice J. , 1944- .
PS558.F6F58 1995
811.008'032759—dc20   95-293
                                                   CIP

First edition
10 9 8 7 6 5 4 3 2 1

Design by Carol Tornatore
Illustrations by Frank Lohan

Printed and bound by Quebecor/Kingsport, Kingsport, Tennessee

C O N T E N T S

12/06

The American Experiment

The Search for Identity

THE VISION OF PARADISE

Contemporary Voices

EPILOGUE: A FLORIDA BESTIARY

The Reptiles of Florida

The Birds of Florida

INTRODUCTION

*F*lorida—the "land of flowers," and of swamps and hurricanes, of alligators and flamingos; the land of spectacular beaches with flaming sunsets; the land of heat and indolence and mosquitoes; the land of the Seminole and the Spaniard, the native Cracker and the midwestern tourist, the runaway slave and the Cuban emigré, the retiree and the job-seeking Northerner—has touched the imagination of poets at least since the first Europeans set foot on her shores. Until very recently, the imaginative response to Florida was that of the observer, the visitor looking at a piece of exotica, bemused by the lushness of what was seen and experienced.

Sometimes visitors find what they are seeking. But more often than not, the objects of their desire, whether Ponce de León's fountain of youth, Albery Whitman's Edenic paradise, or Wallace Stevens's languorous mistress, remain seductively elusive. Often the reaction is ambivalent: fascination mixed with a thorough dose of repulsion. There is something "too much" about Florida: it is too flat, too green, too hot, too stormy, even too beautiful. Except for the real-life reflections found in folk poetry and ballads, it is not until the contemporary poets, those born in Florida or those who have adopted Florida as home, that we begin to see an attempt to accept the landscape on its own terms.

What can be found in these works is, in Kenneth Rexroth's words, "the living voice of memory," a history of the imagination of Florida's past, present, and future. The land begins to have texture and variety, the people faces, and the state a history and a living culture worth preserving.

The earliest poets present the curiosity and ambivalence of strangers encountering an alien but enchanting landscape. Spaniards came seeking gold and the fabled fountain of youth. It was on Easter Sunday (*Pascua florida* in Spanish), 1513, that Juan Ponce de León landed near St. Augustine. Spanish writers credited the date for the name *La Florida* given to the land. But *florida* also means fair or luxuriant, and *Terra Florida* certainly presented such an aspect to the Spaniards. Bartolomé de Flores, who chronicled Menéndez de Avilés' victory over the French at Fort Caroline and Matanzas Inlet in 1565 unhesitatingly attributes such luxuriance to his description of the land. On the other hand, one of the French survivors, Nicholas le Challeux, wrote an octet upon arriving home in Dieppe in the same year. Challeux's "*Huitain, par ledit Autheur arrive en sa maison, en la ville de Dieppe, ayant faim*," together with an account about his experiences, may well be the first poem about North America by someone who had actually lived here. He was less than enchanted by the experience.

Two accounts by those who accompanied the *conquistadores* on their explorations offer striking contrasts. Juan de Castellanos' *Elegias de varones ilustres de Indias* reflects both an appreciation of the land and a desire to exploit and tame it. Only one volume of his vastly panoramic work appeared during his lifetime; the entire work did not reach print until 1886, almost three hundred years later. Perhaps, as scholars have suggested, Castellanos would have achieved wider recognition had his history been in prose. Much less ambivalent was Fray Alonso Gregorio de Escobedo, a Franciscan who served at the Mission Nombre de Dios in St. Augustine between 1587 and 1593. His 21,000 lines of *octaves reales* in *La Florida* reveal the harsh judgment of a strongly traditionalist European and Catholic sensibility.

The Spaniards, impressed by the size and the grace of the native Americans (at that time the tribes included the Calusa in the southwest, the Tequesta and Jeaga in the southeast, the Timucua and Ais in central and northeast Florida, and the Apalachee in the northwest), attempted to convert them to Christianity. The Calusa, particularly, resisted the Spanish incursion. When Ponce de León sailed from Cuba in 1521 with two vessels, two hundred men, and fifty horses to conquer and colonize the west coast of Florida, the Calusa attacked his party at their landing, somewhere between Charlotte Harbor and Tampa Bay. The expedition turned around and sailed back to Cuba, where Ponce de León, wounded by a Calusa arrow, died.

With admirable evenhandedness, Castellanos both describes the strength of the Calusa and eulogizes Ponce de León. The Spaniards, of course, prevailed in colonizing and Christianizing Florida, although European diseases to which the Native Americans had no resistance helped to eliminate opposition. In the twentieth century such writers as Van K. Brock, X. J. Kennedy, William Johnson, and Rosemary and Stephen Vincent Benét have reflected a different ambivalence about those early encounters.

While the power of the Spanish waned in Europe and across the seas during the seventeenth and eighteenth centuries, the British, who had colonized the lands to the north of Florida, began to covet the peninsula. British curiosity about Florida, evidenced in the song "Have you not hard of Floryda," was balanced by a good deal of skepticism, as revealed in Oliver Goldsmith's reference in *The Deserted Village* to the foolhardiness of English villagers who emigrated to America's southern colonies. However, the British moved relentlessly into northern and western Florida and, allied with the Creek Indians of Georgia, began raiding Spanish territory, bringing back cattle and Indians, who were sold as slaves in New England and the West Indies. These raids proved so successful that within a short time the Spanish deserted their villages, and the Creeks moved into the near-empty territories, absorbing the remnants of indigenous tribes and runaway slaves who had fled to Florida. When Florida became a British territory, these Indians, now known as Seminoles ("runaways" or "wild ones"), had banded together in a strong federation.

After the American Revolution, Florida again became a Spanish possession and a refuge for escaped slaves from Georgia and the Carolinas. The Americans, seeking expansion and the recapture of lost slaves, sent Andrew Jackson into Florida to stake America's claim. When Spain ceded Florida to the United States, new settlers encountered Seminole resistance to their incursions. The government decided to relocate all the Indians to reservations west of the Mississippi, but attempts to remove the Seminoles by force resulted in the disastrous Second Seminole War of 1835-42, the most expensive and extensive of all the Indian wars. Most of the Seminoles were finally persuaded or forced to emigrate to Oklahoma where they became one of the Five Civilized Tribes. A few, however, fled to the Everglades and became the ancestors of the two remaining Florida tribes, the Seminole and the Miccosukee. During the Seminole Wars, American soldiers wrote songs celebrating their own officers. But it was the brave and stubborn resistance of the Seminoles that captured the imagination of two American poets, both coincidentally named Whitman.

Walt Whitman, the more famous, eulogized Osceola, the Seminole war leader who died in captivity in 1838 at Fort Moultrie, South Carolina, after being betrayed in a council with the American soldiers. The achievement of Albery Whitman, a nineteenth-century African-American poet, has been unjustly neglected. His epic poem *The Rape of Florida* (1884), reissued in 1885 as

Twasinta's Seminoles, offers an elegy for a lost Edenic Florida inhabited by noble Seminoles gracefully coexisting with the landscape and welcoming runaway slaves and other castoffs from white society into their tribes. The poem laments the forced removal of the Seminoles from Florida and the rape of the virgin land by a more aggressive and greedy people. Although the idyllic Florida of Albery Whitman never actually existed, his poem presents a potent allegory of the sacking of the New World. In the twentieth century, Allen Ginsberg fears for the survival of the remnants of both the native inhabitants and the native species of Florida. After tracing the history of Native Americans on the peninsula, he concludes the remaining inhabitants are "all exotics/ like the Brazilian pepper/ and Australian pine."

When Florida became an American territory in 1819, settlers and visitors began to pour into the northern and central parts of the state. The twenty-seventh state, Florida, with a plantation economy dependent on cotton and slaves to tend it, entered the Union in 1845 as a slave state, balancing the free-state status of Iowa. The experience of slavery in Florida paralleled that in other southern states, and we hear voices of the exploited and exploiters in folk songs of the period. The capture and branding of Jonathan Walker, an abolitionist who had attempted to transport runaway slaves to freedom in the British West Indies, inspired John Greenleaf Whittier's "The Branded Hand." With the election of Abraham Lincoln, Florida became the third state to secede and join the Confederacy. Although many Floridians enlisted in the Confederate Army, little fighting occurred on Florida soil.

The end of the Civil War and Reconstruction saw the decline of Florida's plantation economy and the beginnings of modern Florida. Settlers sang of their work: cattle-raising and sponge-diving, orange-growing and railroad-building, cigar-making and turpentine-tapping. The voices are widely diverse. Crackers, descendents of the first

British settlers, dominated the agricultural scene. The hard labor of the turpentine industry and railroad building rang with the rhythms of African-Americans, while Cubans in Key West and Tampa established the cigar-making industry, adding Hispanic inflections. Greeks in Tarpon Springs and Conchs (Anglo-Saxon settlers from the Bahamas) in Key West sang about diving for sponges.

Those interested in Florida's folk poetry have a number of invaluable resources. Zora Neale Hurston, Frances Densmore, Alton Morris, and Stetson Kennedy must be considered the pioneers in collecting the folksongs and folk poetry of Florida. Hurston, born in Eatonville, the first town incorporated by African-Americans in Florida, was a member of the WPA team that compiled *Florida: A Guide to the Southernmost State* (1939) and the author of *Mules and Men* (1935), a collection of folk stories and songs. Her own occasional poetic efforts, found mostly in her letters, reflect her interest in the folk tradition. During one of her trips collecting Florida folklore, Hurston was accompanied by Langston Hughes, with whom she was collaborating on the play *Mule Bone*.

Also during the 1930s, Frances Densmore, a noted music ethnologist, visited the Florida Seminoles and recorded their songs and stories. Her study *Seminole Music* (1956) was eventually published by the Smithsonian Bureau of American Ethnology. As a young instructor at the University of Florida, Alton Morris began collecting folk songs in 1933. Aided by John Lomax and a number of Florida's high school seniors and college students, he amassed a large collection of folk songs, some of which were published as *Folksongs of Florida* (1950). Stetson Kennedy, editor of *Florida: A Guide to the Southernmost State*, authored *Palmetto Country* (1942), a history of Florida's settlers focusing on three groups: the Cracker culture of the farms and ranches; African-American life as reflected in "Black Magic," a tour of jook joints and the semi-slavery of the turpentine camps; and the

Caribbean presence in cigar factories and seafaring enterprises.

In the latter half of the century, Gloria Jahoda and Wiley Housewright have built upon the work of their predecessors. Jahoda's histories from the 1960s and 1970s reveal a transplanted Northerner journeying into unknown territory and encountering the people and landscape with an unvarnished eye. Housewright's *A History of Music and Dance in Florida, 1565-1865* (1991) offers a formal history of musical culture from the European settlement of St. Augustine until the end of the Civil War. But it is in the words of visitors, lured to the state on the newly built railroads and highways as land was opened to development, that Florida first appears in the mainstream of American poetry.

Convalescing from a lung disease in the 1820s, a young Ralph Waldo Emerson headed south. After stopping first in Charleston, which he found cold and dreary in January, he continued on to St. Augustine where he wintered and recuperated. In Emerson's two poems about St. Augustine, we hear the first note of the New Englander's typical reaction to Florida. Although he found the climate of our oldest city pleasant, he was shocked by the leisure and indolence of the inhabitants. But the land seemed to evoke an imaginative response in him that led from revulsion to ambivalence to fascination and a grudging acknowledgment that in the sand of St. Augustine could be seen "The old land of America/ . . . /The first footprints of that giant grown."

Fifty years later, Sidney Lanier, poet, musician, and occasional journalist, was hired by the Great Atlantic Coastline Railroad Company. He made a three-month tour of Florida and wrote a guidebook to lure tourists to the state. His *Florida: Its Scenery, Climate and History*, published in 1876, remains a classic of travel literature. The following year, Lanier, dying of tuberculosis, returned to Florida on a trip that inspired a handful of poems incorporating Florida's landscape. In his "From the Flats," Lanier finds Tampa too flat,

a monotonous contrast to his native Georgia. However, in "A Florida Sunday," the vista "of earth, sun, air and heaven" brings to him a "divine tranquillity." Still, he recognizes that such tranquillity may be disturbed, and his "Florida Ghost" pokes fun at a speculator whose projected fortune disappeared in a tropical storm. The railroads that Lanier helped to popularize transported tourists farther south to the newly fashionable Miami and to Key West with its bohemian artists' colony.

Two talented Floridians left the state at the turn of the century to escape the limitations of institutionalized racism. Timothy Thomas Fortune, born a slave in Marianna, left to become a journalist in New York where he founded the newspaper *New York Age*. In 1905 he published *Dreams of Life*, a collection of poems that draws on his recollections of life in Florida. Novelist, poet, editor, songwriter, civil rights leader, and diplomat James Weldon Johnson was born in Jacksonville and returned there after attending Atlanta University to found the *Daily American* newspaper and work as a school principal. Moving to New York City at the turn of the century, he wrote musicals with his brother and published his provocative novel *The Autobiography of an Ex-Coloured Man* in 1912. When he became the NAACP's executive secretary in 1920, he helped set the civil rights agenda for the next decade. In addition to his work on civil rights, Johnson became a central figure in shaping the Harlem Renaissance. His book *God's Trombones* (1927), a series of sermons in verse, showed how a distinctively black voice could be conveyed in standard English.

Hart Crane, whose last book of poetry, *Key West: An Island Sheaf*, remained unpublished at his death in 1932, had only a tenuous connection to Florida. He may have stopped in Key West on his journeys to Mexico and to his family's plantation in Cuba. Key West, however, represented the tip end of the industrialized America which he mythologized in *The Bridge* and other poems. Crane seems to be bidding farewell to this America in "Key West," the title poem of his last collection. The poems, with their strong Caribbean imagery, reflect Crane's own demons in the sense of leave-taking and the continuing spectral presence of death. In 1932, on a ship headed from Mexico to New York, he jumped overboard into the Caribbean and was never found.

In the 1920s, 1930s, and 1940s, Florida became a source of inspiration for neo-Romantic poets enchanted by the exotic and still largely unspoiled natural vistas. In Winter Park during the 1920s, Edward Osgood Grover resurrected The Angel Alley Press, originally begun by an ancestor in London in 1674, to publish poems by Floridians. A growing interest in Florida's cultural life led Governor John Martin to appoint Franklin Wood as Florida's first Poet Laureate in 1929.

During the 1930s Vivian Yeiser Laramore Rader edited a series of anthologies containing works that had originally appeared in the *Miami Daily News*. These volumes generally reflect unqualified delight in Florida's Edenic pleasures. Poet Laureate of Florida from 1931 until her death in 1975, Laramore Rader spent her adult life promoting the poetry and poets of Florida. As founder of the Laramore Rader Poetry Group in Coral Gables, she mentored local poets, and for fifteen years she edited a poetry column, "Miami Muse," for the *Miami Daily News*, which featured over 780 poets who lived in or visited Miami.

In a similar neo-Romantic vein, two entrepreneurs—George Graham Currie, a Quebec lawyer and businessman who became mayor of West Palm Beach, and George Merrick, the developer of Coral Gables—published volumes of poetry devoted to the state's beauty and history.

Another businessman who wintered in Key West for a number of years perhaps most completely captured the imaginative possibilities of Florida. It was Wallace Stevens the insurance executive who vacationed for twenty winters in Florida, but it was the poet Wallace Stevens whom Florida seduced. Stevens's first two books of poetry *Harmonium* and *Ideas of Order*, are infused with specific backgrounds and images of the state. Florida evokes in him a need to create artistic order from his sensual response to the overwhelming lushness of her unending nature. But his reaction too is ambivalent. The nature he finds proves at once arousing and monotonous. In "O Florida, Venereal Soil," Stevens accuses his illicit lover: "You come tormenting,/ Insatiable,/ When you might sit,/ A scholar of darkness,/ Sequestered over the sea. . . ." In his poetry, Florida becomes the archetypal "Other." Stevens used Florida to find his poetic voice. But once it was found, he had to return to the more familiar rigorousness of his northern home, and Florida disappears from his later poetry.

A similar sensual response to Florida as a beckoning lover appears in the Cuban poet Alfonso Camín's "A Stop in Miami." Camín's response lacks ambivalence, however, for he is delighted by the invitation offered him. During the same time Juan Ramón Jiménez, Spain's Nobel Poet Laureate, found in Coral Gables a refuge from the Spanish Civil War. His Florida poetry invokes a particular state of mind, perhaps, more than a particular place.

Although the state continued to lure literary visitors from the Northern states, something in the New England soul distrusts tropical charms. Robert Frost, Stevens's friend and neighbor in Key West for many years, never mentioned Florida in his poetry. The man who so brilliantly captured New England's landscape ignored Florida's in his writing, as did Edna St. Vincent Millay, who often wintered on the west coast of Florida. On the other hand, Don Blanding, a native Oklahoman with wandering feet, delighted his popular audiences with whimsical and satiric observations of Florida life in the early 1940s. In recent years, prominent visiting poets, among them the poet laureates of Vermont, New Hampshire, and Connecticut—William Mundell, Pulitzer Prize–winners Richard Eberhart and James Merrill—have employed images of Florida in their works.

Elizabeth Bishop, another Pulitzer Prize–winning New Englander, might be seen as a bridge between the visitor poets and those who claim Florida as home. Bishop, an inveterate traveler, arrived in Key West during the Depression and lived there intermittently until 1948, when she sold her home and moved on. Her view of Florida, however, is far from the romantic muse employed by Stevens, and her poetry expresses no illusions about the state's glamour. Key West in the 1940s was little more than a segregated Southern small town, hard hit by the Depression and facing the Second World War. In her poems, the natural beauty of the landscape is pocked by social ills. Bishop's Florida poems, with their precise descriptions of experience, carry a special importance because they mark a bridge between the Edenic vision of the Florida of "visitor poets" and the more realistic confrontations of contemporary poets.

In the last half of the twentieth century, the population of Florida has grown dramatically. What had been the thirty-second most populous state in 1900 became the fourth in the 1990s: the three million people of 1950 had become over thirteen million by the early 1990s. As the population surged, the number of writers grew proportionally. Today's poets, whether they were actually born in the state or have adopted it as home, come to their work with Florida in their blood. They are obsessed with the history of the state—its people, its land, its traditions, its culture, even its reptiles. In their poems we hear certain questions repeated: Who are we? What is Florida? How can we preserve what is valuable?

These contemporary poets offer a wide range of styles, subjects, and sensitivities. Whether they are "Inventing Poetry in Miami" or arriving on "Flight 318 to Orlando," "Teaching the Miccosukee" or "In Search of Stevens and His Disciples," "Leaving Raiford" or "Being Saved in Daytona Beach," "Looking for God" in Arcadia or "Watching Gators at Ray Boone's Reptile Farm," they sense a need to define the precise quality of their experiences. And they locate those experiences in very real places from Ybor City to Pigeon Key, Wetumpka to Captiva, Cape Canaveral to Key Biscayne, Apalachee to the Ocala National Forest, and the Gandy Bridge to the Palm Beach County Landfill.

Each of their voices is very different; their very diversity celebrates and reflects Florida's potential. The Florida that they inhabit, the state with the longest history of encounters among different people in the United States, continues to speak with many tongues and to reflect a variety of cultures. But these poets share the everyday experiences of living in a part of twentieth-century America that is also Florida.

Sometimes they survey the landscape with a somewhat jaundiced view. A. R. Ammons and David Bottoms look out from garbage dumps and landfills, while Peter Meinke and Alison Kolodinsky examine the tourists in The Magic Kingdom and the bikers at Daytona Beach. The more dangerous edges of Florida life are the subject of examination by Philip Asaph, Geoffrey Philp, and Janet Heller.

Like many of their predecessors, contemporary poets frequently view Florida through a prism. For some, that prism is a place. Just as Fray Alonso Gregorio de Escobedo sees St. Augustine and the Timucua Indians from the perspective of Renaissance Europe and Sidney Lanier remembers Georgia's hills while looking at Tampa's flats, Florida's present Poet Laureate, Edmund Skellings, finds Florida reminding him of the Alaskan woods, and many Cuban-American poets cannot completely separate Miami from Havana. Their Cuba, however, as Ricardo Pau-Llosa suggests, often exists primarily as a matter of imagination rather than reality, a mythic reconstruction by their elders.

For other poets, like Van K. Brock, Yvonne Sapia, Lola Haskins, Suzanne Keyworth, Cynthia Cahn, and Pulitzer Prize–winner Donald Justice, the past offers a lens through which to understand Florida and themselves. Just as their present experiences evoke past memories, that past shapes their present. And for still other writers, a literary heritage can shape a vision. Jean West, for example, describes Orange County as Gerard Manley Hopkins might have; Carolina Hospital searches for Stevens and his disciples; Philip Shultz remembers the Hemingway days in Key West; Stephen Corey satirizes Ted "Crow" Hughes's reading tour in Florida; and Mac Miller imagines Zora Neale Hurston's final interview.

Florida's varied wildlife has also proved to be a rich source of inspiration. Lois Lenski, the Newbery Award–winning author of *Strawberry Girl*, drew her pictures of an alligator and rattlesnake in the same rural Florida environs that she described in the novel. Folksinger Will McLean sings a ballad to the green turtle, and Sylvia Maltzman is bemused by the reptilian ghetto of lizards on her patio. The gorgeous display of the flamingo and the transforming power of the vulture induce varied meditations in Richard Wilbur, May Swenson, Marisella Veiga, and David Bottoms. The act of fishing, whether "Trolling for Blues" or hunting for sharks, creates an intimate connection between the fisher and the fished as revealed in poems by Richard Wilbur, Malcolm Glass, and Greg Pape. A strong concern for the environment can be heard in the voices of contemporary poets. Moses Jumper imparts the traditional Seminole reverence for animals, while Maxine Kumin reminds us of lost and endangered species. From Marjory Stoneman Douglas's silent buzzard swinging in the air to Enid Shomer's elusive panther in the Everglades, the necessity to preserve Florida's natural heritage is a central concern.

The organization of *Florida in Poetry: A History of the Imagination* roughly follows the state's chronology, and the book includes both folk and literary poetry. When we have shifted works to earlier periods, we have done so because of the perspectives they offer. Cynthia Cahn's recent poem "Florida Warns Her Colonists," for example, appears in the first section, The European Contact, even though her vision of colonists goes far beyond the original European explorers. And Marguerite Enlow Barze's ballad of Florida's most famous cowboy, Bone Mizell, seems most appropriate among the cowboy songs of earlier days. Because of the breadth in contemporary writing, this section is the largest; our primary goal with today's poets has been inclusiveness in an attempt to bring together as broad as possible a variety of those voices now being heard in Florida. Although we have attempted to be as representative as possible, we realize that there are many more voices celebrating Florida than we have been able to include. We hope that this collection will encourage readers to explore the variety of those voices.

The book's prologue offers twelve introductory reflections on the state, while the epilogue, "A Florida Bestiary," reflects the poets' continuing fascination with all the varieties of life in Florida. In order to assist students of poetry and those unfamiliar with Florida's history and culture, we have provided some literary and historical background in sidebars to the poems; definitions of bolded words in the sidebars may be found in the Glossary. The Table of Contents includes the available birth and death dates of the poets; the text includes dates of the poems.

The quality of life in Florida depends upon all of her inhabitants recognizing and nurturing her heritage and her environment. We hope that this volume contributes to that awareness.

FLORIDA
IN
POETRY

PROLOGUE

*A Sampling of Florida's Poetry
from the 16th to the 20th Century*

Have You Not Hard of Floryda

*A*s I walked toward St. Pauls
I met a friend of myne
Who took (me) by the hand and sayde
"Com drynk a pynt of wyne,
Wher you shall here
Such news, I fere,
As you abrode will compell,
　　　With hy!

Have you not hard of Floryda
A countree far by west?
Where savage pepell planted are
By nature and be hest,
Who in the mold find glysterynge gold
And yt for tryfels sell:
　　　With hy!

Ye, all along the water syde
Wher yt doth eb and flowe
Are turkeyse found, and wher also
Do perles in oysteres grow;
And on the land do cedars stand
Whose bewty do excell.
With hy! Wunnot a wallet do well?"

The earliest poem in English that mentions Florida, this song appears in a 1564 manuscript at Oxford University's Bodleian Library. Its description of an exotically lush landscape ripe for exploitation reappears over and over again in poetry about the state.

- **here/hard** hear/heard
- **St. Paul's** London cathedral which would burn in 1666 and be rebuilt by Christopher Wren
- **As you abrode will compell** As will compel you to travel abroad
- **be hest** by necessity
- **glysterynge** glittering
- **Wunnot a wallet do well?** Wouldn't a wallet be useful?

Seminole Birth Song

*Y*ou day-sun, circling around,
　　You daylight, circling around,
You night-sun, circling around,
You, wrinkled age, circling around,
You, spotted with gray, circling around.

Songs like this tribal birth song, with its sense of the connection between human life and the natural world, traditionally welcomed newborns into the Seminole community.

SAINT AUGUSTINE

There liest thou little city of the Deep
And always hearest the unceasing sound
Both day & night in summer & in frost
The loud sea lashing thy resounding beach
Great ocean
The roar of waters on thy coral shore.

But in thy gentle clime
Even the rude sea forgets his savageness
Feels the ray of that benignant sun
And pours warm billows up the shelly shore.
O fair befall thee gentle town!
The prayer of those who thank thee for their life.

But much is here
That can beguile the months of banishment
Within the small peninsula of sand
Of present pleasure and romantic past
The faint traces of romantic things
The old land of America
I find in this nook of sand
The first footprints of that giant grown.

—Ralph Waldo Emerson (1827)

We generally associate Ralph Waldo Emerson, the eminent 19th-century poet and essayist, with the spirit and temper of New England. But as a young man in the 1820s, he traveled to Florida to recuperate from a lung ailment. In this poem from his *Journals*, he expresses his gratitude for the healing warmth of the Florida sun. Atypically for a New Englander, he also recognizes the origins of American civilization on Florida's beaches.

ORANGE BUDS BY MAIL FROM FLORIDA

[Voltaire closed a famous argument by claiming that a ship of war and the grand opera were proofs enough of civilization's and France's progress, in his day.]

A lesser proof than old Voltaire's, yet greater,
Proof of this present time, and thee, thy broad expanse,
America,
To my plain Northern hut, in outside clouds and snow,
Brought safely for a thousand miles o'er land and tide,
Some three days since on their own soil live-sprouting,
Now here their sweetness through my room unfolding,
A bunch of orange buds by mail from Florida.

—Walt Whitman (1888)

The enormous growth of railroads in Florida during the last decades of the 19th century began to link the state far more tightly with the Northeast. Marveling over one simple result of that growth, Walt Whitman believed such technology could enrich urban America's experience of nature.

O FLORIDA, VENEREAL SOIL

A few things for themselves,
Convolvulus and coral,
Buzzards and live moss,
Tiestas for the keys,
A few things for themselves,
Florida, venereal soil,
Disclose to the lover.

The dreadful sundry of this world,
The Cuban, Polodowsky,
The Mexican women,
The negro undertaker
Killing the time between corpses
Fishing for crayfish . . .
Virgin of boorish births,

Swiftly in the nights,
In the porches of Key West,
Behind the bougainvilleas,
After the guitar is asleep,
Lasciviously as the wind,
You come tormenting,
Insatiable,

When you might sit,
A scholar of darkness,
Sequestered over the sea,
Wearing a clear tiara
Of red and blue and red,
Sparkling, solitary, still,
In the high sea-shadow.

Donna, donna, dark,
Stooping in indigo gown
And cloudy constellations,
Conceal yourself or disclose
Fewest things to the lover—
A hand that bears a thick-leaved fruit,
A pungent bloom against your shade.

—Wallace Stevens (1923)

A Connecticut insurance executive fascinated with the bohemian freedom of Key West, Wallace Stevens suggests how imagination offers us both pleasure and ways of creating order out of our lives. In the lush, tropical, and seductive environment of the Keys, the Pulitzer Prize winner envisions his ideal *Donna*—the beloved mistress.

- **convulvulus** a family of trailing or twining plants
- **tiestas** possibly a Stevens' variant on *tiestos* or flowerpots

To the Tourists

*H*ere come the tourists . . . the TOURISTS
THE TOURISTS!
The wives and the children of eminent jurists,
The teachers and preachers, reformists and purists,
Artists and writers and caricaturists,
The famous and infamous, snobbish and wealthy,
The sick and the well and the Here-For-Their-Healthy,
Notorious gangsters, the bold and the stealthy,
 Radio crooners and jazz-band basooners,
 After-dark spooners and gay honeymooners,
 Diet fanatics, those Spinach-and-Pruners
 Arctic explorers and famous harpooners,
 Poets and other With-Nature-Communers,
Glamorous movie stars, great ones and hammy,
Having a fling at Palm Beach and Miami
With Café-Society (Don't-Give-A-Dammy)
 Millionaire playboys and other Good-Timers,
 Blue-blooded matrons and rich Social Climbers,
 Hoboes and hoodlums and Haven't-A-Dimers
 Newspaper columnists, syndicate rhymers.
Garden Club Members whose interest is floral,
And men who write volumes on sea-weed and coral,
Evangelists preaching the Good-And-The-Moral,
Parlor-Pink Anti's whose joy is a quarrel.
 Rocking-Chair-Sitters who knit on the porches,
 And soulful eyed girls who are carrying torches,
 And folks who lie out in the sun when it scorches.

Here come the tourists . . . the TOURISTS
THE TOURISTS!
The nudists and prudists and freak Nature-Curists,
Beautiful show-girls . . . are *they* sex-allurists!
Modernist sculptors and painters . . . futurists.
Oil-men from Texas and east Oklahoma
With play-girls who waft an expensive aroma
(what they know didn't come with a college diploma)
And slap-happy drunks in a permanent coma.

A tireless traveler and member of the lecture circuit, Don Blanding spent two years in the state before publishing his *Floridays* (1941). His whimsical catalog of the various visitors to Florida recalls the **catalogs** of Walt Whitman, William Carlos Williams, and Allen Ginsberg.

Some giddy old boys on their way to Havana
They'll have a swell time and swelled head *mañana*,
From Sloppy Joe's mixtures and drinks at Sans Souci,
They'll be sadder but wiser and terribly *wouci*.
There's a second-hand pug with his bottle-blonde floozy.
There are night-club performers and hot rumba dancers,
Professional escorts for lonely romancers,
And hard-boiled patooties who know all the answers,

• **patooties** sweethearts

And folks who tell fortunes and psychic seancers,
There are card-sharps and suckers and I'll-Take-A-Chancers.
There are great merchant princes and small Coats-and-Pantsers.
There are sod-or-grass-widows and sporty divorcees
And people that follow the race-tracks and horses,
And golfers who practically live on the courses,
A spot-lighted deb who for money endorses,
And men who give talks on our Natural Resources.

There's refugee royalty, real or pretenders,
Vacationing husbands on mild little benders,
Traveling aunts, those confirmed Post-Card-Senders,
Plumbers and drummers and radio menders,
Women with banners, convention attenders,
Battle-scarred pugilists, Title-Defenders,
Drifters and grafters and souvenir vendors.
Amorous couples, clandestine week-enders.
Southerners, Westerners, Creoles and Yankees
And girls who wear bathing-suits smaller than hankies.
Britishers, Mexicans, Cubans, Brazilians,
Paupers or people with fabulous millions.
Folks from each city and state of the nation
Seeking beauty or pleasure or wild dissipation.

The tourists ... the TOURISTS ... T H E T O U R I S T S
        are coming!
Their motors are roaring, their tires are humming.
They're coming in limousines, busses or flivvers,

• **flivers** old battered cars or model T Fords

In battered old junk-heaps that jiggle their livers,
They're flocking in planes and in Stratosphere Clippers,
In mobs and in droves and with All-Expense-Trippers,
Hitch-hiking or riding in comfortable trailers,
Private yacht owners and poor Ride-the-Railers,
By Pullman or day-coach or modern stream-liners,
The ones who bring lunches or eat in the diners,

By sail-boat or house-boat or steamer or freighter,
The World-And-His-Wife will come sooner or later.
The TOURISTS ARE COMING! So jack up the prices
And get out the lures and the traps and devices
For snagging their pennies and grabbing their dollars,
And pay no attention to squawkings or hollers,
They've saved up their money intending to spend it,
(the government's waiting to tax and to lend it).

So, join in the chorus . . . you bell-hops and waiters
You folks who sell shell-fish and stuffed alligators,
You Sight-Seeing Busses and doormen and chauffeurs
And swank hotel-keepers and Beach resort loafers
And teachers of dancing and bookies and caddies
And girls who make suckers of big sugar-daddies
And parking-lot owners and swimming instructors
And novelty sellers and Pullman conductors
And permanent wavers and cute manicurists . . .
Hurray for the tourists! The TOURISTS!
 THE TOURISTS!

—Don Blanding (1941)

FLORIDA

The state with the prettiest name,
the state that floats in brackish water,
held together by mangrove roots
that bear while living oysters in clusters,
and when dead strew white swamps with skeletons,
dotted as if bombarded, with green hummocks
like ancient cannon-balls sprouting grass.
The state full of long S-shaped birds, blue and white,
and unseen hysterical birds who rush up the scale
every time in a tantrum.
Tanagers embarrassed by their flashiness,
and pelicans whose delight it is to clown;
who coast for fun on the strong tidal currents
in and out among the mangrove islands
and stand on the sand-bars drying their damp golden wings
on sun-lit evenings.
Enormous turtles, helpless and mild,
die and leave their barnacled shells on the beaches,
and their large white skulls with round eye-sockets
twice the size of a man's.
    The palm trees clatter in the stiff breeze
like the bills of the pelicans. The tropical rain comes down
to freshen the tide-looped strings of fading shells:
Job's Tear, the Chinese Alphabet, the scarce Junonia,
part-colored pectins and Ladies' Ears,
arranged as on a gray rag of rotted calico,
the buried Indian Princess's skirt;
with these the monotonous, endless, sagging coast-line
is delicately ornamented.
Thirty or more buzzards are drifting down, down, down,
over something they have spotted in the swamp,
in circles like stirred-up flakes of sediment
sinking through water.
Smoke from woods-fires filters fine blue solvents.
On stumps and dead trees the charring is like black velvet.
The mosquitoes
go hunting to the tune of their ferocious obbligatos.
After dark, the fireflies map the heavens in the marsh
until the moon rises.

Poems about Florida do not always offer romantic celebrations of a semi-tropical Eden. When Pulitzer Prize-winning New Englander Elizabeth Bishop lived in Key West from 1938 to 1948, her poetry began exploring both the landscape and the culture of her new home. Her precise descriptions of a nature at once extravagant and wasteful contrast with the racially segregated, economically depressed culture of Florida in the 1930s.

Cold white, not bright, the moonlight is coarse-meshed,
and the careless, corrupt state is all black specks
too far apart, and ugly whites; the poorest
post-card of itself.
After dark, the pools seem to have slipped away.
The alligator, who has five distinct calls:
friendliness, love, mating, war, and a warning—
whimpers and speaks in the throat
of the Indian Princess.

—Elizabeth Bishop (1946)

I MUST COME TO TERMS WITH FLORIDA

*I*f you have frost, poinsettias
die for Christmas.

June, with no December freeze,
is a fog of gnats.

You meet someone in the sun and look
through her body.

But this is all classical and I
must come to terms with my life.

Egrets are everywhere
studying egrets in white china water.

Scuba diving, I break off the tails
of lobsters, watching their heads float away.

I look up to see the sun
dissolving flake by flake into the sea.

—William E. Taylor (1968)

Part of becoming a Floridian involves looking at the world differently. William Taylor, a native of New Jersey, taught at Stetson University for over a quarter of a century. As he puzzles over the idiosyncracies of Florida life, he recognizes the need to adjust his Northerner's perspective to Florida's realities.

APALACHEE

*S*ea licked, lapped it, then fell back,
leaving Apalachee dry tide land.

South:

> a sandy plain of palmetto
> cabbage palm and scrub oak
> scattered in pine woods.
> (Along rivers and in swamps
> of map turtle and cottonmouth
> sheltered by yaupon and bay,
> the snakebird perches,
> drying spread wings,
> and ponders the sunken sky.)

North:

> green-brushed gray hills
> red clay
> that lids limestone skeletons
> of a petrified desert, older
> than vegetation.
>   (Water
> has riddled it with caves.
> It swallows rivers
> and spews them out.)

East:

> Wacissa, Aucilla, Suwannee—
> rivers moving in and out
> of the earth in their seams.

Midmost:

>   Wakulla,
> rising from deep water tables
> holding in museum rooms
> the pottery, carvings and tools
> of men whose bones are guarded
> by bones of beasts older than man:
> only the transparency rising
> into the river,
>   Wakulla,
> crossed by a chain-link fence.

In this description of the northern Florida landscape, Van K. Brock, the founder of Anhinga Press, invokes the prehistoric landscapes and inhabitants of the lower Apalachicola watershed. For a derivation of the geographic names in this poem, see Brock's "The Land of Old Fields" and Marguerite Enlow Barze's "Wetumpka, Ocoee, and—"

- **yaupon** an evergreen holly
- **snakebird** the anhinga

West:

Apalachicola, the unitary tongue
of four rivers stammering toward
one mouth as the landscape
slopes toward blue gulf

While Chipola echoes in its caves a Mass
for bats, crayfish and blind, pink salamanders.

—Van K. Brock (1978)

CHILDHOOD

J'ai heurté, savez-vous, d'incroyables Florides. . . .
—Rimbaud

Time: The Thirties
Place: Miami, Florida

How much do we reshape our memories? Here Miami-born Donald Justice, a Pulitzer Prize-winning poet, reconstructs the sights, scents, and sounds of what he has called the "sleepy, middle-sized Southern city" of his youth. As he evokes both the child's world of discovery and the adult's sense of loss in the partially imagined memories of childhood, his use of **ellipsis** and marginal notes help to distance the memories and to suggest their uncertainty.

- **doomed republics**
  Czechoslovakia, e.g.

- **The Katzenjammer Kids**
  for some years the feature comic strip of the Sunday *Miami Herald*.

*O*nce more beneath my thumb the globe turns—
And doomed republics pass in a blur of colors. . .
                    Winter mornings now, my grandfather,
Head bared to the mild sunshine, likes to spread
The Katzenjammers out around a white lawn chair
To catch the stray curls of citrus from his knife.
Chameleons quiver in ambush; wings
Of monarchs beat above bronze turds, feasting . . .
                    And there are pilgrim ants
Eternally bearing incommensurate crumbs
Past slippered feet.—There,
In the lily pond, my own face wrinkles
With the slow teasings of a stick.
                    The long days pass, days
Streaked with the colors of the first embarrassments . . .
And Sundays, among kin, happily ignored,
I sit nodding, somnolent with horizons:
                    Myriad tiny suns
Drown in the deep mahogany polish of the chair-arms;
Bunched cushions prickle through starched cotton . . .

Already

I know the pleasure of certain solitudes.
I can look up at a ceiling so theatrical
Its stars seem more aloof than the real stars;
And pre-depression putti blush in the soft glow
Of exit signs. Often I blink, re-entering
The world—or catch, surprised, in a shop window,
My ghostly image skimming across nude mannequins.
Drawbridges, careless of traffic, lean there
Against the low clouds—early evening . . .

All day

There is the smell of ocean longing landward.
And, high on his frail ladder, my father
Stands hammering great storm shutters down
Across the windows of the tall hotels,
Swaying. Around downed wires, across broken fronds,
Our Essex steers, bargelike and slow . . .

Westward now,

The smoky rose of oblivion blooms, hangs;
And on my knee a small red sun-glow, setting.
For a long time I feel, coming and going in waves,
The stupid wish to cry. I dream . . .

And there are

Colognes that mingle on the barber's hands
Swathing me in his striped cloth Saturdays, downtown.
Billy, the midget haberdasher, stands grinning
Under the winking neon goat, his sign—
And Flagler's sidewalks fill. Slowly
The wooden escalator rattles upward
Towards the twin fountains of a mezzanine
Where boys, secretly brave, prepare to taste
The otherness trickling there, forbidden . . .
And then the warm cashews in cool arcades!
O counters of spectacles!—where the bored child first
Scans new perspectives squinting through strange lenses;
And the mirrors, tilting, offer back toy sails
Stiffening breezeless towards green shores of baize . . .

How thin the grass looks of the new yards—
And everywhere
The fine sand burning into the bare heels
With which I learn to crush, going home,

- **a ceiling so theatrical** the Olympia Theater

- **storm shutters** the hurricane season

- **Essex** obsolete make of car

- **smoky rose of oblivion** the Everglades on fire
- **on my knee** my osteomyelitis-anesthesias

- **barber's hands** the Capitol Barber Shop—M. DuPree, proprietor
- **Billy** Billy's Men's Shop

- **Flagler** the principal east-west street
- **The wooden escalator** in Cromer Cassell's (later Richards') Department Store
- **twin fountains** the shameful "white" and "colored" drinking fountains of those days and that region—against which we reacted in our own way
- **counters** the 5-and-10 ¢ stores—a tray of unsorted eyeglasses in Grant's—a toy display at Woolworth's

- **new yards** the N.W. section, still under development

The giant sandspurs of the vacant lots.
Irridescences of mosquito hawks
Glimmer above brief puddles filled with skies,
Tropical and changeless. And sometimes,
Where the city halts, the cracked sidewalks
Lead to a coral archway still spanning
The entrance to some wilderness of palmetto—

Forlorn suburbs, but with golden names!

> —*Dedicated to the poets of a mythical childhood—*
> *Wordsworth, Rimbaud, Hart Crane and Alberti*

> —Donald Justice (1979)

- **golden names** Sunny Isles, Golden Glades, Buena Vista, Opa-Locka

INVENTING POETRY IN MIAMI

*L*ooking rather unhappy,
my mother sits in a chair
in the lobby of a South Beach hotel.
Her ankles are swollen.
My stepfather takes no interest.
He is trying to nap in the sun.
My mother hates the light
grazing on his stubbled face.

The warm air droops over them.
They are both gray-haired.
Their mouths are firm.
They began to look alike long ago.

Tomorrow they will go home
to Deltona where they must
be left alone
with the ghosts of their words.

My stepfather wants to divorce my mother.
I know a good lawyer, I tell him.

He buys me a cup of Cuban coffee
as we mull over his choices.
The old waiter tells us

Communicating across generations has become an important issue in the state with the largest percentage of older citizens. A native New Yorker of Puerto Rican descent, Yvonne Sapia attended Florida universities and now teaches at Lake City Community College. Much of her poetry focuses on the complexities of contemporary family life and illustrates how personal truths may alter objective reality.

this is what it is like
for something to die.

When I return to my hotel room,
I begin
to write the words truth creates,
not the real story,
but the story I recall.
My mother and stepfather
wait for me in the lobby,
silence spread between them
like an empty guestbook
of a place no one dares to visit.

—Yvonne Sapia (1983)

ZEN WALK
IN THE AFTERMATH OF
HURRICANE ANDREW

*H*ow all things must come to rest—
the rake screeches with stones
and leaves singed by mildew.
And there, a solemn point
where balance halves the empty world
into mates: the metal shell
of the boat leaning against the railing
near the roofless gym embraces its hollow,
and the branch finds its stillness
after parrots light on its nakedness
and their green cries are swallowed
tide-like by the hum of motors gardening
and the rattling of sweaty foreign tongue.

How all things yearn to be restored
from the disasters of stillness,
yearn to leave themselves:
the concrete U's of benches tossed
leaf-like by August weather,
the stammered urgencies

The ravages of Hurricane Andrew in August, 1992, led many Floridians to a new sense of community in the face of disaster. Cuban exile Ricardo Pau-Llosa, a professor at Miami-Dade Community College, describes a walk he took with his creative writing class to contemplate the effects of the storm.

of headlines caught in their journey
to trashdom, snared on the pruned branches
of the gardener's obedient shrubs.

How the buildings mock the roughness
of what was once fluid sand and virgin stone
and celebrate, "Here, among our geometries,
lie the destinies of shell and rock,
lumber and desire, for there is no rest
without the hand-made shadow, the roof
that says to us, 'This is your space—
you who never knew what it was
to live simply among the gifts and lights.'"

How all things demand to remind.
The dragonfly pinning itself to the air's lapel,
its wings haloed by velocity, is somewhat like
the green parrots in the perfect rectangle
of the branch-strewn plaza behind us,
in turn evoking the order of trailing students
strange in their re-mapping of the familiar
and thinking, What should I notice to excel?
and so miss the point, much as I have,
failing again to see how little kinship
I've endured for others' wounds, how the easy
noble thing the storm inspired
was to compare its passing ravages with history
and say, 'But over there is my island
torn by decades of tyranny, and what could it matter
that this suburb bleed when that nation drowns?'
Except that this freshly pierced shell
has become less exile than home.
Close. Closer still. Even as my back is turned.
My eyes slide up the careful walls
minutely, the hourglass sand of new love.

—Ricardo Pau-Llosa (1993)

<table>
<tr><td>

HUITAIN, PAR LEDIT AUTHEUR
ARRIVÉ EN SA MAISON, EN LA
VILLE DE DIEPPE, AYANT FAIM.

</td><td>

OCTET, BY THE AUTHOR UPON
ARRIVING IN HIS HOME, IN THE
TOWN OF DIEPPE, HUNGRY.

</td></tr>
</table>

One of the few survivors from the 1564-65 French Huguenot expedition to Fort Caroline, Nicholas Le Challeux wrote an account of his adventures after returning home to Dieppe. His **octet** appears to be the first poem about North America by a European who had actually visited the continent. It is probably fitting that this man, described as a carpenter and lay minister, brought back a piece of wood as his only souvenir of the New World.

<table>
<tr><td>

*Q*ui veut aller à la Floride,
Qu'il y aille i'y ay esté:
Et revenu sec & aride,
Et abbatu de poureté.
Pour tous bien i'en ay rapporté
Un beau baston blanc en ma main.
Mais je suis sain, non degouté:
Ca à manger: je meurs de faim.

</td><td>

*W*hoever wishes to go to Florida,
Let him go where I have been,
And return dry and arid,
And worn out by rot.
For the only good I have brought back—
A single silvery stick in my hand.
But I am safe, not defeated:
It's time to eat; I die of hunger.

</td></tr>
</table>

—Nicolas Le Challeux (1565)

Translated by Maurice O'Sullivan

This Fertile Paradise

In 1571 Bartolomé de Flores wrote *Obra nuevamente compuesta* (*Newly Composed Work*), a poem of 375 lines celebrating the victory of Pedro Avilés de Menéndez over the French Huguenots at Fort Caroline. In this section he extols the beauties of the land, perhaps to attract colonists to the new settlement that Menéndez was nurturing at St. Augustine.

Y por dar mejor aviso
quiero contar la grandeza
la hermosura y belleza
deste fértil paraiso:
su gente y naturaleza.
es un nuevo mundo lleno
de deleites y frescuras
con muy diversas pinturas
prado florido y ameno
con aves de mil hechuras.

*A*nd in order to better describe it
I wish to tell of the expanse,
of the beauty and loveliness
of this fertile paradise,
of its people and its nature.
It is a new world
full of charms and comely
with many diverse colors,
a flowered and delightful meadow
with birds of a thousand kinds.

—Bartolomé de Flores, (1571)

Translated by William Richard Jackson

On Ponce de León

In his *Elegias de varones illustres de Indias (Elegies on the Illustrious Men of the Indies,* 1589), Juan de Castellanos, a veteran of numerous Spanish expeditions to the New World, describes Ponce de León's quest for the fountain of youth. Castellanos relates the legends about the fountain but scoffs at the search as "such foolish nonsense." De León, of course, never found the fountain of youth, but he did reach the Floridian peninsula on Easter Sunday, 1513. Castellanos's descriptions of those who might come to drink from the fountain of youth and the fortune to be made from such an attraction are, indeed, prophetic of the flocking of retirees to Florida in the 20th century.

Vuelvo pues á Joan Ponce, poderoso
En los dones de Juno y Belona,
Que de mayor empresa codicioso,
Y de servir á la real corona:
Nunca quiso jamàs tomar reposo
Pudiendo ya gozallo su persona;
Y ansi fuera del cargo de justicia,
Quiso sacar á luz esta noticia

     Entre los mas antiguos desta gente
Habia muchos indios que decian
De la Bimini, isla prepotente,
Donde varias naciones acudian,
Por las virtudes grandes de su fuente,
Do viejos en mancebos se volvian,
Y donde las mujeres mas ancianas
Deshacian las rugas y las canas.

     Bebiendo de sus aguas pocas veces,
Lavando las cansadas proporciones,
Perdian fealdades de vejeces
Sanaban las enfermas compexiones;
Los rostros adobaban y las teces,
Puesto que no mudaban las faiciones
Y por no desear de ser doncellas
Del agua lo salian todas ellas.

     Decian admirables influencias
De sus floridos compos y florestas;
No se vian aun las apariencias
De las cosas que suelen ser molestas,
Ni sabian que son litispendencias,
Siao gozos, placeres, grandes fiestas:
Al fin nos la pintaban de manera
Que cobraban alli la edad primera.

I return, then, to Juan Ponce
strong in the gifts of Juno and Belona,
in quest of greater undertakings
and service to the royal crown.
He never wished to live in ease,
although his station permitted it;
and being free of his office,
he wished to seek out this tale.

     Among the aged of this people
there were many Indians who told
of Bimini, prepotent island
where several peoples resorted
for the great benefits of its fountain;
where old men were turned into youths,
and where the most aged women
lost their wrinkles and the gray in their hair.

     Having drunk its water a few times,
bathing their sagging figures,
they lost the ugliness of old age;
their sickly constitution was mended,
their faces and complexion beautified
although their features unchanged;
and because they did not want to be maidens
all of them emerged from the water as such.

     They told of the admirable effect
of its flowered fields and woods.
No stringency was yet known
of those things which are troublesome.
Nor were lawsuits known,
only joys, pleasures and feasting:
all in all such was it painted
that they were again in the Golden Age.

Estoy agora yo considerando,
Segun la vanidad de nuestros dias,
¡Qué de viejas vinieran arrastrando
Por cobrar sus antiguas gallardias,
Si fuera cierta como voy contando
La fama de tan grandes niñerias!
¡Cuán rico, cuán pujante, cuán potente
Pudiera ser el rey de la tal fuente!
¡Que de haciendas, joyas y preseas
Por remozar vendieran los varones!
¡Qué grita de hermosas y de feas
Anduvieran aquestas estaciones!
¡Cuán diferentes trajes y libreas
Vinieran a ganar estos perdones!
Cierto no se tomara pena tanta
Por ir á visitar la tierra santa.

　　　La fama pues del agua se vertia
Por los destos cabildos y concejos.
Y con imaginar que ya se via
En mozos se tornaron muchos viejos:
Prosiguiendo tan loca fantasia
Sin querer ser capaces de consejos;
Y ansi tomaron muchos el camino
De tan desatinado desatino.

　　　Al norte pues guiaron su corrida,
No sin fortunosisimos rigores,
Bien lejos de la fuente referida
Y de sus prosperados moradores;
Mas descubrió la punta que Florida
Llamó, porque la vió pascua de flores;
Volvióse hecho tal descubrimiento,
Y pidióla por adelantamiento.

....
• **Adelanto** colonial governor

Now comes to my mind,
considering the vanity of our day,
the number of old women who would come
　　　adragging
to recover their former charms,
if that I am telling were true,
as I relate these childish tales:
how important, how rich, how powerful
might be the ruler of such a fountain.

　　　What treasures, jewels and valuables
the men would sell to regain their youth:
what a clamor of beauty and homeliness
seeking to obtain these indulgences:
for certain so much trouble would not be taken
to go to visit the Holy Land.

　　　The fame, then, of these waters
flowed among those of these parishes and towns,
and in their mind many were seen
to turn from old age to childhood;
heeding such a crazy fantasy,
incapable of heeding counsel.
And thus, many set out on the road
in search of such foolish nonsense.

　　To the north, then, they turned their
　　　course,
accompanied by great difficulties,
far indeed from the famed fountain
and the prosperous dwellers in its land:
but he discovered the peninsula which he named
　　　Florida
because he sighted it on Easter Sunday.
Having made this discovery, he returned
and asked to be made its ADELANTO.

　　　　　　—Juan de Castellanos, (1589)

　　　　　Translated by William Richard Jackson

On the Indians of Florida

In this section from his *Elegias*, Castellanos describes the warlike Calusa of Florida's Gulf Coast, the natives who drove Ponce de León and his men from Charlotte Harbor in February, 1521. De León later died in Cuba from a wound received during the attack. Castellanos admires the remarkable skills of the Calusa in the water—although the whales he alludes to are probably manatees—and respects their ability to survive in an alien landscape which the Spaniards found inhospitable.

No nada con tal impetu sirena,
Ni por las bravas ondas tan esperta,
Pues eada cual y no con mucha pena
Entre voraces peces se despierta;
Matan en alta mar una ballena
Para la repartir después de muerta,
Y aunque ella se zabulla, no se ciega
El indio, ni de encima se despega.

    No puede con sus fuerzas no ser flacas
Desechallo de encima las cervices
El indio lleva hechas dos estacas
De durisimas ramas ó raices,
Y en medio de las ondas ó resacas
Se las mete de dentro las narices,
La falta del resuello la desmaya,
Y ansi la hacen ir acia la playa.

    Son las cazas y pescas sus usanzas,
Y en aquesto consisten sus primores,
Aqui suelen poner sus esperanzas,
Los niños y mancebos y mayores;
Ausi se curan poco de labranzas,
Y entre ellos hay muy pocos labradores,
Sus usos á las noches y mañanas
Son mazas, arcos, flechas y macanas.

    La tierra con verdores se matiza,
Y desde lejos buen color esmalta;
Por ser de bastimentos toda falta;
En su mayor compás anegadiza
Sin parte que podamos decir alta;
Hay por estas distancias y caminos
Cantidad de nogales y de pinos

Not even the sirens swim so swiftly
nor are so expert among the wild waves,
since every one of them with little trouble
disports among voracious fishes;
they kill whales on the high sea,
and when dead apportion them,
and when it dives the Indian is not daunted
nor does he leave his post on its back.

    It cannot withal its great strength
rid him from its back.
The Indian carries two stakes
fashioned of hard branches or root,
and in the middle of the waves and swell
puts them in its nose.
The lack of breath weakens it
and thus drives it on the shore.

    Fishing and hunting is their living,
and that is the best thing in their life;
on this, base their future
the elders, children and youths.
So, they care little for farming,
and there are among them few farmers;
their implements for night or day
are maces, bows, arrows and cudgels.

    The land is tinted with green,
and from afar with good color adorned;
but disappointment awaits you if you tread
there because victuals are completely lacking.
Its greater breadth is in swamp,
and there is no part that can be called high.
In these expanses and byways
walnut trees and pines abound.

—Juan de Castellanos (1589)

Translated by William Richard Jackson

FROM LA FLORIDA

A Franciscan priest, Alonso Gregorio de Escobedo arrived in Florida in 1587 and worked at the Nombre de Dios mission in St. Augustine for about ten years. His epic poem, *La Florida*, completed in Spain around 1609, presents a series of historical, biographical, and descriptive vignettes of Spanish Florida and the Greater Antilles.

*E*s tan perdida que al cristiano admira
    cuyo invincible animo suspende,
    y con mucha razón gime y súspira
    y el cielo con sus lagrimas enciende,
    suplicandole a Dios cese su ira
    si destruir idolatras pretende,
    porque toda la gente de la costa
    al infierno camina por la posta.
Es costa la Florida peligrosa,
    cercada de montañas y pantanos.
    La gente que la ocupa es belicosa
    enemiga rabiosa de cristianos,
    de suerte que si alguno salir osa
    por el monte sin miedo de paganos,
    si acaso vuelve vivo trae el pecho
    lleno de flechas, harto a su despecho.
Aunque no es cual solía su fiereza,
    ya el pueblo infiel se finge mas piadoso.
    La pólvora rompió su fortaleza,
    que suele dar jucio al alevoso.
    Ella cuando dio acaso en la cabeza
    del hombre más valiente y animoso
    hace tenga virtud si es insolente,
    y obediencia el varón inobediente.

*I*t is so lost that the Christian marvels
    awed by its invincible spirit,
    and with great reason moans and sighs
    and heaven with his tears inflames,
    begging God to cease his wrath
    if he wants to destroy pagans,
    since all peoples of the coast
    walk to hell along the post-road.
The coast of Florida is perilous,
    fenced by mountains and swamplands.
    The people who live there are warlike,
    furious foes of Christians,
    so that anyone who dares set out
    for the hill, heedless of pagans,
    if he returns alive, will have a heart
    full of arrows and heartlessness.
Although of an accustomed ferocity,
    the infidel fakes great piety.
    Gunpowder, rendering the treacherous
        prudent,
    breaks their resolve.
    Powder, when it lands on the head
    of the bravest, most spirited man
    gives him virtue if he is insolent,
    and obedience to the inobedient man.

—Fray Alonso Gregorio de Escobedo
    (c.1598)

Translated by Rebeca Daniels

FROM THE DESERTED VILLAGE

Through torrid tracts with fainting steps they go.
Where wild Altama murmurs to their woe.
Far different there from all that charm'd before,
The various terrors of that horrid shore.
Those blazing suns that dart a downward ray,
And fiercely shed intolerable day;
Those matted woods where birds forget to sing,
But silent bats in drowsy clusters cling,
Those poisonous fields with rank luxuriance crowned
Where the dark scorpion gathers death around;
Where at each step the stranger fears to wake
The rattling terrors of the vengeful snake;
Where crouching tigers wait their hapless prey,
And savage men more murderous still than they;
While oft in whirls the mad tornado flies,
Mingling the ravaged landscape with the skies.

—Oliver Goldsmith (1770)

In contrast to Bartolomé de Flores's description of Florida's "fertile paradise," designed to lure colonists to the New World, Oliver Goldsmith's passage from *The Deserted Village* attempts to warn English colonists off with descriptions of the terrors that await: intense heat, bats, scorpions, rattlesnakes, "crouching tigers" (panthers and bobcats?), savages, and tornadoes.

THE FOUNTAIN OF YOUTH

The font the Spaniard sought in vain
Through all the land of flowers
Leaps glittering from the sandy plain
Our classic grove embowers.
Here youth, unchanging blooms and smiles,
Here dwells eternal spring,
And warms from Hope's eternal isles
The winds their perfume bring.

Here every leaf is in the bud
Each singing throat in tune,
And bright o'er evenings silver flood
Shines the young crescent moon.
What wonder age forgets his staff
And lays his glasses down,
And gray-haired grandsires look and laugh
As when their locks were brown!

As Dean of the Harvard Medical School, Holmes first gained recognition for *Old Ironsides* (1830), a poem which blocked the government from dismantling the frigate *USS Constitution*. Unlike de Castellanos, Holmes's enthusiastic, patriotic vision of the fountain of youth reflects Victorian America's belief in the limitless possibilities of the future.

With ears grown dull and eyes grown dim
They greet the joyous day
That calls them to the fountain's brim
To wash their years away.
What change has clothed the ancient sire
In sudden youth? For, lo!
The Judge, the Doctor, and the Squire
Are Jack and Bill and Joe.

And be his titles what they will,
In spite of manhood's claim
The gray beard is a school-boy still
And loves his school-boy name;
It calms the ruler's stormy breast
Whom hurrying care pursues,
And brings a sense of peace and rest,
Like slippers after shoes.

And what are all the prizes won
To youth's enchanted view?
And what is all the man has done
To what the boy may do?
O blessed font, whose waters flow
Alike for sire and son,
That melts our winter's frost and snow,
And makes all ages one!

I pledge the sparkling fountain's tide
That flings its golden shower
With age to fill and youth to guide,
Still fresh in morning flower.
Flow on with ever-widening stream,
In ever brightening morn,
Our story's pride, our future's dream,
The hope of times unborn.

—Oliver Wendell Holmes (1873)

TIMUCUAN CADENZA

I crush the same dried leaves
rotting on the game trail
to the mangrove mound—
the sound of walking tingles
ghost-stained oaks, pink lichen
graying, ageless in decay.
From the brown lagoon

our people dredged the great carved owl,
your resurrected spectre
enlightened after centuries of dark,
staring into blue, sun scanning
brackish murk for signs
of your disappearance,
the shudder we call history.

Smallpox?
Spanish missionaries?
A clash of empires
over how light glances from a body,
falls on a girl's raven hair
somewhere along the river?
How did your leaving begin?

Scholars patched and painted
your totem; it stands
in a manicured park, cemented
near the screened concession.
Few take the path through steamy rain
along the edge of pine flat
where the fish-eagle stitches

a stick-eyrie in the white tree,
plunges talons-first
to its prey; where the buck
scents ritual death in the scrub,
the spear unbroken, unburned,
unthrown to the river.
Your absence echoes in the woodpecker's knock.

A walk to a Timucuan shell mound in a mangrove lagoon induces a reverie about the indigenous peoples who inhabited the northern Atlantic coast of Florida. The Timucua, a relatively peaceful community, welcomed and aided the French colonists at Fort Caroline. Like all the other inhabitants of Florida at the time of the European encounter, they disappeared, victims of European diseases and colonial expansion.

In what moon did you mound
the shells of river snail
over your fallen dead? For burial
alone, for riding out the hurricane?
We find no bones, but sand . . .
We too are afraid of storm.
We have raised no mound for listening to our dead.

You answer in a shadowy scuttle,
armadillo clicking under ragged brush,
the rasp of saw palmetto,
a spring-gold web dangling
across the trail. I stand on the bank,
trapped in fragile calm,
the pause of the bittern before flight.

—William Johnson (1984)

- **bittern** a wading bird
  related to the heron

Hernando De Soto

*H*ernando De Soto was Spanish,
an iron-clad conquistador.
Adventure he knew in the sack of Peru,
but it just made him anxious for more.

Hernando De Soto was knightly,
Hernando De Soto was bold,
like most of his lot,
he'd be off like a shot
wherever he heard there was gold.

With priest and physician and army,
not to speak of a number of swine,
at Tampa he started a quest, fiery hearted,
for the gold of a fabulous mine.

From Florida way out to Texas,
this Don of the single-track mind,
went chasing his dream over prairie and stream,
and the pigs kept on trotting behind.

Although born in California, Pulitzer Prize-winning poet Stephen Vincent Benét traced his ancestry back to Florida's 18th-century immigrants from the Mediterranean island of Minorca. With his wife, Rosemary, he wrote *A Book of Americans* (1933), a series of poems about people who have shaped the country for good and ill. Their exuberant **anapests** and ironic juxtapositions of words and ideas create a lighthearted portrait of de Soto's brutal and bloody expedition through Florida in 1539.

He discov'red the great Mississippi,
he faced perils and hardships untold,
and his soldiers are bacon, if I'm not mistaken,
  but nobody found any gold.

They buried De Soto at midnight,
where the wide Mississippi still jigs.
he was greedy for gain but a soldier of Spain.
(I hope someone looked after the pigs.)

  —Rosemary and Stephen Vincent Benét (1941)

FORT DESOTO

Ponce de León hoisted sail
  Returned to Mullet Key
The year was 1521.
  He met his destiny.

Eight years before, careened off-shore
  His ship was scraped and cleaned.
The bottom shone in full moonlight
  And Spanish armor gleamed.

But thrumming strings drove feathered shafts
  That stung like angry bees.
A Spaniard died upon the sand—
  Was given to the seas.

So Ponce de León found no youth
  In springs—but met his doom.
An arrow from an Indian's bow
  Did lay him in his tomb.

  —Will McLean (1980)

Folksinger and balladeer Will McLean chronicled the history and ecology of Florida in over 3,500 poems and songs about the state. In this **ballad** he relates the history of Ponce de León's death.

PONCE DE LEÓN

*C*upped brackish water in his fingers, held
His breath in hope. Attending him, his men
Gaped for the promised miracle. But his skin
Had lost no wrinkle, not one liver spot—
Another false
Fountain that sprang from earth, not from God's Garden.

These Everglades.
Dissolved his bones, rusted the cutlass blades.
He felt the night wind harden—
Arthritic raindrops dabbled at his tent.
Was his resolve now, like the wine casks, spent?

Destroying him, the Angel begged his pardon.

—X. J. Kennedy (1994)

Does the fountain of youth symbolize hope or delusion? Popular poet, satirist, and anthologist X. J. Kennedy offers an alternative view to the one presented earlier by Oliver Wendell Holmes. Kennedy's ironic tone, concrete detail, and harsh language contrast sharply with Holmes's upbeat and generalized images and diction.

CHRIST IN THE SUN

(A Spanish padre is sick with fever in the New World.)

*S*ince in our great forests we have no roads
Nor cities, we have dreamed of a land of sun
Merely; though a paradise with neither Christ
Nor a Christian is Satan's work, an illusion of lust
That stirs fantasies as fever stirs my blood
And tempts to conquest, a test for Christian man.

The primitive men we find here are, to us, new men,
Though old world men are also new here. These roads
Bewilder my brain. The vessels of my blood
Are inflamed by the naked savages and their sun.
God tempts us with false freedom; the rank lust
Of old Adam, my enemy, hopes to win me from Christ.

Within the traditional repetitive pattern of the **sestina,** Van Brock finds an ideal form to represent an examination of conscience. In his feverish hallucinations, a Spanish missionary questions his traditional religious beliefs after encountering an Edenic culture.

But I will preach them Christ! Christ! Christ!
As the stern fathers did me, from boy to man,
Until I, until they, are stronger than our lust,
Or Christ is stronger in us than these false roads—
And these pagan chants, these dances to the sun,
Like these tempers, are purged from our dark blood.

"O Father, take this darkness from my blood
And brain, make bright for me, in me, Christ's
Pure Light. The simple light of their sun
Must be our darkness. O what is man
That delusion in him can take such subtle roads
He cannot know love from a lie, faith from lust?"

They did receive us freely, despite their lust
For the flesh. Though crude, they have a gentle blood,
A child's pulse for earth and creatures. Their roads
Leave no scars. They have small property. Like Christ
They would rather give than receive. Their shamans
Say they walk in the light of two worlds, two suns.

Yet it is like Eden, this place, with its warm sun,
Its flowers, flesh, fruit, fresh streams. Is it lust
To breathe too deeply, is the faith that cools my blood
Then also false that it can enrage a man
Against such outward grace in the joined names of Christ
And that dreamed life to which death is the one road.

Here, where the one road is the sun's road,
Spain, torn between goldlust and Christ lust,
Drives its two-edged sword into every man's blood.

      —Van K. Brock (1979)

FLORIDA WARNS HER COLONISTS

f the land itself could speak, what would it say about all these human invaders? Cynthia Cahn, who died shortly after her prize-winning chapbook *The Day the Sun Split* was published, shows little sympathy for those who exploit the land. Although she uses language associated with the 16th and 17th centuries, her warning rings as true today as 400 years ago.

*Y*ou have come to pluck the sun
from its blue branch, suck
its glowing pulps till your palms
bleed gold. I know. You see
me a brace of huge bronze thighs
to pry open with cannons,
Bibles, fat bags of coin. I shall splay
with diamonds, you pray; shall
rain crowns, palaces, slaves.

I bear enough inhabitants,
thank you. They dance in rounds
to honor my ways, the planet's,
heaven's. Thrive circumscribed
in my woodlands, hills, pale crescents
of beach. Thank me for animals, fruits
I yield to their hands.
I show you the perfect pentacle:
air, fire, earth, water,
mind. You have come to smash it.
I shall bring you bare larders, bloodshed.
I shall bring you bellowing
winds that whirl as fiercely as sun's
atoms. I tell you again and
again, though I can't speak
and you won't listen:

    Stay off me.
    Stay off
    me.

    —Cynthia Cahn (1982)

RUINS OF STREETS OF STONE . . .
(St. Augustine, 1827)

Ruins of streets of stone unpeopled town
Pillars upon the margin of the Sea
With worn inscriptions oft explored in vain.
The motley population—Hither come
The Forest families timid & tame
Not now as once with stained tomahawk
And at the council fires painting haughtily
His simple symbols for your fears to read
But in unclean & sloven apathy
Brings venison from the woods with silly trade
And here the dark Minorcan sad & separate
Wrapt in his cloak strolls with unsocial eye
All day basks idle in the sun then seeks his food
By night upon the waters stilly plying
His hook & line in all the moonlit bays.
Here steals the sick with uncertain gait
Looks with feeble spirit at things around
As if he sighing said What is it to me
I dwell afar, far from this cheerless fen
My wife my children strain their eyes to me
And oh in vain wo wo is me I feel
These wishful eyes no more
Shall see New England's wood crowned hills again.

—Ralph Waldo Emerson (1827)

During his stay in St. Augustine, the young clergyman Ralph Waldo Emerson recorded a variety of impressions in his *Journals*. In contrast to his idealized "St Augustine" in the Prologue, his unsympathetic description of the Native Americans and Minorcans reflects the New England values that would later inspire such essays as "Self Reliance." The Minorcans, immigrants from an island off Spain, came first to New Smyrna in 1767 and later migrated to St. Augustine.

THE SEMINOLE REMOVAL

*T*hey are taking us beyond Miami,
They are taking us beyond the Caloosa River,
They are taking us to the end of our tribe,
They are taking us to Palm Beach, coming back beside
      Okeechobee Lake,
They are taking us to an old town in the west.

SONG FOR THE DYING

*C*ome back.
Before you get to the king tree, come back.
Before you get to the peach tree, come back.
Before you get to the line of fence, come back.
Before you get to the bushes, come back.
Before you get to the fork of the road, come back.
Before you get to the yard, come back.
Before you get to the door, come back.
Before you get to the fire, come back.
Before you get to the middle of the ladder, come back.

Susie Tiger recorded these two songs for the noted musical ethnologist Frances Densmore's collection *Seminole Music* (1956). During the Second Seminole War (1835-42), over 3,800 Seminoles were removed to reservations in the western Indian territories in Oklahoma. The images in "Song for the Dying" refer to various stages in the journey of death.

OSCEOLA

[When I was nearly grown to manhood in Brooklyn, New York (middle of 1838), I met one of the return'd U.S. Marines from Fort Moultrie, S.C., and had long talks with him—learn'd the occurrence below described—death of Osceola. The latter was a young brave, leading Seminole in the Florida war of that time—was surrender'd to our troops, imprison'd and literally died of "a broken heart," at Fort Moultrie. He sicken'd of his confinement—the doctors and officers made every allowance and kindness possible for; then the close:]

*W*hen his hour for death had come,
He slowly rais'd himself from the bed on the floor,

Drew on his war-dress, shirt, leggings, and girdled the belt
        around his waist,
Call'd for vermilion paint (his looking glass was held before
        him,)
Painted half his face and neck, his wrists, and back-hands,
Put the scalp-knife carefully in his belt—then lying down,
resting a
        moment,
Rose again, half sitting, smiled, gave in silence his extended
                                                hand
        to each and all,
Sank faintly low to the floor (tightly grasping the tomahawk
        handle,)
Fix'd his look on wife and little children—the last:

(And here a line in memory of his name and death.)

        —Walt Whitman (1892)

After the artist George Catlin gave Walt Whitman a print of his famous portrait of Osceola, the poet recalled hearing an account of the warrior's death more than a half century earlier. The parenthetical final line suggests that the poem remained unfinished, even though Whitman included it in his *Leaves of Grass*.

IN THE FLORIDA WAR

*O*h, jolly brave knight was Benjamin Beall
        In the Florida War;
As many a jolly bright camp-fire could tell
        In the Florida War.
Oh! the stories he told that never grow old
And the songs that he trolled until reveille rolled,
        In the Florida War.
Made chiefs and subalterns as merry as bold
        In the Florida War.

Who was brave as a lion, yet soft as a child
        In the Florida War?
Who could swim the Suwannee when waters were wild
        In the Florida War?
Who could harass Sam Jones till he ached in his bones,
Rap a redskin whilst laughing, then weep o'er his groans
        In the Florida War?

Soldiers have traditionally romanticized their heroes in popular camp songs. Here, the captain of the Second Dragoons during the Second Seminole War epitomizes the courage, humor, and humanity of the 19th century's ideal warrior.

• **Sam Jones** is the nickname given to a Miccosukee leader who fought in all three Seminole wars. Adamantly refusing to emigrate West, he led a band into the Everglades where he remained until his death at well over 100 years old.

Then chant him a requiem in reverent tones,
  In the Florida War?
Who, when shattered and broken, from scouting and toils,
  In the Florida War?
Could smile at grim death as he felt its cold coils,
  In the Florida War?
Who but valiant old Ben—beau ideal of men,
Who wore gay soldier's togs in the days that we ken,
  In the Florida War?
God rest his old head where his blanket is spread
Far from toil and cold lead
  In the Florida War?

Two Songs from *The Rough and Ready Songster*

These songs appear in a collection praising General Zachary Taylor for his leadership in the War of 1812, the Indian Wars, and the Mexican War. Known as "Old Rough and Ready" for his simple uniform, personal courage, and stocky build, Taylor was elected president in 1849, only to die of cholera the following year.

I knew him first, the soldier said,
  Among the Everglades
When we gave the savage red-skins
Our bayonets and our blades.
I think I hear his cheerful voice:
"On column!" Steady! Steady!
So hardy and so prompt was he
We called him Rough and Ready.

II

*I*n eighteen twelve 'gainst twelve to one,
He bravely saved Fort Harrison.
And made Miami's red-skins fly,
From the lead of his guns, and the fire in his eye,
  Hurrah, Hurrah.

At Florida in thirty seven,
With five hundred men—the foe eleven,
He burnt "red alligators" Toby,
And conquered Lake Okeechobee.
  Hurrah, Hurrah.

Invocation

IV

*S*ay, then, of that too soon forgotten race
That flourished once, but long has been obscure
In Florida, and where the seas embrace
The Spanish isles; say, if e'er lives more pure
Warmed veins, or patriots could more endure
Around the altars of their native bourn!
Say, when their flow'ry landscapes could allure,
What peaceful seasons did to them return,
And how requited labor filled his golden urn!

V

How sweet their little fields of golden corn!
How pleasure smiled o'er all the varying scene!
How, 'mid her dewy murmurs dreamt the morn,
As Summer lingered in the deep serene!
How nibbling flocks spread on the hillsides green,
And cattle herded in the vales below;
And how wild meadows stretched in bloom-sweet sheen,
Beneath unconquered shades, where lovers go
When comes the evening star above the dark to glow!

VI

In this delightful valley of the isle,
Where dwelt the proud Maroon, were not deeds done
Which roused the Seminole and fierce exile
To more than savage daring? Here begun
The valiant struggles of a forest son;
And tho' by wrong's leagued numbers overborne,
Hid deeds of love and valor for him won
The envied wreath by heroes only worn,
And which from manhood's brow oppression ne'er hath torn!

Twasinta's Seminoles; or The Rape of Florida, published by the African-American poet Albery Whitman in 1885, is an **elegaic epic**, written in **Spenserian stanzas**, mourning the loss of what Whitman envisioned as an Edenic Florida. The poem chronicles the defeat of the Seminoles by the U.S. Army and their forced removal from Florida to Oklahoma in 1842. In the poem, Twasinta is the tribal chief; his son Atlassa, the warrior chief, is married to Ewald, daughter of Palmecho, a Spanish landowner, and a Maroon mother.

- **bourn** boundary meaning homeland

In his Invocation, Whitman calls upon the voice of his Muse in a vision of Florida as an ideal multiracial community in which Seminoles, runaway slaves, and the descendants of early Spanish settlers peacefully coexisted.

- **Maroon** an escaped slave who lived in the forest

Canto I

XX

Later in Canto I he contrasts the heroic Atlassa with Osceola, an embittered warrior seeking revenge against the American soldiers for the enslavement of his wife.

So with our young Atlassa, hero-born—
Free as the air within his palmy shade,
The nobler traits that do the man adorn,
In him were native; Not the music made
In Tampa's forests or the everglade
Was fitter, than in this young Seminole
Was the proud spirit which did life pervade,
And glow and tremble in his ardent soul—
Which, lit his inmost self, and spurned all mean control.

XXV

Not so with Osceola, thy dark mate;
The hidden terror of the hummock, he
Sat gloomily and nursed a bitter hate,—
The white man was his common enemy__
He rubbed the burning wounds of injury,
And plotted in his dreadful silent gloom;
As dangerous as a rock beneath the sea.
And when in fray he showed his fearless plume,
Revenge made sweet the blows that dealt the white man's doom.

XXVI

The pent-up wrath that rankled in his breast,
O'er smould'ring embers shot a lurid glare,
And wrongs that time itself had not redrest,
In ghost-like silence stalked and glimmered there.
And from the wizzard caverns of despair,
Came voice and groan, reminding o'er and o'er
The outrage on his wife so young and fair;
And so, by heaven and earth and hell he swore
To treat in council with the white man never more.

Canto II

LXXIII

If e'er the muse of history sits to write,
And Florida appear upon her page,
This nation's crimes will blush the noonday light,
And * * * * * *'s name will lead her criminal age!
Of all the cruel wars she e'er did wage,
The cruelest will be to him assigned!
The hardened soldier's lust, the bloodhound's rage,
And San Augustine's church and prison joined,
Will be fit monuments for his chivalric mind!

LXXIV

Extermination was his highest creed,
Bondage the one provision of his will,
The blood of innocence marred not the deed,
He knew no art of warfare but to kill:
Slaying was sweet, but slaughter sweeter still!
A human monster, traced thro' tears and blood
From Blount's poor fort on Apalachi's hill,
To Tampa's waters and the Mexic flood, —
But, to forget him, is perhaps a common good!

LXXV

Heard ye not in the cypress come a troop?
Saw ye not by the gray old battlement,
In fear's deep anguish hurdled exiles stoop;
Wife, mother, child within the stockade pent,
As down the angry Apalachi went
The steamy monitor, to belch out death,
While savage Creeks rushed thro' the bloody rent
Made by the iron havoc of its breath,
To massacre the wounded that did shriek beneath?

—Albery A. Whitman (1884)

In Canto II Whitman recalls the devastation visited upon the Seminoles by Colonel Clinch who had allied his soldiers with 200 Creek mercenaries in July 1816. They invaded Spanish Florida in order to recapture runaway slaves living with the Seminoles. About 300 Seminoles and slaves took refuge in Fort Apalachicola, which became known as Fort Negro. An American warship bombarded the fort, killing 270 people; the survivors were taken to Georgia and enslaved. This First Seminole War ended in 1818 when the U.S. purchased Florida from Spain.

• **monitor** Whitman uses the term **anachronistically** to refer to any iron-clad warship

*L*awless men, they were to blame.
From the Georgia line they came.
Burning, killing, stealing slaves,
From the Seminole Indian braves.

Major Dade and his hundred
Were marching along,
By the edge of a thick swamp.
It was shortly before dawn.
Through scrub and palmetto
Their harnesses did ring.
They were marching from Tampa
On the way to Fort King.

Oh the sun's rays were burning,
Dade's temper was short!
His scout had deserted
Somewhere to the north.
The men had a feeling.
The land was too quiet.
They held their guns tightly
Their eyes showed their fright.

Well, it came of a sudden,
That wild cry of craze,
From the screaming throats
Of the Seminole braves.
Black smoke, thudding bullets
From Indian guns.
I'll tell you, the Dade
Massacre had begun.

Major Dade, he fell first
With a deep mortal wound.
'Twas from Jumper's rifle
That he met his doom.
His men were all killed
Without mercy or plea.
This legend lives ever
In our history.

On December 28, 1835, Osceola and a band of Seminoles ambushed a regiment of American soldiers under the command of Major Francis L. Dade. Increasing demands by settlers seeking more land and by plantation owners demanding the return of runaway slaves who had joined the Seminole tribe led the government to pressure a small number of Seminole leaders into signing the Treaty of Payne's Landing in 1832. The treaty stipulated that the Seminoles would move voluntarily to Oklahoma and unite with the Creeks, who had earlier been forced westward. Most of the Seminoles rejected the Treaty and resisted its enforcement.

• **John Jumper**, a Seminole chief.

Now the land is all serene.
  There's a marker at the scene,
Where Major Dade sleeps
  Among his hundred men.

   —Will McLean (1980)

MAJOR DADE

*M*ajor Dade, Major Dade,
What happened to your Brigade?

It seems sir you have taken the wrong turn,
And now it seems that it's your time to burn.
You have tried to chase the Native from His land.
You killed, captured and tried to shame
the people of the Seminole Band.

Major Dade, Major Dade,
This is where your body is laid!

Your family will weep, but do they really know
why?
Or did you tell them about the Native women and
children you made cry.
You led the Bluecoats against the Native and made
many a fatherless son.
But today Major Dade, the medicine too strong,
you can't shoot what you can't see with your
mighty gun.

Major Dade, Major Dade,
What happened to the Bluecoats' raid?

Did you think the Red Man had run out of time?
When you marched those hundred men from the
Florida state line?
Were you going to rid Florida and cause the
Seminole to fall?
Pesky Indians! Let's kill them all!

When is a massacre a heroic act of self-defense? Word choices invariably reflect points of view. Here a Seminole poet challenges the tradition of the "massacre" of Major Francis L. Dade and his men, one of the actions which ignited the Second Seminole War.

Major Dade, Major Dade,
The name in the history books you've made.

Oh yes, it's there in Black and White,
And we know who really won the fight!
In your books you win a great battle, and it
becomes historical lore.
The Indian wins and it's a massacre or the
Heathens have started another Bloody War!

Major Dade, Major Dade,
The truth we must never let fade!

Major Dade, Major Dade!
This is where your body is laid!

—Moses Jumper, Jr. (1990)

SEMINOLE SLEEP SONG

*S*wing, Jonny-Willie, in your pretty red hammock,
  Frog in swamp make glad night song;
Alligator bay down in Big Cypress,
  Hammock hide Jonny when bear trot along.

Dark come quick when sun go down,
  Wind make music in tall pine tree;
Hammock swing out and hammock swing in,
  But sleep catch Jonny, he no can see.

Screech owl laugh and wildcat snarl,
  Bat swoop low, but Jonny no afraid,
Big chief tell: "No harm can come
  To Seminole baby in deep Everglade."

Swing, Jonny-Willie, in your pretty red hammock,
  Mockingbird call come low and sweet;
Stars make crown for your moss pillow,
  Moonbeam gild your little brown feet.

—Carrie Blaine Yeiser

In this gentle lullaby, Yeiser presents the **neo-Romantic** view of Seminole life in the Everglades as connected to nature in a way that modern civilization has lost.

TEACHING THE MICCOSUKEE: LATER

The Medicine Man at Big Cypress hates me.
He has sliced Annie's ears.
Others come now, but the children of Big Cypress
look down when they see me at the post.
With his potion of nettle and bitter oak
the Medicine Man has shriveled
the child I would have grown.
In dreams he tells me what he has done.

The Medicine Man at Big Cypress
buys nothing here.
Others come, with their pigs and their dogs
and their chickens with muddy feathers.
The Medicine Man stays in his chickee,
built with none of our nails,
sharpening his knives for little ears.
They cannot keep the knowledge from him.
Let an ibis cross the swamp
five miles away, ten miles,
and he knows.

—Lola Haskins (1984)

In her **poetic sequence** "Julia O'Halloran (b. 1880 Orange City, d. 1970 Gainesville)," Lola Haskins creates a historical character based on the oral histories spoken by the real Julia Stranahan, Fort Lauderdale's first school teacher. In this poem, Julia recounts her frustration in trying to teach the Miccosukee at Big Cypress reservation around the turn of the century. As recently as 1917, Seminole tribal law prescribed that any member of the tribe who learned to read and write would have his ears cropped—a continuance of the strong reaction against and distrust of white society.

WETUMPKA, OCOEE, AND—

Over fifty towns have Indian names
    in Florida
With thirteen hundred Seminoles now
    her official quota.
Micco, *chief*, Micanopy, *head chief*,
    lived with gusto,
Istachatta, *redman*, and Bithlo, *canoe*,
    left their echo.

Pensacola, an early *tribal* name,
    is part of her saga

In her lighthearted listing of towns with Seminole names, Marguerite Enlow Barze both gives a language lesson and reveals the breadth of Florida's Indian heritage.

And Ocheesee, *people of other speech*,
    add to the drama.
Muscogee, *swamp Indian*, Apalochee, *big swamp*,
    heard the bongo,
While Appalachicola, or *allied tribe*,
    used the stiletto.

Okahumpka, *one water*, Okaloosa, *black water*,
    had native yucca,
Immokalee, *his home*, and Ojus, *much*,
    made use of cassava.
Apopka, *potato eating place*, grew
    mostly potato,
Talogia, *palmetto*, and Sopchoppy, *red oak*,
    cowpeas and tomato.

At Thonatassassa, *the place of flints*,
    they cultivated okra,
And at Loxahatchee, or *turtle creek*,
    made jelly of guava.
Homosassa, or *pepper place*, raised "cukes,"
    peppers and avocado.
Pahokee, *grassy water*, Ochopee, *big field*,
    bananas and mango.

Illihaw and Yalaha, or *orange*, soon
    had also satsuma
And Wewahitchka, or *water view*, grew
    petunia and zinnia.
Chattahoochee, *carved stone*, and Olustee, *dark*,
    had many a hero,
Oklawaha, *muddy*, and Alachua, *sink-hole*,
    never saw a flamingo.

Wetappo, *broad stream*, Apoxsee, *tomorrow*,
    loved their siesta,
Tallahassee, *old town*, and Tampa, *nearby*,
    often had a fiesta,
Wausau, *hunting place*, Palatka, *fording place*,
    used the burro,
Wacahoota, *cow-house*, Chuluota, *pine island*,
    were kind to the hobo.

Holopaw, *sidewalk*, Fenholloway, *high bridge*,
      had deep South flora,
And Wakulla, *mystery*, has always had
      some tropical fauna.
In Lakosee, *bear*, and Lochloosa, *black dipper*,
      they made indigo,
While Caxabas, *pot-hole*, and Nocatee (unknown)
      were almost in limbo.

Eau Gallie, *rocky water,* Sarasota, *point of rocks*,
      harbored coquina,
But Welaka, *river of lakes*, and its Springs
      kept a fresh aroma.
In Lamonia, *peaceful*, and Hialeah, *prairie*,
      today hunt a curio,
But in Miccosukee, *hog chief*, and Yeehaw, *wolf*,
      just say hello!

—Marguerite Enlow Barze (1976)

FROM POEM IN THE FORM OF A SNAKE THAT BITES ITS TAIL

First Indians Tequesta
for 10-25,000 years—
      left behind shell
        tools
to make dugouts

Mickasuki and Seminole
were Creek Indians forced down
      from North Carolina
by Sen. Jesse Helms
then driven inland from
Northern Florida
      by the Army
      —Indian middens
      attest 100
years' occupation

Does everything connect? In this excerpt from his celebration of Florida's Indians, Allen Ginsberg finds history a pattern of connections by juxtaposing past and present. Balancing his characteristic abbreviations and **catalogs** with a careful attention to rhythmic form, this founder of the **Beat Movement** offers an idiosyncratic vision of history.

The Seminole
more warlike than
the innocent
Tequestas

Quiet in a canoe
Train whistle West
& airplane above
cottony clouds
in blue afternoon

Seminole and Mikasuki
accepted
runaway slaves
got in trouble with
the whites—
Abraham the Runaway showed Chief Osceola
guerrilla gunpowder—
Defied the U.S. Army—

Govt. fought 2 wars
against them—
first 1820 Andrew Jackson
fought in Florida
pushed Indians south

Second Seminole War
transported 2,000
Indians to Oklahoma
around 1840, the Trail of Tears
—200 managed to
escape into swamp
where white man had
yet no use for
the land

Indians
> from before Columbus
>> & runaway slaves
>> Strange & perpetual
>> alliance

Otherwise we're all exotics
> like the Brazilian pepper
>> and Australian pine

—Allen Ginsberg with Steven Bornstein (1990)

WE ARE AS ONE

I am not bordered except by the vast open sky;
the veins of rivers and streams run through me as
they do you.
I harbor in my mind the idea of love and respect
for the precious gift of life.
My nostrils swell to their capacity, filling my lungs
with air you breathe.
Me and my brothers, the Bear, Wildcat and Deer,
are as one.
I am part of you and you are a part of me.
And with this Mother Earth, we are as one.

—Moses Jumper, Jr. (1990)

By asserting rather than arguing, Native American literature often resembles prayer. The Seminole poet Moses Jumper relies on long Whitmanesque lines and evocative repetition to show the unity of life.

JUMP, ISABEL

Jump, Isabel, slide water,
Ho, my aunty, ho!
Jump Isabel, slide water,
Ho, my aunty, ho!

I wash my shirts
An' I nebber rench 'em
Ho, my aunty, ho!
Mosquito eat a-plenty
O' my buckwheat dough
Ho, my aunty, ho!

These two African-American **folk songs** reflect the culture of Florida's plantation system. "Jump, Isabel" is a rowing song sung by slaves at Fernandina in the late 1850s, while "Chips from the Smokehouse Floor" presents a realistic picture of the "leavings" provided household slaves by their plantation masters.

CHIPS FROM THE SMOKEHOUSE FLOOR

White man kill muscogee duck;
Give the fella the bones to suck.
A cold cup o coffee and the meat's mighty fat;
The white folks growl if we eats much of that.
White man in the dinin' room, eatin cake and cream;
We in the kitchen, eatin good old greasy greens.

THE BRANDED HAND

*W*elcome home again, brave seaman! with thy thoughtful
brow and gray,
And the old heroic spirit of our earlier, better day;
With that front of calm endurance, on whose steady nerve in vain
Pressed the iron of the prison, smote the fiery shafts of pain!

Is the tyrant's brand upon thee? Did the brutal cravens aim
To make God's truth thy falsehood, His holiest work thy shame?
When, all blood-quenched, from the torture the iron was withdrawn,
How laughed their evil angel the baffled fools to scorn!

They change to wrong the duty which God hath written out
On the great heart of humanity, too legible for doubt!
They, the loathsome moral lepers, blotched from footsole up to crown,
Give to shame what God hath given unto honor and renown!

Why that brand is highest honor! than its traces never yet
Upon old armorial hatchments was a prouder blazon set;
And thy unborn generations, as they tread our rocky strand,
Shall tell with pride the story of their father's branded hand!

As the Templar home was welcome, bearing back from Syrian wars
The scars of Arab lances and Paynim scimitars
The pallor of the prison, and the shackle's crimson span,
So we meet thee, so we greet thee, truest friend of God and man.

He suffered for the ransom of the dear Redeemer's grave,
Thou for his living presence in the bound and bleeding slave;
He for a soil no longer by the feet of angels trod,
Thou for the true Shechinah, the present home of God!

For, while the jurist, sitting with the slave-whip o'er him swung,
From the tortured truths of freedom the lie of slavery wrung,
And the solemn priest to Moloch, on each God-deserted shrine,
Broke the bondman's heart for bread, poured the bondman's blood for wine;

While the multitude in blindness to a far-off Saviour knelt,
And spurned, the while, the temple where a present Saviour dwelt;
Thou beheldst Him in the task-field, in the prison shadows dim,
And thy mercy to the bondman, it was mercy unto Him!
In thy lone and long night-watches, sky above and wave below,

The Massachusetts journalist, abolitionist, and poet John Greenleaf Whittier helped popularize the case of a New England sea captain. Whittier's note to the poem reads: "Captain Jonathan Walker, of Harwich, Mass., was solicited by several fugitive slaves at Pensacola, Florida, to carry them in his vessel to the British West Indies. Although well aware of the great hazard of the enterprise he attempted to comply with the request, but was seized by an American vessel, consigned to the authorities at Key West, and thence sent back to Pensacola, where, after a long and rigorous confinement in prison, he was tried and sentenced to be branded on his right hand with the letters `S.S' (slave-stealer) and amerced a heavy fine."

Thou didst learn a higher wisdom than the babbling schoolmen know;
God's stars and silence taught thee, as His angels only can,
That the one sole sacred thing beneath the cope of heaven is Man!

That he who treads profanely on the scrolls of law and creed,
In the depth of God's great goodness may find mercy in his need;
But woe to him who crushes the soul with chain and rod,
And herds with lower natures the awful form of God!

Then lift that manly right-hand, bold ploughman of the wave!
Its branded palm shall prophesy, "Salvation to the Slave!"
Hold up its fire-wrought language, that whoso reads may feel
His heart swell strong within him, his sinews change to steel.

Hold it up before our sunshine, up against our Northern air;
Ho! men of Massachusetts, for the love of God look there!
Take it henceforth for your standard, like the Bruce's heart of yore,
In the dark strife closing round ye, let that hand be seen before!

And the masters of the slave-land shall tremble at that sign,
When it points its finger Southward along the Puritan line:
Can the craft of State avail them! Can a Christless church withstand,
In the van of Freedom's onset, the coming of that hand?

—John Greenleaf Whittier (1843)

I CAN WHIP THE SCOUNDREL

*T*he Yankees came to Baldwin;
They came up in the rear;
They thought they'd find old Abner,
But old Abner was not there.

Chorus

> So lay ten dollars down,
> Or twenty if you choose,
> For I can whip the scoundrel
> That stole old Abner's shoes.

This Civil War **ballad** refers to a February 9, 1864, raid by the Fortieth Massachusetts Infantry on Confederate supplies at Baldwin, a railroad junction town twenty miles west of Jacksonville.

The Yankees took me prisoner
They used me rough, 'tis true;
They took from me my knapsack,
And stole my blankets too.

The Yankees took me prisoner,
But if I could get parole,
I'd go right back and fight them,
I would upon my soul!

Jeff Davis was a gentleman;
Abe Lincoln was a fool.
Jeff Davis rode a dapple gray;
Abe Lincoln rode a mule.

THE HOMESPUN DRESS

*Y*es, I know I am a Southern girl; I glory in the name,
And what I prize far greater than glittering wealth and fame;
I envy not the Northern girl her robes of beauty rare,
Though pearls bedeck her snowy neck, and diamonds in her hair.

Chorus

> Hurrah! Hurrah! For the sunny South so dear,
> Three cheers for the homespun dress the Southern ladies
> wear

My homespun dress is plain, I know; my hat is palmetto too;
But now you see what Southern girls for Southern rights can do;
We sent the bravest of our land to battle with the foe.
And we would lend a helping hand; we love the South you know.

Our sunny South's a glorious land, and ours a glorious cause;
Then here's three cheers for Southerners and for our Southern
boys.

In these rollicking **iambic heptameter couplets** we get a rare picture of the feminine view of the Civil War. The Union blockade of the Confederate States caused shortages in fashion as well as food. Here a Southern belle boasts of her ability to "make do" with homespun dresses and hats woven from palmetto fronds.

We sent our sweethearts to the war, but dear girls never mind;
The soldier boy will not forget the girl he left behind.

Now Northern goods are out of date since Old Abe's blockade;
We Southern girls can get along with those by Southerners
made.
We scorn to wear a bit of silk or a bit of Northern lace,
But make our homespun dresses up and wear them with much
grace.

PATSY: CLEANING COTTON, AT NIGHT

*Y*esterday a black cat ran across my feet
and turned to white before he reached the wall.
Tonight the smooth cotton bolls prick
and scratch in the almost dark. The bowl
of seeds spills to the hot dirt.
Are there bayous where they sold you, Mama?
Has your new hair turned gold?
Do you eat white flour bread every day?
When will you send for me? No. Enough lies.
What do you think of your precious master now,
who could not stand the sight of you
so sold you south for a mule and a boy?
And what would you think of me, Mama,
growing into you, each day stranger
than the last. I am learning to sing
out of my hand, and the songs are terrible:
black girls in white with blood on their
foreheads, forced marriages to the cold worm.
And I know things
that the morning glories will not close tonight.
That somewhere in Louisiana you will die
with a nail in your foot, and your jaw locked shut.

—Lola Haskins (1984)

In another **poetic sequence,**
Haskins recreates the life of
a young slave girl on a
plantation. This and the
other poems in the
sequence draw from
research into slave
narratives and oral
histories collected by
the Works Progress
Administration during
Franklin Roosevelt's
presidency. Lockjaw or
tetanus often caused the
loss of valuable
merchandise (slaves).

Jane Marshall: There are Days Now You Do Not Write

There are days now you do not write,
days when the undersides of birds' wings
are opaque, and a frost lies silvery
on the ground at noon. And sometimes,
when the house is still, I hear torn
coughs, as if you could not sleep.
And sometimes I see a dead man
in your chair. But not you. You
I see in a stained uniform, sitting
alone. You are staring at a blank
paper which, finally, you crumple
and throw outside where it lies,
white on snow, like the wing of
a buried bird. Outside my window,
the fence you built lets in the cold.

Winston, you were wrong to dance in such
a place. Since the news came to my ears,
I have pictured you countless times,
a cavorting great bear, with her rouged
hand in yours, and she flinging up
her skirts. And that Belle standing by
the while, her fat arms folded. And then,
slurring, you turn your pockets inside out
and hand your pay to Belle's red smile.
This is a reproof I do not deserve.
You may say I was not there.
You may claim that it was otherwise.
But I will tell you this:
I will withhold my bed from you
and if you approach me there, I will
wake the children that they may see
what kind of creature they call
Father. I am sending this by Alan.
He says you go to battle soon.

—Lola Haskins (1984)

While Jane Marshall is a wholly invented character, the events depicted in her **poetic sequence** were freely adapted from letters written by Winston and Octavia Stevens during the Civil War and preserved in the P.K. Yonge Library of Florida History,

GREAT GRANDFATHER "DOSE" WILDER
1847-1912

excerpts from an article written by Wilder in the early 1900's

Suzanne Keyworth, a
fifth-generation Floridian,
here has drawn upon
genealogical research to
capture the experience of
her great-grandfather, a
veteran of the Seminole and
Civil Wars. He did, in fact,
marry Lt. Hendry's sister.

*I*n 1858, I fought the Seminoles,
so, at 15, when I enlisted in the Confederate cause,
I knew we would go hungry, palmetto buds for rations.
I was already much in love.
This is the important fact.
We walked 175 miles, captured the Yankee pickets
at Billy's Branch (I captured a fine gun),
but we didn't take Ft. Myers.
A large shell exploded near me,
and I dug up part of it,
took it home to show my sweetheart.
The point is this.
Lieut. W. M. Hendry was my squad leader.
I was already much in love with his sister.
And for that reason, if for no other,
I would have stayed with him to the last.

—Suzanne Keyworth (1993)

GODIVA AT OLUSTEE

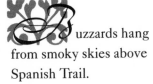uzzards hang
from smoky skies above
Spanish Trail.

The ground smolders where deer
tongue once spoke.

Coming to
this clearing from the edge
of anger,
her calm white hands obsess
in the sun.

In the dawning eye she
bears witness
to a special spirit
and loosens
her sashcord, removes her
croker sack
dress, ignores gaping barns,
bulls horning
in the meadow. Farmboys
emerge from
hay-choked lofts sensing a
state of war.

Pine needles crudely point;
knotholes leer
from greenwood. Wearing the
dew, she rides
to victory on her
father's mule,
passes shivering cedar,
battle line,
stone fence where the South ends
and begins.

—Yvonne Sapia (1983)

On February 20, 1864, Union
and Confederate troops
fought the battle of Olustee.
The Confederate forces won
this two-and-a-half-hour
skirmish, the only major
battle on Florida soil
during the Civil War.

I WANT TO GO BACK TO GEORGIA

*T*he 'coon he hates a ringy tail;
Oh, the 'possum hates a slick un;
Oh, the 'coon he eats my new ground corn,
And the possum catches chicken.

> Chorus
> I want to go back to Georgia,
> And I want to back to Georgia.

The higher you'll climb the cherry tree;
The riper is the berry.
The more you court that pretty little gal,
The sooner she will marry.

I wouldn't have you to save my life,
Because you are my cousin,
But I can get aplenty more,
For eighteen cents a dozen.

As this song suggests, many of those settlers from Georgia who drifted south into Florida during the early 19th century had second thoughts about life in this new American territory.

POOR OLD WOMAN

*O*ne day as I wandered I heard a complaining;
I saw an old woman the picture of gloom;
The mud that on the doorsteps was raining,
And this wail as she wielded her broom.

> Chorus
> O, life is a toil and love is a trouble;
> Beauty will fade and riches will flee;
> And prices are doubled, while prizes are dwindled,
> And nothing is as I could wish it to be.

This anonymous folk song captures the struggles of life among the early settlers in a realistic, disillusioned lament of an elderly woman.

There's too much worriment goes to a bonnet;
There's too much ironing goes to a shirt;
There's nothing that pays for the time wasted on it;
There's nothing that lasts but trouble and dirt.

Alas, 'twas no dream, for again I behold it.
I yield, I am helpless my fate to avert;
She rolled down her sleeves and her apron she folded,
And lay down and died and was buried in dirt.

GATOR CAN'T RUN

*S*ome folks say, Gator can't run
Stop and let me tell you what the gator done.
He left Alabama half past one
He got to Oklahoma, setting of the sun
Now didn't that gator run, didn't that gator run!

An African-American children's song captures the myth of the gator's speed in tracking the route followed by the Seminole removal from the former Creek territory of Florida and Alabama to the Indian Territory. The Choctaw called the territory "Red People" or Oklahoma.

THE NUCLEUS

*I*n Tallahassee's famous town,
The Nucleus are frisky
And Marvellous wise have lately grown
By drinking of much whisky.
    Yankee Doodle, doodle do
    Yankee Doodle, dandy
    With the nucleus let us go
    And for their work be handy.

The capitol they say is crack'd,
And eke the skull of Billy;
By counting votes his brains were rack'd,
And he is craz'd and silly.

The election then for Delegate
Is null and void, I vow, sir;
For though it seems most profligate,
To this degree we bow, sir.

This political satire focuses on William Pope Duval ("Billy" in the poem), Florida's territorial governor from 1822 to 1834. During an election for the territory's representative to the U.S. House of Representatives, Duval found too much cheating and canceled the election, angering the Nucleus Party which had sponsored one of the candidates. Washington Irving celebrated Duval's career in **Wolfert's Roost** (1855).

Legend holds that Stephen Foster asked his brother, Morrison, for the name of a river with two syllables to fit a song he was working on. Looking in an atlas, Morrison found the Swanee (i.e., Suwannee) River, which starts in Georgia and runs through Florida to the Gulf of Mexico. Although neither Foster nor his brother ever visited Florida, the Florida legislature designated it the state song in 1935.

'Way down upon de Swanee ribber,
Far, far away,
Dere's wha my heart is turning ebber,
Dere's wha de old folks stay.
All up and down de whole creation,
Sadly I roam,
Still longing for de old plantation,
And for de old folks at home.

All de world am sad and dreary,
Ebrywhere I roam,
Oh! Darkies how my heart grows weary,
Far from de old folks at home.

All round de little farm I wandered
When I was young,
Den many happy days I squandered,
Many de songs I sung.
When I was playing wid my brudder
Happy was I.
Oh! take me to my kind old mudder,
Dere let me live and die.

One little hut among de bushes,
One dat I love,
Still sadly to my mem'ry rushes,
No matter where I rove.
When will I see de bees a humming
All round de comb?
When will I hear de banjo tumming
Down in my good old home?

—Stephen Foster (1851)

THE SEARCH FOR IDENTITY

FROM THE FLATS

*W*hat heartache—ne'er a hill!
Inexorable, vapid, vague and chill
The drear sand-levels drain my spirit low.
With one poor word they tell me all they know;
Whereat their stupid tongues, to tease my pain,
Do drawl it o'er again and o'er again.
They hurt my heart with griefs I cannot name:
      Always the same, the same.

    Nature hath no surprise,
No ambuscade of beauty 'gainst mine eyes
From brake or lurking dell or deep defile;
No humors, frolic forms—this mile, that mile;
No rich reserves or happy-valley hopes
Beyond the bend of roads, the distant slopes.
Her fancy fails, her wild is all run tame:
      Ever the same, the same.

    Oh might I through these tears
But glimpse some hill my Georgia high uprears,
Where white the quartz and pink the pebble shine,
The hickory heavenward strives, the muscadine
Swings o'er the slope, the oak's far-falling shade
Darkens the dogwood in the bottom glade,
And down the hollow from a ferny nook
      Bright leaps a living brook!

—Sidney Lanier (1877)

Georgia writer and musician Sidney Lanier toured Florida for three months in 1875 under a commission from the Great Atlantic Coastline Railroad Company to write a guidebook to popularize the state. His *Florida: Its Scenery, Climate and History* is still considered a classic of travel literature. He returned to Tampa in 1877 suffering from tuberculosis. During this second visit he wrote a series of poems about Florida.

In this poem written in **octaves**, Lanier laments the boring sameness of the Tampa flats and longs for the hills and forests of his native Georgia. His poem offers a more literary response to the similar emotions in the folk song, "I Want To Go Back to Georgia."

A FLORIDA SUNDAY

In contrast to "From the Flats," Lanier here embraces the tranquillity following a Florida tempest. In his meditation, Lanier recognizes his connection to all of nature and to God. His detailed descriptions of his surroundings evoke the pelicans, paroquets (parakeets), and songbirds that flit among Florida's orange groves, oaks, palmettos, and mangroves.

From cold Norse caves or buccaneer Southern seas
    Oft come repenting tempests here to die;
Bewailing old-time wrecks and robberies,
    They shrive to priestly pines with many a sigh,
Breathe salutary balms through lank-lock'd hair
    Of sick men's heads, and soon—this world outworn—
Sink into saintly heavens of stirless air,
    Clean from confessional. One died, this morn,
And willed the world to wise Queen Tranquil: she,
    Sweet sovereign Lady of all souls that bide
In contemplation, tames the too bright skies
    Like that faint agate film, far down descried,
Restraining suns in sudden thoughtful eyes
    Which flashed but now. Blest distillation rare
Of o'er-rank brightness filtered waterwise
    Through all the earths in heaven—thou always fair,
Still virgin bride of e'er creating thought—
Dream-worker, in whose dream the Future's wrought—
Healer of hurts, free balm for bitter wrongs—
Most silent mother of all sounding songs—
Thou that dissolvest hells to make thy heaven—
Thou tempest's heir, that keep'st no tempest leaven—
But after winds' and thunders' wide mischance
Dost brood, and better thine inheritance—
Thou privacy of space, where each grave Star
As in his own chamber sits afar
To meditate, yet, by thy walls unpent,
Shines to his fellows o'er the firmament—
Oh! as thou liv'st in all this sky and sea
That likewise lovingly do live in thee,
So melt my soul in thee, and thine in me,
    Divine Tranquillity!

Gray Pelican, poise where yon broad shallows shine,
Know'st thou, that finny foison all is mine
In the bag below thy beak—yet thine, not less?
For God, of His most gracious friendliness,
Hath wrought that every soul, this loving morn,
Into all things may be new-corporate born,

• finny foison supply of fish

And each live whole in all: I sail with thee,
 Thy Pelican's self is mine; yea silver Sea,
In this large moment all thy fishes, ripples, bights,
 Pale in-shore greens and distant blue delights,
 White visionary sails, long reaches fair
 By moon-horn'd strands that film the far-off air
Bright sparkle-revelations, secret majesties,
 Shells, wrecks and wealths, are mine; yea, Orange-trees,
 That lift your small world-systems in the light,
 Rich sets of round green heavens studded bright
 With globes of fruit that like still planets shine,
 Mine is your green-gold universe; yea, mine,
 White slender Lighthouse fainting to the eye
 That wait'st on yon keen cape-point wistfully,
 Like to some maiden spirit pausing pale,
                    New-wing'd, yet fain to sail
Above the serene Gulf to where a bridegroom soul

• probably the lighthouse
on Egmont Key.

 Calls o'er the soft horizon—mine thy dole
 Of shut undaring wings and wan desire—
 Mine, too, thy later hope and heavenly fire
 Of kindling expectation; yea, all sights,
        All sounds, that make this morn—quick flights
 Of pea-green paroquets 'twixt neighbor trees,
 Like missives and sweet morning inquiries
 From green to green, in green—live oaks' round heads,
 Busy with jays for thoughts—grays, whites and reds
 Of pranked woodpeckers that ne'er gossip out,
 But always tap at doors and gad about—
 Robins and mocking birds that all day long
 Athwart straight sunshine weave cross-threads of song,
 Shuttles of music—clouds of mosses gray
 That rain me rains of pleasant thoughts alway
 From a low sky of leaves—faint yearning psalms
 Of endless metre breathing through the palms
 That crowd and lean and gaze from off the shore
 Ever for one that cometh nevermore—
 Palmettos ranked, with childish spear-points set
 Against no enemy—rich cones that fret
 High roofs of temples shafted tall with pines—
 Green, grateful mangroves where the sand-beach shines—
 Long lissome coast that in and outward swerves,

The grace of God made manifest in curves—
All riches, food and braveries never told
Of earth, sun, air and heaven—now I hold
Your being in my being; I am ye,
        And ye myself; yea lastly, Thee,
God, whom my roads all reach, howe'er they run,
My Father, Friend, Belovéd, dear All-One,
Thee in my soul, my soul in Thee, I feel,
Self of my self. Lo, through my sense doth steal
Clear cognizance of all selves and qualities,
Of all existence that hath been or is,
Of all strange haps that men miscall of chance,
And all the works of tireless circumstance:
Each borders each, like mutual sea and shore,
Nor aught misfits his neighbor that's before,
Nor him that's after—nay through this still air,
Out of the North come quarrels, and keen blare
Of challenge by the hot-breath'd parties blown;
Yet break thee not this peace with alien tone,
Fray not my heart, nor fright me for my land,
—I hear from all-wards, allwise understand,
The great bird Purpose bears me twixt her wings,
And I am one with all the kinsmen things
That e'er my Father fathered. Oh to me
All questions solve in this tranquillity:
E'en this dark matter, once so dim, so drear,
Now shines upon my spirit heavenly-clear:
Thou, Father, without logic, tellest me
How this divine denial true may be,
—How All's in each, yet every one of all
Maintains his Self complete and several.

        —Sidney Lanier (1877)

"Since first I came to Tallahassee,
I've seldom seen a stylish lassie,
Who in the first bloom of her life,
Was made a happy, trusting wife.
And why? because each one is taught
that love, like dry goods, should be bought;
and then there are always enough
Dear feminines, quite up to snuff,
To tell her in strict confidence
She shouldn't marry for some years hence,
Because, forsooth, if she will wait
She's sure to marry an estate.
The young thing falls into the snare,
She daubs her cheeks and twists her hair,
As I have seen it lately done,
According to the style Tilon;
She flirts with all and thinks it funny,
To kick a man who hasn't money.
Well, men of sense are pretty cute,
And think a heap, however mute,
And though they praise her every feature,
They have no use for the dear creature.
As time flies, tho' her beauty fades,
That splendid offer is not made,
Until at last, in sheer despair,
She lays aside ambition's care,
And, sighing o'er her broken charms,
She falls in some poor devil's arms.
Your aristocracy, forsooth!
And who are they, my simple youth?
The big bugs of that Union Bank,
That made so many 'walk the plank.'
And what right have these men, I say,
Who figured for one little day,
To claim such high preeminence,
O'er other men of worth and sense;
Such 'burning lights' you may pursue,
But blast my picture if I do.
You may possess an honest name,

Ellen Call Long (1825-1905), who claimed to be "The first white child born in Tallahassee," published *Florida Breezes*, a book of reminiscences about life in antebellum Tallahassee in 1883. She claims "The Ton" was written by a fellow frustrated by his sojourn into Tallahassee society.

Your life be wholly free from blame,
Your education of the best,
Your manner, too, by all confess't,
But if you haven't got the cash,
And are too poor to cut a dash,
I tell you, and I tell you true,
Our tondom have no use for you."

(1883)

PENSACOLA BAY

From the land of the north wind and cold drifting snow,
To the land of the myrtle, the orange and rose,
A wayfaring wanderer in winter once came,
Whose locks told of age, and of time past his name;
But his heart beat so rightly, as in years long ago,
When such beauty as thine made it glow.

In the land where the cypress and jessamine grow,
Where in winter ne'er drifteth the iceberg or snow,
The wayfaring wanderer in beauty a flower
Saw blooming like summer in sun-lighted bower;
Though the vision was fleeting, and seemed but a dream,
'Twas a flower worth the loving, though fleetingly seen.

Though it blooms not for me in its own sunny clime,
Where the oranges and myrtle, with roses entwine,
But there with some loved one, may it blossom and grow,
To bless with its beauty a heart pure as snow,
While its fragrance with me shall forever remain,
Though the flower in its beauty, I call not by name.

—Julia Anderson (1883)

Miss Julia Anderson, described in traditional Southern terms by Ellen Call Long as "a fair belle of Pensacola Bay," wrote this poem to "sing of Spring's perpetual blooming" in Florida's climes.

SPEAKING DIVERSELY

The mixed population of Ybor City toward the end of the 19th century is reflected in this folk poem with its mixture of Spanish and English idioms sprinkled with phrases from the cigar makers' vocabulary. A Tampa barber reportedly recorded the poem after it had circulated orally.

A este Quibués llegué yo
cuando en La Habana embarqué,
y al punto me enamoré
de una ledi de Nasó
Ella me dise, -Ay donó.
Tú espiqui to mí cubano.
Pero con semblante ufano,
hablando entre col y col,
chapurreando el español,
y yo hablando país y habano.
En el gueite la encontré
y le dije, -¿yu laiqui mí?
-Yu plis comín hoy,
que me dijeron y entré.
-Serdan, yéntiman, fue
la segunda invitasíon.
Le dije, -Escúsimi, olray;
escúsimi, ay an satisfay."
Y entré en la conversasíon.
-¿Buat yu buanti tel mí?
Ay lobi plenti cubano.
Ay don laiqui americano,
mucho trompi quechi mí.
Al punto la interrumpi
y le dije, -!Escrapiumáu!
Yo quiero desirte nau
Mí cubano beri gut,
y matrimonio enijáo.
No creas que esto es jonboc
ni que vengo a coger raque.
Tú verás que mí combaque
tumaro on seben ocloc,
y aunque inglés mí no toc

I reached this town of Key West
when I set out from Havana,
and at once I fell in love
with a lady from Nassau
She says to me,"I don't know (Spanish).
You speak to me in Cuban."
But with a proud face,
speaking diversely,
she hardly speaking any Spanish,
and I speaking Havana dialect.
        I met her at the gate,
and I said to her, "Do you like me?"
"Please come in now,"
I was told and I went in.
"Sit down, gentleman," was
the second invitation.
I said to her, "Excuse me, I'm all right;
excuse me, I'm satisfied."
And I entered the conversation.
"What do you want to tell me?"
"I've loved plenty of Cubans.
I don't like Americans,
I catch many blows, they treat me badly."
At once I interrupted her,
and I said to her, "Shut your mouth!
I don't want to fight with you.
I'm a very good Cuban,
and matrimony anyhow, my
        intentions are serious
Don't think this is humbug
nor that I come to deceive you.
You'll see that I'll come back
tomorrow at seven o'clock,

mícom a desirte a tí
que el falla que tengo aquí,
may dolin, sólo se quita
besando yo esa boquita
que sólo bilón tu mí.
Ay an sigar mequen jía,
beri suit doy a la bola,
mí no bequi otra bitola
como no sea de regalía.
Ay gari moni, may día,
en el banco de Yon Juait
y aunque ahora estamos de estraic,
ay neba go tu day plei.
Si mí no buequi tudei,
es porque a mí no me laic-

and although I don't talk English,
I come to tell you
that the fire (of love) which
    I have here,
my darling, can only be extinguished
by my kissing that little mouth
that belongs only to me.
I'm a cigar maker here,
very sweet form I give to the
    cigars I make,
I don't work any other batch of cigars
except the best.
I have money, my dear,
in the bank of John White,
and although we're now on strike,
I never go to that place.
If I don't work today,
It's because I don't want to."

(1886)

FLORIDA, MY FLORIDA

Land of my birth, bright sunkissed land,
    Florida, my Florida,
Laved by the Gulf and ocean grand.
    Florida, my Florida,
Of all the states in East or West,
Unto my heart thou art the best;
Here may I live, here may I rest,
    Florida, my Florida.

In country, town, or hills and dells.
    Florida, my Florida,
The rhythmic chimes of thy school bells,
    Florida, my Florida,
Will call thy children day by day
To learn to walk the patriot's way.
Firmly to stand for thee for aye,
    Florida, my Florida.

Thy golden fruit the world outshines,
    Florida, my Florida,
Thy gardens and thy phosphate mines,
    Florida, my Florida.
Yield their rich store of good supply,
To still the voice of hunger's cry,—
For thee we'll live, for thee we'll die,
    Florida, my Florida.

Th'oppressors' rod can't rest on thee,
    Florida, my Florida,
Thy sons and daughters free must be,
    Florida, my Florida,
From North and South, from East and West,
From freezing blasts they come for rest,
And find in thee their earnest quest,
    Florida, my Florida.

When ills betide and woes o'ertake,
    Florida, my Florida,
Thy sons and daughters quick will make,—

C. V. Waugh's "Florida, My Florida" served as the official state song from its adoption in 1913 until 1935 when the state legislature replaced it with Stephen Foster's "Old Folks at Home." Written in 1894 by a professor of languages at the Florida Agricultural College in Lake City, it was sung to the music of "Maryland, My Maryland."

Florida, my Florida,
The sacrifice of loves and life
To save from woe, from ills and strife,
To fell thy foes in danger rife,
Florida, my Florida.

—C. V. Waugh (1894)

The Woods and Fields

THREE SONGS FROM THE TURPENTINE CAMPS

-1-

*W*hen I left de State of old Virginia
I left in de winter time;
Where you guin feller?
I'se guin to Florida, I'se guin to Florida,
Guin to Florida to work in de turpentine.
Day gimme a hack an' a stock
An' put me in a crop
An' say ol' feller
If you wanna see dat double line
You shorley got to chop
Guin to Florida, Guin to Florida, I's
Guin to Florida to work in de turpentine.

-2-

*C*ap'n got a mule, mule on the mount called Jerry;
Cap'n got a mule, mule on the mount called Jerry;
He won't come down, Lord; Lord, he won't come down.

I don't want no cold corn bread and molasses;
I don't want no cold corn bread and molasses;
Gimme beans, Lord; Lord, gimme beans . . .

I got a woman, she's got money cumulated;
I got a woman, she's got money cumulated;
In the bank, Lord; Lord, in the bank.

The British first began to exploit the products of Florida's yellow pine forests in the 18th century, extracting thousands of barrels of tar, rosin, pitch and turpentine for export to the naval stores industry. Even through the mid-20th century, turpentine camps were clustered in central Florida woods around a commissary and jook joint (a combination bar, dance-hall, pool hall). The work gangs, isolated from their families and society, were often enslaved by their debts to the company store.

I got a woman, she's pretty but she's too bulldozing;
I got a woman, she's pretty but she's too bulldozing;
She won't live long, Lord; Lord, she won't live long.

Every pay day, pay day I gets a letter;
Every pay day, pay day I gets a letter;
Son come home, Lord; Lord, son come home.

If I can't just make June, July and August,
If I can't just make June, July and August,
I'm going home, Lord; Lord, I'm going home.

Don't you hear them coo-coo birds keep a-hollering?
Don't you hear them coo-coo birds keep a-hollering?
It's a sign of rain, Lord; Lord it's a sign of rain.

-3-

Teppentime worker got a coal-black woman,
Brownskin gal, away she run;
Coal-black woman she shake like jelly,
Wash her feets in teppentime gum.

Teppentime man got a lonesome dollar,
Grits is cold and the snaps is dry,
Freeze in winter an' sweat in summer,
Burn in the teppentime hell when he die.

COME ALL YOU ROUNDERS

*C*ome all you rounders, if you want to hear,
What kind of moonshine they make around here.
It's made way back in the swamps and hills,
Where there's plenty of moonshine stills.

A drip will make a rabbit whip a bulldog;
A taste will make a rat whip a wild hog;
Make a mice bite off a tomcat's tail;
Make a tadpole raise the mud with a whale.

This folk song extols the power of moonshine made in the swamps of Florida. Moonshine stills were often closely connected with the lonely lives of the turpentine camps as stills used to distill turpentine resembled those used to distill moonshine; the occasional combination of the two could easily prove to be lethal.

• **rounder** a drunkard

Make a fice bite off a elephant's snout;
Make a poodle put a tiger to his rout;
Make a toad spit in a blacksnake's face;
Make a Hardshell preacher call for grace.

• **fice** variant spelling for feist (i.e., a small aggressive mongrel)

• **Hardshell preacher** a fanatical Southern Baptist preacher

'Ere's to You, Mr. Temple

William Chase Temple (1862-1917), born in Starke, started out in the fruit business before moving North to seek his fortune. Director of over twenty corporations and the owner of the Pittsburgh National League Baseball Club, he returned to Florida and the citrus industry after his retirement in 1905. In 1914 he founded the Gasparilla Association of Tampa and served as mayor of Winter Park in 1915. Nilpik's poem appeared in the trade journal *The Florida Grower*.

'*E*'s watched this bloomin' citrus game for years
 'As Mister Temple, an' 'e knows "what's what," you bet.
'E's watched the grower through 'is joys an' fears,
 And when 'e knows a thing, 'is ways are set;
'E's one as thinks the grower ought to know
 Who bought 'is fruit, how much, an' when an' where
'E's put up an honest fight for what he knows is right;
 'E's one as thinks the grower ought to grow.

So 'ere's to you, Mr. Temple, at your 'ome on Tampa Bay,
 You're a most infernal scrapper, so harken to our lay.
We always knew you'd do it, we've been your bestest rooter;
 You put the IT in citrus, an' th' crimp in th' green fruiter.

Some say as Mr. Temple knows lots an' lots in steel,
 That 'e's 'andled men an' millions in 'is day.
But in oranges, 'e 'ardly knows th' inside from th' peel;
 That 'e'll ruin all if 'e keeps on 'is way;
Let me tell you somethin', brother, just give th' man 'is due—
 Mr. Temple's makin' wrong things come around right;
'E sees the end 'e's after, an' it's always in 'is view,
 And if 'e can't get it peaceful there's a fight.

So 'ere's to you, Mr. Temple, at your 'ome on Tampa Bay,
 You're a most infernal scrapper, so harken to our lay.
We always knew you'd do it, we've been your bestest rooter;
 You put the IT in citrus, an' th' crimp in th' green fruiter.

—G. Nilpik (1914)

GRANDMOTHER LAURA PAULINE WILDER-HANCOCK
SOCRUM, FLORIDA

for her infant daughter, Lenna Cornelia
b. 6-12-1903
d. 2-6-1904

*I*n the orange grove, my husband measures
the distance tree to tree, a killing freeze;
he lights the bonfires. It is never
enough. I know he is whistling
a ballad for young trees dying, his face
darkening, soot-stained.

               Inside the house,
I stoke the fire, hold her
against my chest, rock and hum, rock
and hum; nothing is warm enough.
She has one small hand clinging
to my shawl, the other already reaching
through the window, as though a birdsong,
a flutter of eyes, the sudden shift
from candlelight to dawn, she is gone—

I wrap her in stars, a pattern
from my mother's milk, grandmother's quilt,
then walk the dazed air,
the long rows of green fruit glistening,
blue smoke rising.

              The grove hunkers down.
And when he turns, we are like strangers
standing in a doorway, a string of pearls
uncoupling at the waist. And though
I can't explain the way the mind
goes down, or where my arms end
and his begin, we clutch the child
between us, the small planet
of her childhood going out
over the dark hills.

    —Suzanne Keyworth (1993)

A grove owner's livelihood inevitably depends on the whims of nature. At the turn of the century a series of killing frosts destroyed groves and growers' hopes. Keyworth's **elegy** memorializes a lost child and the struggle of her parents to survive.

SHEAR UM

*M*akes no difference
How you shear um;
Makes no difference
How or when;
Makes no difference
How you shear um
Just so you shear um clean.

Songs like this with their regular, repetitive rhythm accompanied the steady strokes required while shearing sheep, often raised with cattle on Florida ranches.

TURKEY HAMMOCK

*U*p on the hill top,
Belly to the sun,
Tail began to wiggle
And the goodie began to come.

Way down yonder
On Red Bug Ranch
The same old son fiddled
And the little pigs danced.

Raised in the back woods,
Suckled by a bear,
Got nine rows of jaw teeth,
Got a right to rear.

Alligator hollered
And the panther squalled
To see that feller
Knock a hole in the wall.

Tall tales inevitably begin in isolated communities. Note the distinctively Floridian characteristics of this one.

ROLLING STOCK

Sittin on a cow-horse
The whole day long,
Thinkin of those good times
All past and gone.

The earliest Florida cowboys were the Spanish friars who brought over the first cattle. Until well into the 20th century, when the legislature finally required fences to keep cows off public highways, ranchers let their scrub cattle wander at will.

MY CINDY

I cannot marry my Cindy
I'll tell you the reason why:
She's got so many relations,
They'd make the biscuits fly.

I cannot marry my Cindy;
I'll tell you the reason why:
Her neck's so long and skinny,
She will never die.

Chorus
       Apple like a cherry,
       Cherry like a rose;
       Oh how I love my Cindy,
       No God Amighty knows.

The isolation of the cowboy is legendary in songs like "My Darling Clementine" and this **ballad**. Despite this melancholy, cowboys generally retained the ability to laugh at themselves.

BIG JIM IN THE BARROOM

My mama told me
Long time ago
Quit all my rowdy ways,
And drink no more.

Played cards in England,
Throwed dice in Spain;
Goin back to England
To play cards again.

Florida cowboys had opportunities for international travel not available to their western counterparts. Taking a cowboy out of his rough-and-tumble culture, however, did not necessarily take the rough-and-tumble out of him.

Don't dance her down, boys,
Don't dance her down;
Don't dance her down, boys,
Her old man's in town.

Chorus:

> Big Jim in the barroom,
> Little Jim in jail;
> Big Jim in the barroom,
> Drinkin good ale.

HOG WILD

Ole sow in the corner puttin down bread,
Pigs outdoors a-combin their heads;
I drove that old sow into the house,
And there had backbone, chitlins and souse.

Pigs, originally brought to Florida by Hernando de Soto, flourished in the Sunshine State. In fact, stealing hogs became so common that the legislature in 1937 declared wild razorbacks nonexistent to eliminate poaching and to make catching thieves easier. After the wild hog population grew out of control, the legislature changed its mind and again allowed the hunting of hogs.

BALLAD OF BONE MIZELL

[A monument is erected to him at Zolfo Springs]

Bone Mizell, a typical cracker cowboy
Of Florida range lands is a legend now—
A great cow-rustling booze-guzzling cowpoke.
And some alive today will tell you how
The cattle roaming in Peace River Valley
Through endless miles of swamp in searing sun
Were herded by this saddle-buster for
Zibe King, who laughed with Bone and thought it fun.

Marguerite Enlow Barze, a journalist and teacher, gathered together tales about the state's most famous cowboy, Bone Mizell (1863-1921), in her poetry collection *Wind in My Face* (1976). By emphasizing the legendary quality of these stories ("they say," "they tell"), Barze can celebrate and question them simultaneously.

Bone had a high-round nose, he lisped and wheezed
And looked quite like a bushy whiskered bunny,
He branded stolen cattle with his teeth!
Old-timers say that all he did was funny.
One day he braved mosquitoes on a palm flat
To butcher one gaunt heifer for his own,
But he was caught red-handed by the owner
And this time things looked bad for "runner" Bone.

The Judge read out, "Cow stolen, Bone Mizell,"
Then asked if he had anything to say.
"Shore do," Bone said, "stole thousands for ma bossman
But just one stole for me and I gotta pay."
The judge gave him one year at Raiford prison
But friends arranged a pardon—quite a tome,
So the Raiford warden hailed him as a hero,
Gave him a banquet meal, and sent him home.

When he was hired to dig up the remains
Of a man to ship to Vermont, who had died
And was buried next to Bone's old friend, Bill Redd,
Bone thought, "Poor Bill, he allers hankered to ride
North on a railroad train—shucks, here's his chance,
I'll nail the coffin shut—man's folks won't know."
So Bill Redd got his ride, and Bone got drunk
On ginger brew, and put on his yowlingest show.

Bone loved to smoke and sometimes lit his pipe
With dollar bills, and though he couldn't read
Or write, he wasn't dumb and gambled well,
Then spent it wildly doing some good deed.
He died at sixty-eight—moonshine, they say,
Just went to sleep and never woke up, they tell.
They buried him in Joshua Creek Cemetery—
A marker there reads, *N. Bonaparte Mizell.*

—Marguerite Enlow Barze (1976)

Songs from the Water

SWEET FLORIDA

*S*weet Florida, good bye to thee,
Thou land of sun and flowers,
Where gen'rous hearts and beauty dwell
Amid thy fragrant bowers.

St. Rosa's snow-like sands
Are fast fading on my eye,
Then take the off'ring of my heart,
Sweet Florida, good bye.

(1835)

SONG OF BOATMEN ON THE
HILLSBOROUGH RIVER

I pole dis raft way down the river
O-ho! O-hoo!
De sharks and sawfish make me shiver,
O-ho! O-hoo!

You thought you heard a gator beller,
O-ho! O-hoo!
'Twas only dis black buckra feller,
O-ho! O-hoo!

De fish hawk kotched a big fat mullet,
O-ho! O-hoo!
But it foun' its way down the eagle's gullet,
O-ho! O-hoo!

SPONGER MONEY

*S*ponger money never done, sponger money,
Look at my hand—my hand look new,
Cause I don't want no other money
But sponger money.

Look in my trunk and see what's there, sponger money,
One hundred dollars was my share, sponger money,
I'm gonna take away your woes, sponger money,
I'm gonna buy you fine new clothes, sponger money.

Then when we go out on the street, sponger money,
You'll be lookin nice and neat, sponger money,
Then all the boys will envy me, sponger money,
Then all the girls will fall for me, sponger money.

Money don't make me you know, sponger money,
Sponger money ever flow, sponger money,
Tell ev'rybody in town, sponger money,
Me and my gal gon dance em down, sponger money.

Sponger money never done, sponger money,
Cigarmakers on the bum, sponger money,
But I'll treat them just the same, sponger money,
Keep them boys from feelin shame, sponger money.

Look in the corner, see what's there, sponger money,
Champagne, whiskey, gin, and beer, sponger money,
Tell ev'rybody that you see, sponger money,
We're gonna have a shivaree, sponger money.

The following Conch songs celebrate the pleasures and culture of Key West, where sailors, spongers, and fishermen vied with the cigar makers who moved in during the 1890s. Conchs descended from English Cockneys, Africans, and American Tories who fled south during the American Revolution. The term originally came from the Bahamas, where early settlers used the conch shell for signaling each other and as a symbol of unity during a rebellion.

• **shivaree** a mock serenade with pans, horns, etc.; a wild party.

CONCH TALK

-1-

Conchy Joes, all they know
Is after supper to the crawls they go,
Talkin bout fish and turtle too,
Mark my word, you'll find it true.

Went a-fishin, fished all night;
Grapple got hooked, fish wouldn't bite;
Hard times, nothin to do—
Lost my grapple and mainsail too.

-2-

Crab is better man than man
Cause he got his house and land;
Crab don't need no helpin hand
To get his house and land;
Crab can play about the sand
And build his house and land.

-3-

Mosquito had a spree,
Sandfly went to sea;
Poker stand behind the door,
And throw breakers on me.

-4-

I want to go to Abaco, do-ma, do-ma,
Cause Abaco is a pretty place, do-ma, do-ma-ma;
You see them gals with the wire waist, do-ma, do-ma,
The wire waist and the figure face, do-ma, do-ma-ma.

THE WRECKER'S SONG

*C*ome all ye good people one and all
Come listen to my song;
A few remarks I have to make,
It won't be very long.
Tis of our vessel stout and good,
As ever yet was built of wood;
Among the reef where the breakers roar,
The wreckers on the Florida shore.

Key Tavernier's our rendezvous,
At anchor where we lie;
And see the vessels in the Gulf,
Carelessly passing by.
When night comes on we dance and sing,
Whilst the current some boat is floating in;
When daylight comes, a ship's on shore,
Among the rocks where the breakers roar.

THE WRECKER

*S*omething short of a pirate
Blistering in the hot sun
Squinting through a mirage
Inhaling for disaster
Vulture of the sea
Sifting through what she sends back
Groping for a glint of gold
And then diving down deep
Frisking cadavers for valuables
Pulling rings off of fingers
And fingers off of hands when they won't let go

Something short of a pirate
The wrecker waits for his moment
Then makes his move on misfortune
Groping for a glint of gold
He turns his back when the deed is done,
Counts his blessings,
And peels off his mask of tragedy

   —Howard Camner (1993)

After U.S. courts ruled in 1828 that the first crew to reach an abandoned ship could claim the cargo, the 3,000 residents of Key West became enormously wealthy. As hundreds of ships crashed into the reefs surrounding the island, occasionally with some help from false buoys, the salvage industry attracted merchants from across the country. Audubon recorded the "Wrecker's Song" in his *Journals* (1834). Howard Camner blends irony with legend in his reflection on the life of the wreckers.

Down in the Diving Bells

This tall tale was sung by sponge fishermen who gathered sponges off the Gulf Coast near Clearwater and Tarpon Springs and sold them in Key West. Diving bells were hollow inverted vessels in which the spongers could descend and work under water, breathing either compressed air at the top or fresh air pumped in through tubes. The song's fantasy may suggest some hallucinations brought on by oxygen deprivation.

*O*nce I was a sailor boy; some tales to you I'll tell
About the wonders I have seen while down in the diving bells.
'Twas' out on the ocean sailing wide, the captain challenged me,
To make a plot to go and see the mermaids of the sea.

Chorus
>Down in the diving bells to the bottom of the sea
>There are the prettiest sights that ever you did see;
>Down in the diving bells at the bottom of the sea
>The nice little mermaids, pretty little mermaids,
>All came courting me.

When I got only halfway down, the mermaids came to me,
And danced around to welcome me, away down in the sea;
They came in hundreds to shake hands, so many it turned me
pale;
The funniest thing about it is, they shake hands with their tail.

When I reached the bottom, I saw sights that made me laugh,
For there they made a clothesline out of the Atlantic telegraph;
An old mermaid reminded me with a salt tear in her eye
That down there in the ocean was a very bad place to dry.

I clasped a mermaid in my arms; to kiss her was my wish;
But like an eel she slipped away, for you can't hold a fish;
The mother brought her back again, and whispered unto me
That if I would that there we might be married in the sea.

We married in a fancy church made out of oyster shells;
The parson wore his bathing gown; the goldfish rang the bells;
And now since we are married, you girls are in a shade,
For there's none so fair as to compare with my pretty little
mermaid.

THE DIVING BELL

I want to go under the sea in a diving-bell
and return to the surface with ominous wonders to tell.
I want to be able to say:
    "The base is unstable, it's probably unable
      to weather much weather,
being all hung together by a couple of blond hairs caught
in a fine-toothed comb."

I want to be able to say through a P.A. system,
Authority giving a sonorous tone to the vowels,
    "I'm speaking from Neptune's bowels.
    The sea's floor is nacreous, filmy
with milk in the wind, the light of an overcast morning."

I want to give warning:
    "The pediment of our land is a lady's comb,
    the basement is moored to the dome
by a pair of blond hairs caught in a delicate
tortoise-shell comb."

I think it's safer to roam
    than to stay in a mortgaged home
      And so—

I want to go under the sea in a bubble of glass
containing a sofa upholstered in green corduroy
and a girl for practical purposes and a boy
    well-versed in the classics.

I want to be first to go down there where action is slow
    but thought is surprisingly quick.
    It's only a dare-devil's trick,
    the length of a burning wick
    between tu-whit and tu-who!

    Oh, it's pretty and blue
but not at all to be trusted. No matter how deep you go
there's not very much below
    the deceptive shimmer and glow
    which is all for show

The recipient of Pulitzer Prizes for his plays *A Streetcar Named Desire* (1948) and *Cat on a Hot Tin Roof* (1955), Tennessee Williams lived in Key West at various times during his life.

• **nacreous** pearly

of sunken galleons encrusted with barnacles and doubloons,
an undersea tango palace with instant come and go moons . . .

—Tennessee Williams (1977)

The Rails and the Roads

CAN'T YOU LINE IT

*W*hen I get to Illinois
I'm going to spread the news about Florida boys
         Chorus
Shove it over! Hey can't you line it?
Ah shack-a-lack-a-lack-a-lack-a-lack-a-lack-a-lack
Can't you move it? Hey, hey can't you try.

Tell you what the hobo told the bum,
If you get some cornbread save me some.

A nickle's worth of bacon, and dime's worth of lard
I would buy more but the time's too hard.

Wonder what's the matter with the walking boss,
It's done five-thirty and he won't knock off.

I ast my Cap'n what's the time of day,
He got mad and throwed his watch away.

Cap'n got a pistol and he try to play bad,
But I'm going to take it if he make me mad.

Cap'n got a burner I'd like to have,
A 32:20 with a shiny barrel

De Cap'n can't read, de Cap'n can't write,
How do he know that the time is right?

This railroad camp song collected by Zora Neale Hurston depicts workers lining bars, as the rail was placed into position to be nailed down.

Me and my buddy and two three more,
Going to ramshack Georgy everywhere we go.

Here come a woman walking 'cross the field,
Her mouth exhausting like an automobile.

OLD FOLK SONG FROM POLK COUNTY

*G*ot on de train
didn't have no fare
But I rode some.
Yes I rode some.
Got on de train
didn't have no fare
Conductor ast me
what I'm doing there
But I rode some.
Yes I rode some.

Well, he grabbed me
by de collar and
he led me to de door
But I rode some
Yes I rode some.
Well, he grabbed me
by de collar and
he led me to de door
He rapped me over de head
with a fourty-four
But I rode some.
Yes I rode some.

African-Americans not only
provided much of the labor
for building railroads, as
this comic dialect poem
illustrates, they found trains
an effective if sometimes
frustrating mode of
transportation.

HERLONGS TRAIN

Herlongs Train ran from Gainesville through Rocky Point and Micanopy to Fairfield. The line, originally chartered as the Gainesville, Rocky Point, and Micanopy Railroad before 1894, ran until 1942 under various names and owners.

*H*and me down my walking cane this morning;
O, hand me down my walking cane this morning so soon;
Hand me down my walking cane,
See if I can't catch old Herlong's Train,
This morning, this morning so soon.

I got me a wife and a sweetheart too, this morning
I got me a wife and a sweetheart too, this morning so soon
I got me a wife and a sweetheart too;
My wife don't love me but my sweetheart do.
This morning, this morning so soon.

FOLLOW THE CROWD

Henry B. Plant, a transplanted Connecticut businessman, built both a railway from Jacksonville to Tampa and the exotically Moorish Tampa Bay Hotel (today the University of Tampa). George Graham Currie, a poet as well as mayor of West Palm Beach and treasurer of Dade County, playfully speculates on what might have passed between these two titans of development.

*I*n Jacksonville station once, Flagler met Plant
Each on his way South for a Winter time jaunt;
Said Plant unto Flagler in jocular speech:
"Where, sir, can you tell, is the place called Palm Beach?"
Then Flagler retorted most woefully loud:
"If you're really in earnest, sir, 'follow the crowd.'"

—George Graham Currie (1921)

Consummatum Est

Far down the sunlit golden sands
  Lie gleaming rails—the twin steel bands
    Of commerce—spanning verdant isles,
      Running o'er the sea miles on miles;
        In old Key West their mission ends.
          Dreadnoughts to he each nation sends—
            And wealth and game all this portends.

Each year was wrought through storm and strife
  Another link in the railway's life;
    Safe and strong was each great arch made
      That bore the rails from grade to grade.

Cities, hamlets like magic grew
  Out of jungles the road went through,
    And fertile farms now meet the eye,
      Seen as the train goes roaring by
        To old Key West, 'neath tropic sky.

Rearing an empire—man of might,
  A toast I give. You've won the fight
    In spite of odds—and they were great:
      "Long may you live, high be your state;
        Wealth, health, honor may you enjoy
          All your life through, without alloy.
            Yours to the end may God defend!"

        —J. B. Killibrew (1912)

J. B. Killibrew's **acrostic** on the Florida East Coast Railway celebrated the completion of Henry Morrison Flagler's line from St. Augustine to Key West on January 22, 1912. The brilliant and dangerous engineering feat of building 128 miles of rail cost $20 million and up to seven hundred lives.

Henry Flagler's Song

I invented Florida when I was old.
We lived in New York City in the cold.

I was retired from oil, I had some wealth;
Mary, my first wife, was in poor health.

Robert Watson's account of Flagler's reminiscences follows his career, capped with the extension of his railroad 522 miles from Jacksonville to Key West. A partner of John D. Rockefeller, Flagler used his fortune to build a series of luxury hotels from the Ponce de León in St. Augustine to the Breakers in Palm Beach, where he also built a mansion for his third wife. The Ponce de León is now Flagler College.

We rode in my private railroad car.
Ah, the warm south surely would be her cure.

That winter we steamed into Jacksonville
Where I drew up Florida like my will:

I said I would bequeath to future men
Of wealth and station a temperate garden

By the sea which they could reach by yacht or rail
Where they could toast the sun with ginger ale.

Now in my holy city of St. Augustine,
My hotel Ponce de Leon can be seen:

Its many courts and cool retreats with fountains,
Water spraying from the mouths of dolphins.

That my civilization would prevail,
That all Florida could be coasted by rail

I built my roadbeds, bridges down the entire state.
Now its length my hotels punctuate.

My conquest is a land of orange trees,
Palms, Bougainvillaea, and warm salt seas.

After God, as artist, I have created most and best:
St. Augustine, Palm Beach, Miami, Key West.

It did not matter much that Mary died,
In Florida I found a younger bride.

—Robert Watson (1980)

CHAIN GANG THEME SONG

*W*ha'd you do, Boy, to get so long?
Wha'd you do, Boy, to get so long?
I was highway robbin, Lord, I know I was wrong.
Lord, Lord, I know I was wrong.

I asked Mister Police to turn me loose,
I asked Mister Police to turn me loose,
But he said, I gon turn you every way *but* loose.
Lord, Lord, every way but loose.

Like many of its southern neighbors, Florida relied on convict labor for chain gangs to work on the state's roads. The gangs often worked to rhythmic chants like this one.

I'm gonna drink my likker every place I go,
I'm gonna drink my likker every place I go,
Cause it makes me feel good from my head to my toe,
Lord, Lord, from my head to my toe.

I'm so bad I don't never want to be good,
I'm so bad I don't never want to be good,
I wouldn't go to heaven even if I could,
Lord, Lord, if I could.

They say I'm a poor lost boy, Lord,
They say I'm a poor lost boy, Lord,
Lost for evermore,
Lord, Lord, lost for evermore.

But I'm goin to live anyhow, Lord,
But I'm goin to live anyhow, Lord,
Until I die,
Lord, Lord, till I die.

I told my Baby not to worry a-tall,
I told my Baby not to worry a-tall,
Cause I'm gonna go to heaven or not at all,
Lord, Lord, or not at all.

Oh, looka yonder: hot boilin sun turnin over,
Oh, looka yonder: hot boilin sun turnin over,
And it won't go down,
Lord, Lord won't go down.

I asked the Capm, What's the time of day?
I asked the Capm, What's the time of day?
But he shook his head and sadly walked away,
Lord, Lord, sadly walked away.

This old hammer, Lord,
This old hammer, Lord,
Gets heavier and heavier,
Lord, Lord, heavier and heavier.

But I'm gonna lay it, Lord,
But I'm gonna lay it, Lord,
To save my hide and feet,
Lord, Lord, to save my hide and feet.

I don't want no cornbread nor no molasses,
I don't want no cornbread nor no molasses,
For supper-time,
Lord, Lord, supper-time.

Ev'ry mail-day I gets a letter,
Ev'ry mail-day I gets a letter,
Sinnin son, come home,
Lord, Lord, son come home.

But this old chain gang, Lord,
But this old chain gang, Lord,
Aint gonna let me go,
Lord, Lord, aint gonna let me go.

I'm gonna write one more letter to the Guvnor,
I'm gonna write one more letter to the Guvnor,
About my time,
Lord, Lord, 'bout my time.

My Capm's a mighty big man,
My Capm's a mighty big man,
He the biggest man I ever see,
But I don't bar him,
Lord, Lord, don't bar him.

My Capm's got a big gun that shoots mighty long,
My Capm's got a big gun that shoots mighty long,
But Capm, I'm gonna run,
Lord, Lord, run by sun-down.

Did you hear bout the chain gang breakin up in Georgia?
Did you hear bout the chain gang breakin up in Georgia?
I'm goin back home,
Lord, Lord, goin back home.

One of the founders of the Harlem Renaissance, Langston Hughes developed a poetry based on the rhythms of jazz and blues. He wrote primarily about the African-American workers he met during his extensive travels through the United States. Zora Neale Hurston served as his guide during his exploration of Florida's folk life.

FLORIDA ROAD WORKERS

*I'*m makin' a road
For the cars
To fly by on.

Makin' a road
Through the palmetto thicket
For light and civilization
To travel on.
Makin' a road
For the rich old white men
To sweep over in their big cars
And leave me standin' here.

Sure,
A road helps all of us!
White folks ride—
And I get to see 'em ride.
I ain't never seen nobody
Ride so fine before.
Hey buddy!
Look at me.
I'm making a road!

—Langston Hughes (1931)

THE DINKY LINE

July lay heavy between a shower
of stars and a carpet of crickets
scratching the palmettos with raw
zither music. The squeal and whine
of the late night local train sailed
over scrub pines and water oaks—
the bitter complaint of greaseless
axles. The "dinky," we called it,
though we weren't sure why. Every
night it dragged strings of coal
cars loaded with oranges, grapefruit,
tangelos from the groves in Oviedo,
from the farthest reaches of my known
world, to the Atlantic Coast Line
linking with those Ohio freights,
Chesapeake, Baltimore, to haul citrus
gold into the north. Through picking

The tiny Orlando and Winter
Park Railroad, better known
as the Dinky Line, ran
between the two cities
from 1889 to 1967.

season, the whole town could hear it
shriek across midnight, telling us
how great a load it had to bear.

I always wanted to go out and hop
that train one night, to take
the thirty-mile ride rumbling
along on the clatter and raucous
wailing of wheel, axle, and rail,
wrapped in humid perfume, orange
blossoms thickening dime store
scent around me. I would sit high
on those vast dunes of oranges,
dig into skin with my fingernails
to let the juice strike my eye,
and bite down into the pungent
shiver of sugar laced with acid.
I would be king of the mound,
and no one would have such heavy
wealth to transport him, no one
would ride carried along on such
dense, harsh music, no one would
look up to see the stars in the same
configuration; I would lie basking
under new constellations, constant
in their changing as I travelled
eastward, fabulous patterns shifting
across my eye. I have lived another
life since, yet that dream, like so
many, holds in my cells, stains and stays.

—Malcolm Glass (1992)

The Storms

This **ballad**, written in **rhyming couplets**, tells the story of fishermen lost during an 1894 hurricane that swept along the West Coast, destroying several small towns. The fishermen were on the east arm of St. Andrews Bay near Apalachicola.

THE LOST BOYS OF EAST BAY

*T*here's a story so sad I'm about to relate,
Of a ship that has left here and gone to her fate,

Of the fatherless children and the mothers who wait
The news of their loved ones and their hard cruel fate.

Chorus

    Oh, your hearts will turn towards them in pity, I know,
    When the surf beats loud and the stormy winds blow.
    Let their friends look towards Heaven, where their spirits today
    Look down on their sad homes on the shores of East Bay.

'Twas the year '94 on an October day
They sailed from their homes on the shores of East Bay.
Not a thought of their fate as the farewell they say
As each kissed some loved one and sailed from the Bay.

But the saddest of all is the tale I now tell,
How the storm swept Sand Island like the furies of Hell,
How each raging sea claimed its victims that day,
Those sixteen brave lads from the shores of East Bay.

Oh, that mother who's left without husband or son
To cheer her at evening when the day's work is done.
But those kind-hearted men will go out never more,
In struggle to drive the grim wolf from the door.

    —Harry Evans (1894)

A FLORIDA GHOST

*D*own mildest shores of milk-white sand,
    By cape and fair Floridian bay,
Twixt billowy pines—a surf asleep on land—
    And the great Gulf at play,

Past far-off palms that filmed to nought,
    Or in and out the cunning keys
That laced the land like fragile patterns wrought
    To edge old broideries,

The sail sighed on all day for joy,
    The prow each pouting wave did leave
All smile and song, with sheen and ripple coy,
    Till the dusk diver Eve

This long **ballad** introduces the reader to the ghost of an entrepreneur who thought to make a fortune by building a sanitarium to lure Northern patients to his Gulf Coast key.

Brought up from out the brimming East
        The oval moon, a perfect pearl,
In that large lustre all our haste surceased,
        The sail seemed fain to furl.

The silent steersman landward turned,
        And ship and shore set breast to breast.
Under a palm wherethrough a planet burned
        We ate, and sank to rest.

But soon from sleep's dear death (it seemed)
        I rose and strolled along the sea
Down silver distances that faintly gleamed
        On to infinity.

Till suddenly I paused, for lo!
        A shape (from whence I ne'er divined)
Appeared before me, pacing to and fro,
        With head far down inclined.

A wraith (I thought) *that walks the shore
        To solve some old perplexity.*
Full heavy hung the draggled gown he wore;
        His hair flew all awry.

He waited not (as ghosts oft use)
        To be *dearheaven'd*! and *oh'd*!
But briskly said: "Good-evenin'; what's the news?
        Consumption? After boa'd?

"Or mebbe you're intendin' of
        Investments? Orange plantin'? Pine?
Hotel? or Sanitarium? What above
        This yea'th *can* be your line?

"Speakin' of sanitariums, now,
        Jest look'ee here, my friend:
I know a little story,—well, I swow,
        Wait till you hear the end!

"Some year or more ago, I s'pose,
        I roamed from Maine to Floridy,
And,—see where them Palmettos grows?
        I bought that little key,

"Cal'latin' for to build right off
      A c'lossal sanitarium:
Big surf! Gulf breeze! Jest death upon a cough!
      —I run it high, to hum!

"Well, sir, I went to work in style:
      Bought me a steamboat, loaded it
With my hotel (pyazers more'n a mile!)
      Already framed and fit,

• **pyazers** piazzas or large
covered porches

"Insured 'em, fetched 'em safe around,
      Put up my buildin', moored my boat,
Com-plete! then went to bed and slept as sound
      As if I'd paid a note.

"Now on that very night a squall,
      Cum up from some'eres—some bad place!
An' blowed an' tore an' reared an' pitched an' all
      —I had to run a race

"Right out o' bed from that hotel
      An' git to yonder risin' ground,
For, 'twixt the sea that riz and rain that fell,
      I pooty nigh was drowned!

"An thar I stood till mornin' cum,
      Right on yon little knoll of sand,
Frequently wishin' I had stayed to hum
      Fur from this tarnal land.

"When mornin cum, I took a good
      Long look, and—well, sir, sure's I'm me—
That boat laid right what that hotel had stood,
      And hit sailed out to sea!

"No: I'll not keep you: good-bye, friend.
      Don't think about it much,—preehaps
Your brain might git see-sawin', end for end,
      Like them asylum chaps,

"For here I walk, forevermore,
      A-tryin' to make it gee,
How one same wind could blow my ship to shore
      And my hotel to sea!"

      —Sidney Lanier (1877)

Miami Hairikin

*G*od A'mighty moved on the water
And the peoples in Miami run.
And the lady left Miami;
She left in lightning speed.
Ev'ry time the lightnin' flash
She thinks about her dirty deeds.

God A'mighty moved on the water
And the peoples in Miami run.
Ships swam down that ocean,
It was almost too sad to tell;
Ten thousand peoples got drownded,
And all went to Hell but twelve.

God A'mighty moved on the water
And the peoples in Miami run.
Yon stan' the lady,
Stan'ing in the back do'
Singing, "If I get back to Georgia,
I won't go to Florida no mo'."

God A'mighty moved on the water
And the peoples in Miami run.
The rich white folks and the well-to-do
Were playing five-up and pool;
God A'mighty got angry in glory,
And they forgot each other's move.

God A'mighty moved on the water
And the peoples in Miami run.
Some was floatin' on the sea;
And some was cryin' on bended knee,
"Lord, have mercy on me."

(1928)

These two folk songs recount the events of the South Florida hurricane of September 1928, in which the Red Cross reported 1,810 people killed and 1,849 injured. Other reports raised the death toll as high as 4,000. Most deaths occured from the flooding of farms and the settlements of Belle Glade, Pahokee and South Bay along the shore of Lake Okeechobee where African-American laborers worked in the truck farms and cane fields. Zora Neale Hurston described this hurricane in her novel *Their Eyes Were Watching God* (1937).

WEST PALM BEACH STORM

On the sixteenth day of September,
In nineteen twenty-eight,
God started riding early,
He rode 'till very late.

Chorus
       In the storm, oh in the storm;
       Lord, somebody got drowned in the storm.

He rode out on the ocean
Chained the lightning to his wheel,
Stepped on land at West Palm Beach,
And the wicked hearts did yield.

Over in Pahokee,
Families rushed out at the door,
And somebody's poor mother
Hasn't been seen anymore.

Some mothers looked at their children
As they began to cry,
Cried, "Lord, have mercy,
For we all must die."

I tell you wicked people,
What you had better do;
Go down and get the Holy Ghost
And then you live the life too.

Out around Okeechobee,
All scattered on the ground,
The last account of the dead they had
Were twenty-two hundred found.

South Bay, Belleglade, and Pahokee,
Tell me they all went down
And over at Chosen,
Everybody got drowned.

Some people are yet missing,
And haven't been found they say.

But this we know, they will come forth
On the Resurrection Day.

When Gabriel sounds the trumpet,
And the dead begin to rise,
I'll meet the saints from Chosen,
Up in the heavenly skies.

(1928)

HOLD BACK THE WATERS

*T*he Seminole left there in haste and with speed.
Their wise words of warning were given no heed.
When the waters receded, Great God what a sight!
Men, women and children turned black as the night.

Chorus:
>   Lord hold back the waters of Lake Okeechobee
>   For Lake Okeechobee's blue waters are cold.
>   When wild winds are blowin' across Okeechobee
>   They're calling and seeking for other poor souls
>   Oh Lake Okeechobee's blue waters are cold.

Now Lake Okeechobee is calm and serene.
The land all around it is fertile and green.
But the people get fearful when the wild winds do roam.
They look at the earth dam and they think of their home.

—Will McLean (1980)

Will McLean's song about the hurricane of 1928 relates the belief that the Seminoles can predict hurricanes by noting "when the sawgrass blooms," a phenomenon in which the atmospheric condition makes pollen visible several days before the hurricane strikes. The last stanza warns that the earthen dikes raised after the hurricane to hold in the lake's waters probably could not withstand a storm of similar magnitude.

THE HURRICANE

*L*o, Lord, Thou ridest!
Lord, Lord, Thy swifting heart

Nought stayeth, nought now bideth
But's smithereened apart!

Hart Crane marvels at the power of the hurricane, likening it to a divine gallop across the sky. His complex imagery, coupled with strained syntax and strong rhythmic beats, emphasizes the force of the storm.

Ay! Scripture flee'th stone!
Milk-bright, Thy chisel wind

Rescindeth flesh from bone
To quivering whittlings thinned—

Swept, whistling straw! Battered,
Lord, e'en boulders now outleap

Rock sockets, levin-lathered!
Nor, Lord, may worm outdeep

                                            • **levin** lightning

Thy drum's gambade, its plunge abscond!
Lord God, while summits crashing

                                            • **gambade** an upward leap

Whip sea-kelp screaming on blond
Sky-seethe, dense heaven dashing—

Thou ridest to the door, Lord!
Thou bidest wall nor floor, Lord!

      —Hart Crane (1931)

HURRICANE SEASON

𝒱oices crackle out coordinates
and scalpers hawk batteries
in the street.

We are bunkered in again
for a storm: oil lamps,
sterno, bathtub full of water,

antenna disconnected
to the TV snows
in the August heat. Still,

we dream of it coming
the way a child turns
the idea of his mother's death

in his mind. Something in us
longs to try the tragedy on
for size: barometer plunging,

Hurricane warnings invari-
ably inspire preparation
and anticipation. Balancing
description with **metaphor**
and **simile**, Enid Shomer
evokes our dread and
perverse longing for
the disaster.

wires slapped down, fish
in trees, the beach quarried
to a cliff where we teeter

as with a childhood fever.
In the churn of the wind's
blades, in the swollen

waves, there is this sidelong
wish, this trigger we finger,
a breath we hold for days.

—Enid Shomer (1987)

HEIRLOOMS

*T*hrough the garbled signals
of a transistor radio
my mother kept for hurricanes like this,
but never like this,
we scan for the next location
of ice, water, food and catch
the edge of a Caribbean tinged
station, fragments of a Marley tune
"No woman, nuh cry, everything's
gonna be all right," and my son,
barely nine months, who cut a tooth
while Andrew gnawed through the Grove,
dances with his mother
by the glow of a kerosene lamp,
preserved through airport terminals,
garage sales, and, as the window
splintered, the house glittered
for a moment before the walls
fell flat, stood on the mantle
of the fireplace we never used.
In the midst of the rubble
these, our only heirlooms, bind us
against the darkness outside,
all that she could ever give,
all that we could ever pass on
or possess: this light, this music.

—Geoffrey Philp (1994)

The results of Hurricane
Andrew's strike in south
Florida in August, 1992,
remind the poet of the
essence of fragile
heirlooms. His per-
sonal reaction contrasts
sharply with Ricardo
Pau-Llosa's more social
response to the same
hurricane in "Zen Walk
in the Aftermath of
Hurricane Andrew."

FABLIAU OF FLORIDA

*B*arque of phosphor
On the palmy beach,

Move outward into heaven,
Into the alabasters
And night blues.

Foam and cloud are one.
Sultry moon monsters
Are dissolving.

Fill your black hull
With white moonlight.

There will never be an end
To this droning of the surf.

—Wallace Stevens (1923)

Wallace Stevens's odd use of the term **fabliau** for this elegant, intensely visual description of a beach scene suggests that the sounds of words and the **images** they convey may have more to do with the poem's meaning than any traditional meaning of the words. One of his personal favorites, the poem reflects Stevens's fascination with contemporary painters and their sense of color and texture.

NOMAD EXQUISITE

As the immense dew of Florida
Brings forth
The big-finned palm
And green vine angering for life,

As the immense dew of Florida
Brings forth hymn and hymn
From the beholder,
Beholding all these green sides,

And blessed mornings,
Meet for the eye of the young alligator,
And lightning colors
So, in me, come flinging
Forms, flames, and the flakes of flames.

—Wallace Stevens (1923)

INDIAN RIVER

The trade wind jingles the rings in the nets around the
    racks
    by the docks on Indian River.
It is the same jingle of the water among the roots under the
    banks of the palmettoes,
It is the same jingle of the red-bird breasting the orange-
    trees
    out of the cedars.
Yet there is no spring in Florida, neither in boskage perdu,
    nor
    on the nunnery beaches.

—Wallace Stevens (1923)

FAREWELL TO FLORIDA

I

*G*o on, high ship, since now, upon the shore,
   The snake has left its skin upon the floor.
Key West sank downward under massive clouds
And silvers and greens spread over the sea. The moon
Is at its mast-head and the past is dead.
Her mind will never speak to me again.
I am free. High above the mast the moon
Rides clear of her mind and the waves make a refrain
Of this: that the snake has shed its skin upon
The floor. Go on through darkness. The waves fly back.

II

Her mind had bound me round. The palms were hot
As if I lived in ashen ground, as if
The leaves in which the wind kept up its sound
From my North of cold whistled in a sepulchral South,
Her South of pine and coral and coraline sea,
Her home, not mine, in the ever-freshened Keys,
Her days, her oceanic nights, calling
For music, for whisperings from the reefs.
How content I shall be in the North to which I sail
And to feel sure and to forget the bleaching sand . . .

III

I hated the weathery yawl from which the pools
Disclosed the sea floor and the wilderness
Of waving weeds. I hated the vivid blooms
Curled over the shadowless hut, the rust and bones,
The trees like bones and the leaves half sand, half sun
To stand here on the deck in the dark and say
Farewell and to know that that land is forever gone
And that she will not follow in any word
Or look, nor ever again in thought, except
That I loved her once . . . Farewell. Go on high ship.

The introductory poem for
his Pulitzer Prize-winning
collection *Ideas of Order*
heralded Stevens' decision
to reject the sensuous, erotic
world of Key West and return
to the cold, harsh realities of
the North. As he leaves the
tropical garden, complete
with serpent, he travels
through a series of deathlike
images toward the public,
social order of the North.
What seems most important
as he turns his back on the
seductive lure of Florida is
his capacity to choose.

IV

My North is leafless and lies in a wintry slime
Both of men and clouds, a slime of men in crowds.
The men are moving as the water moves,
This darkened water cloven by the sullen swells
Against your sides, then shoving and slithering,
The darkness shattered, turbulent with foam.
To be free again, to return to the violent mind
That is their mind, these men, and that will bind
Me round, carry me, misty deck, carry me
To the cold, go on, high ship, go on, plunge on.

—Wallace Stevens (1936)

THE CLIME OF MY BIRTH

*O*h, take me again to the clime of my birth,
The dearest, the fairest, to me on the earth,
The clime where the roses are sweetest that bloom,
And nature is bathed in the rarest perfume!

Where the songs of the birds awake us at morn
With a thrill of delight and pleasure new born;
For the mocking bird there is loudest in hymn,
With notes ever changing, none fettering him.

When the hills of the North are shrouded in snow,
When the winds of Winter their fiercest do blow—
Then take me again to the clime of my birth,
Dear Florida—dearest to me on the earth.

—Timothy Thomas Fortune (1905)

Born a slave in Marianna, Fortune attended a freedman's school and Howard University after the Civil War. He moved to New York City, began publishing a newspaper, wrote a series of highly influential and critical books on race in the United States, and collected his poems in *Dreams of Life*. Fortune's use of **anapests** and his images of life and freedom help establish the poem's sense of romantic nostalgia.

THE EDEN ISLE

Oh come, oh my love! I have found now a place
Where old romance dawns ever a-new:
Where the Spirit of Love unveils her fair face;
And fairies trip over the blue.

'Tis an isle in the seas of Tennyson's dream
When he sang of the Eden isles:
And the waters surrounding so crystal they seem,
As to mirror the heavenly aisles.

Ah listen, my love! As we fly to this isle
Where luscious fruits ripen on lustrous tree,
We'll sail the Gulf waters for purple-pale mile,
—To the bounds of a Parrish sea.

When we glide through the gates of that velvet bay blue,
—Gates—that like corraline lions brown stand—
In our Parrish-white ship, with our fairy-brown crew—
We will beach on the Eden strand.

So come, oh my love, to this far-away place
Where sweet romance dawns ever a-new!
Where the Love of all Ages is seen in the face
That Nature here shows unto you.

—George Merrick (1920)

A founder of the University of Miami and the developer of Coral Gables, George Merrick remained a visionary romantic all of his life. With his fondness for Maxfield Parrish, a painter famous for his brilliant use of color, Merrick offers this dream of escape to a fantastic, Edenic island.

LAKE TOHOPEKALIGA

A rude, uncouth, outlandish word it seemed,
    Which on our Saxon tongues had little grace;
In nowise fitting for the lake that dreamed
    Away the days in this enchanted place.

The homing curlew toward the sunset swept
    Above the mirror of the placid lake;
The swamp blackbirds their ringing chorus kept
    Vibrant with courage in the sedge and brake.

When to an Indian guide we spoke the word,
    No sign of recognition crossed his face.
It was no name that he had ever heard,
    To him conveyed no thought of any place.

"What name you call this lake?" we asked the guide.
    And then with liquid notes he spoke the song

"To-ho-pe-ka-liga," and open wide
    Were swung the gates of vision, closed so long.

In tone and in inflection he had voiced
    The very spirit of the bird's brave song.
This was the name in which the lake rejoiced
    In vanished years, while yet his tribe was strong.

We saw the ancient peoples who had passed
    And under his stoic mask, the love
Wherewith he loved unto the very last,
    His lake beneath us and his sky above.

—Stephen Cochran Singleton (1924)

PRAYER

𝒴ou are de same God, Ah
Dat heard de sinner man cry.
Same God dat sent de zigzag lightning tuh
Join de mutterin' thunder.
Same God dat holds de elements
In uh unbroken chain of controllment,
Same God dat hung on Cavalry and died,
Dat we might have a right tuh de tree of life—
We thank Thee that our sleeping couch
Was not our cooling board,
Our cover was not our winding sheet . . .
Please tuh give us a restin' place
Where we can praise Thy name forever,

Amen.

—Zora Neale Hurston (1934)

Zora Neale Hurston's fasci-
nation with African-American
religion resulted in a number
of dialect poems. In this
prayer by a central charac-
ter in her first novel *Jonah's
Gourd Vine* (1934), she
recreates the sermons of
her childhood in Eatonville.

THE CREATION

𝒜nd God stepped out on space,
And he looked around and said:
I'm lonely—
I'll make me a world.

And far as the eye of God could see
Darkness covered everything,
Blacker than a hundred midnights
Down in a cypress swamp.

Then God smiled,
And the light broke,
And the darkness rolled up on one side,
And the light stood shining on the other,
And God said: That's good!

As executive secretary of
the NAACP and editor of *The
Book of American Negro
Poetry* (1922), Jacksonville-
native Johnson helped
shape the Harlem
Renaissance. Author of
"Lift Every Voice and Sing"
(1900), often called the
Negro National Anthem,
he attempted in poems
like "The Creation" to
recreate the African-
American sermons he
had heard as a child.
The simple but powerful
imagery creates a very
human and very appealing
image of God.

Then God reached out and took the light in His hands,
And God rolled the light around in His hands
Until He made the sun;
And he set that sun a-blazing in the heavens.
And the light that was left from making the sun
God gathered it up in a shining ball
And flung it against the darkness,
Spangling the night with the moon and stars.
Then down between
The darkness and the light
He hurled the world;
And God said: That's good!

Then God himself stepped down—
And the sun was on His right hand,
And the moon was on His left;
The stars were clustered about His head,
And the earth was under His feet.
And God walked, and where He trod
His footsteps hollowed the valleys out
And bulged the mountains up.

Then He stopped and looked and saw
That the earth was hot and barren.
So God stepped over to the edge of the world
And He spat out the seven seas—
He batted His eyes and the lightnings flashed—
He clapped His hands, and the thunders rolled—
And the waters above the earth came down,
The cooling waters came down.

Then the green grass sprouted,
And the little red flowers blossomed,
The pine tree pointed his finger to the sky,
And the oak spread out his arms,
The lakes cuddled down in the hollows of the ground,
And the rivers ran down to the sea;
And God smiled again,
And the rainbow appeared,
And curled itself around His shoulder.

Then God raised His arm and He waved His hand
Over the sea and over the land,
And He said: Bring forth! Bring forth!
And quicker than God could drop His hand,
Fishes and fowls
And beasts and birds
Swam the rivers and the seas,
Roamed the forests and the woods,
And split the air with their wings.
And God said: That's good!

Then God walked around,
And God looked around
On all that He had made.
He looked at His sun,
And He looked at His moon,
And He looked at His little stars;
He looked on His world
With all its living things,
And God said: Im lonely still.

Then God sat down—
On the side of a hill where He could think;
By a deep, wide river He sat down;
With His head in his hands,
God thought and thought,
Till He thought: I'll make me a man!

Up from the bed of the river
God scooped the clay;
And by the bank of the river
He kneeled Him down;
And there the great God Almighty
Who lit the sun and fixed it in the sky,
Who flung the stars to the most far corner of the night,
Who rounded the earth in the middle of His hand;
This Great God,
Like a mammy bending over her baby,
Kneeled down in the dust
Toiling over a lump of clay
Till He shaped it in His own image;

Then into it He blew the breath of life,
And man became a living soul.
Amen. Amen.

—James Weldon Johnson (1927)

ROYAL PALM

For Grace Hart Crane

$\mathcal{G}$reen rustlings, more-than-regal charities
　Drift cooly from that tower of whispered light.
Amid the noontide's blazed asperities
I watched the sun's most gracious anchorite

Climb up as by communings, year on year
Uneaten of the earth or aught earth holds,
And the grey trunk, that's elephantine, rear
Its frondings sighing in ætherial folds.

Forever fruitless, and beyond that yield
Of sweat the jungle presses with hot love
And tendril till our deathward breath is sealed—
It grazes the horizons, launched above

Mortality—ascending emerald-bright,
A fountain at salute, a crown in view—
Unshackled, casual of its azured height
As though it soared suchwise through heaven too.

—Hart Crane (1931)

KEY WEST

*H*ere has my salient faith annealed me.
Out of the valley, past the ample crib
To skies impartial, that do not disown me
Nor claim me, either, by Adam's spine—nor rib.

The oar plash, and the meteorite's white arch
Concur with wrist and bicep. In the moon
That now has sunk I strike a single march
To heaven or hades—to an equally frugal noon.

Because these millions reap a dead conclusion
Need I presume the same fruit of my bone
As draws them towards a doubly mocked confusion
Of apish nightmares into steel-strung stone?

O, steel and stone! But gold was, scarcity before.
And here is water, and a little wind. . . .
There is no breath of friends and no more shore
Where gold has not been sold and conscience tinned.

—Hart Crane (1931)

As he rows off the coast of Key West, does the poet find peace from his sense of isolation and his frustration with materialism? Or does the poem suggest the sense of loss that drove Crane to commit suicide by leaping off a ship while leaving Mexico?

- **salient** conspicuous, noticeable; protruding, jutting out

- **anneal** to temper metals by slow regulated cooling

Sonnets

A Pulitzer Prize-winning poet and editor of *Poetry* magazine, George Dillon shaped his highly disciplined, elegant language into traditional forms. These matched **Shakespearean sonnets**, offering a dialogue with different ways of viewing the future, provide an interesting contrast in **imagery**.

Fear not to die, though you must feel the cold
Shadow of all things that the sun has shown:
The body with its bright excess of gold
Blowing to silver ere the sun goes down;
The earth and the wild issue of her womb—
The ape that drags its knuckles from afar,
The pulsing fish, the bird on rigid plume.
You bear their blindness, being what you are.
Being the weariest creature and the last,
The sigh of God upon the seventh day,
You keep the bestial chrysalis uncast
And the wing folded that would fly away.
What do you fear of dying? That will be
To drop the world like fetters and go free.

Fear not to live, for life is proud and long
Past the grave's ignominy to undo.
As men peered outward when the earth was young
Dreaming of shores unsailed for, so may you.
So of the timeless mystery may you take
Your amorous will—though nevermore from Spain
The little ships with laughter in their wake
Will sail to the Americas again.
This is your home, the hemisphere they won:
It is a lovely land—so high, so wide,
You may ascend its mountains to the sun
And step into the sea on either side.
Yet even now, in the enamoured mind,
This were another port to put behind.

—George Dillon (1931)

TAMPA

*L*ow, rambling docks along tidewater ways,
Delicious sunlight, spilling down the street
In shallow golden pools: the fragrant, sweet
Perfume of oleanders, lazy days
Beneath old palms, are memories that blaze,
When through a northern blizzard's stormy sleet
I seem to hear the warm gulf's pulsing beat,
And mocking birds, in madrigals of praise.

When like a full blown rose the sun drops down,
In dreams, I see you, glamorous port of call,
With sapphire sea and glorious evening star.
Within the Spanish quarter of the town
In fancy, I can hear, behind a wall,
The tinkling of a troubadour's guitar.

—Franklin N. Wood (1931)

Appointed Florida's first Poet Laureate in 1929, Franklin Wood paints highly sensual, richly detailed portraits. His **Petrarchan sonnet** evoking Tampa's exotic, musical appeal and his lush description of the close of day both suggest the gentle, private quality of the poet's sensibility and his acute sensitivity to sound.

FLORIDA DUSK

*T*he purple feet of dusk steal through the skies,
Cooling the heated path of day's vast disk,
While through the shadows, myriad fireflies
Slide down the dark. High in a tamarisk
A mocking bird, his *Nunc Dimitis* sings;
An allamander's scent perfumes the breeze;
I hear the flutter of homecoming wings
And silence sits among the orange trees.

—Franklin N. Wood (1931)

• *Nunc Dimitis* the Song of Simeon, Luke 2.29-32, used as a hymn; part of Evening Prayer in the Anglican Church; dismissal

EVERGLADES

*T*he slow hot wind is trying to explain
Just why the sun is like a stab of pain,
The shadow of a buzzard circling low
Outlines the rotting carcass of a doe,
And where a sulpher pool has puckered through
Quick hyacinths have flung a blur of blue.

Its endlessness an ache against the eyes
The sawgrass marches on to meet the skies,
The gaunt and twisted mangrove-root parades
The vastness men have called the Everglades,
And legs absurdly long support the crane
That looks upon the whole with fine disdain.

—Vivian Yeiser Laramore Rader (1931)

During a period in which most writers described Florida as an exotic but alien place, Vivian Laramore Rader described home. The Poet Laureate of Florida from 1931 until her death in 1975, Laramore Rader's musical and imagistic poetry shows the influences of Emily Dickinson and Edna St. Vincent Millay.

A fine irony in these **heroic couplets** acknowledges the intertwining of life and death in the remorseless nature of the Everglades.

FLORIDA LANDSCAPE

*M*y land is wild lantana in the wind,
A puff-cloud over sawgrass bending low,
And where the scrub-palmetto has been thinned,
The philosophic gopher and the crow.
It is the deep survival of a need
For endless giving, endless overflowing,
The cradle for that energetic seed
Which beauty in a spendthrift mood is sowing.
Here cypress-knees that press against blue space
Were old when Lincoln wept for his lost Ann,
And moss that hangs like elemental lace
Is poetry too beautiful to scan;
And here the sea forgets all minor shades
To concentrate upon the source of blue
Which merges with the sapphire Everglades

Aware of the criticisms that northern poets had laid against Florida's landscape, Laramore Rader rejoices in the ancient and native foliage that provides a backdrop for the flight of egrets and flamingos.

• **lantana** a flowering bush that grows wild

And brings the heart of heaven close to you.
And here the sun is like a righteous man
Who hurls his wrath upon an erring race,
And then, grown gentle as a guardian,
Protects the fledgling wings of purple space.
There are no hills in this, my native land,
No jagged cliffs that tear the sky asunder,
But level miles of fertile jungle fanned
By leaves that clap their jeweled hands in wonder.
Monotonous, they call this land of mine
Who do not know its sameness is a song,
Who have not sensed the fact that its design
Is but a sweeping curve the tides prolong.
They say that it is lush and overgrown,
In need of winter with its wand of death;
But they have never walked in groves alone
Where petalled snow came down with every breath,
And they have never seen the startled flame
Of great flamingoes rushing toward the sun,
Or traced along the quiet path they came
White egrets homing when the day is done.
My land is flight and flame and rooted laughter.
With orchids dripping from its topmost rafter.

  —Vivian Yeiser Laramore Rader (1932)

BISCAYNE BAY

A poet and composer, Aleda
Davis, a winter resident of
Coral Gables, uses imagistic
language and syllabic verse
to capture her vision of
Biscayne Bay.

*T*he bay
At sunset is
An old silver mirror
In which Evening looks to apply
Her rouge.

The bay
At mid-day is
A zircon, its blue-green
Eyes quick to catch the tropic skies
At play.

—Aleda Norma Davis (1931)

MOSS-HUNG OAKS

Lakeland poet Etta Murfey
captures the image of
Spanish moss hanging from
native oaks in a series of
metaphors that evoke
nature's tapestry.

*I*n ghostly benediction,
Weird fingers
Caress the rich dark verdure
Of the ageless oaks.
A twilight veil,
Woven on unseen looms
And flecked with misty radiance,
Garlands them
With eerie beauty,
Entwining
Its blue-gray fibres
With the living green.

—Etta Josephean Murfey (1931)

THE MANGROVES DANCE

*T*he mangroves dance in the light of the moon,
(Three feet, four feet, more feet, many feet)
Dance and prance in the light of the moon,
Dance and prance to the swishing-tune
Of wind on the waves in the light of the moon.
Gnarled old mangroves, bent and marred,
With crooked arms—
With bodies scarred by wind and wave,
When the sea mounts high,
And through the sky the tearing storm goes shrieking by.
Gray old mangroves, awkward and stumbling,
Twisted legs—tortuous—tumbling on to a shuffling tune,
As they dance and prance in the light of the moon.

The mangroves dance in the light of the moon,
Dance in a trance as the tide mounts high.
And only the moon in the southern sky
Can see them groping, loping by,
(Three feet, four feet, more feet, many feet)
Can hear the drone of the muffled tune
As the mangroves dance in the light of the moon.

—Rose Strong Hubbell (1932)

The dance of the mangroves on the shores of the sea prevents the tides from stealing the land. Rose Hubbell's weird and whimsical **charm** relies on **internal rhyme, assonance,** and **alliteration** to exercise its spell.

FLORIDA NIGHT

*G*o dip your body in the night and find
　　A beauty too refulgent for the mind;
Feel it with your swift fingertips, your hair,
Your vibrant being,—breathe it in with air.
Sing it with heartbeats; do not pause to think;
Run down the lucent paths of night and drink
Of forest-filtered water, moonlight-cool,
The molten darkness lying like a pool.
Watch phosphorescent fishes, see the gleam
Of starlight laid like gold leaf on a stream;
Reach up and catch the comets as they fall;
Mock the enchanted night-birds when they call;
Gather the jasmine in a great festoon
And offer it as incense to the moon.
Stay not for thought, live only to be glad—
The night and firmament are going mad!

　　　　—Marlise Johnston (1932)

Published while she was still a student at Rollins College in Winter Park, Marlise Johnston's enchanted Florida night evokes a glowing fairy landscape. Like George Merrick's, her vision of Florida as a fairyland owes a good deal to British Romantic and Victorian poets and artists.

- **refulgent** radiant
- **lucent** transparent

A MILLION YEARS TO COME

*W*hen they excavate Miami
　　In a million years to come,
All the wonders of Pompeii
　　Will be overshadowed some!
When compared with all her splendors
　　Theirs will seem a little stale,
For the city we are building
　　Is on such a mammoth scale.

When they exhume Coral Gables
　　Old King Tut won't stand a show,
His was but a minor venture,
　　Though he let the whole world know

A proud Miami citizen here extols the marvels of her city's grand architecture, comparing it with the wonders of the ancient world.

He had builded once an empire
      Which was mighty in its day,
But compared with Coral Gables
      It was nothing but child's play.

When they make their excavations
      'Round the Biltmore Country Club
And disclose the Casa Loma
      In the ultra social hub,
Men afar will note the tidings
      And will marvel at the place,
Filled with everlasting beauty
      Left by such a noble race.

      —Elaine Duncan Sigler (1932)

SUNSET

*T*he sunset is reflected
In mirroring sands.
Two herons rest immobile
By the water's edge.
Seeing a strange traveler,
Affrighted, they rise
To seek shelter underneath
A flowering rose.
So does my too timid soul
Circumvent sorrow.

      —Eleanor Anderson Fay (1935)

How does a traveler understand an exotic sunset? Eleanor Fay's striking image ends with personal reflection.

FLORIDA JUNGLE

In this rhythmic **chant** written in strongly accented lines, Maxeda Hess plays with repetition and **assonance** to evoke the wilderness of the Florida swamp threatened by civilization's encroachments.

In the shadows of the jungle,
Deep and cool, deep and cool,
There a panther, black and purple,
Pads the trail to red-deer pool;
There the white owl cries his challenge
In the swamp, in the bog,
Cries above the castanets
Of the silver-bellied frog;
There the mocker courts in moonlight,
Pleading love, constant love,
To his moss-grey mate coquetting
In the cypress high above;
There the early stars are searching
Path of moon, maiden moon,
As the night wind in the grasses,
Stirs a jungle tune;
Then the healing of the Dark
Hides the earth, ancient earth,
Comes to cover scars that Man
Has inflicted since dawn's birth;
There a river starts its journey,
Lazy journey to the sea,
And the trade winds through the forest
Blow a murmurous melody;
Fathoms deep in shell-locked harbors
Of the dead, there softly swells,
Chant of ghostly shrouded sailors
Tolling muffled galleon bells.

—Maxeda Hess (1935)

FLORIDA

*C*ypress,
old ... old.
Countless ages have passed
While you, with calm and tolerant gaze,
surveyed all,
Scornfully amused.
How can you stand
hugging the gray tatters
of wistful moss,
knowing all and revealing nothing?
I wonder ...
Were you born old?

Spanish moss
fluttering in the wind,
you are the ghosts of old men
who have always been old.
You draw back from the sharp curve
of the wind's sickle,
forlorn and afraid.
But what have ghosts
to fear?

Red flamingoes,
sure and stately,
each standing on a thin leg,
too thin to support a bubble,
are you as proud and bored as you look?
A vague background of dusty cypress
for your flame loveliness,
And blue water
for your haughty reflections.
Purple wisteria,
growing in the warm huskiness of a southern night,
heavy with bloom,
you are like giant bunches of wild grapes.
But tomorrow
the purple bloom in my hair
will be lifeless.

—Peggy Hudgings (1935)

Florida's primeval cypress and moss provide a backdrop for the proud flamingo and ephemeral wisteria, as Peggy Hudgings connects ancient wisdom and modern life.

MIAMI

O, young Miami, glorious Miami!
Your winters gentle as lambs, your colors gemmy
Like coronation garb of Maharani.
Dreamy Miami, flowery Miami,
Perennially blossoming Miami.
Oh, most enticing, most glamorous mermaid!
All metaphors fade,
All superlatives are used in vain,
To tell of your fame. Your very name
Has a caressing sound. You are crowned
With more exalted lights than eye can bear.
You are an exotic fair, a constant holiday.
It isn't the palms that sway
In eternal rhythm, fringing your dazzling beaches.
It isn't the sun that teaches
New joy to those tired of life. It isn't even
Your generous people.
I can't define what nameless gift is given
To anyone who enters the City of Magic.
My Slavic soul, always verged on the tragic,
Began to glow with steady merriment for the first time
When it spread its cramped wings in Miami.

—Maria Moravsky (1935)

Maria Moravsky's vision of Miami rivals the streets of gold in many immigrants' visions. Like Elaine Sigler, Moravsky's Miami is young and promising and joyful— a breath of life to a disillusioned and tragic Eastern European soul.

SEA GRAPES

*M*ad and mad forever is he
    Who drinks of sea grape wine,
And madder far from grapes of a tree
    Than grapes that grow on a vine.

The juice is pressed from lush black pearls
    By the tread of the sun's bare feet,
And flagoned in jade on a shore that swirls
    In the gauze of tropic heat.

Who sips of the wine is sea-enchanted
    In a crystal bowl of light,
And doomed by the grape the Trade Winds planted
    By a sea of malachite.

And wild is the dawn within his eyes
    That rends the night asunder
And hammers down the copper skies
    To beat the hot stars under.

And mad is he who leans his ears
    On the turquois walls of noon
Where fiddler-crabs file by in tiers
    To scrape of their own march tune.

When light and dark are the tangled fret
    Of a mad glass blower's dream,
Flamingos wade in silhouette
    Like fire on a jungle stream.

—Anita Austerman (1936)

The **Dionysian** frenzy of Anita Austermann's celebration of the distillation of the sea grape invokes both the mythic divinity of wine and the particularity of a Floridian vision.

LIME PIE

*L*ime Pie! Oh, my!
How I like my lime pie.
Every so often I up-and-go
Down to the keys where the wild limes grow,
Cool and green like the soul of spring,
Tart and sharp with a zestful zing.
I look for a certain drift-wood shack
With the road in front and the Gulf out back,
With these letters scrawled in a clumsy way
On a home-made sign, "LIME PIE TODAY."
There's a gaunt lean woman, weathered brown
With a pleasant smile and a thoughtful frown.
She's not a beauty . . . her genius lies
In the way she makes those wild lime pies,
With a crust as light as a flake of snow
And the filling made just thus-and-so,
Rich and smooth and as soft as down
Like the floating wings of an angel's gown,
With a clean perfume that is tart and cool.
When I think of it I start to drool.
It's quite a gang that is waiting there,
A bent old man with snow-white hair,
A fisherman and a husky buck
Who drives a big old battered truck,
A silent man with a pale scarred face
And a couple of fellows I can't quite place.
But all of us watch with hungry eyes
While the woman cuts those wild lime pies.
I eat one piece and ask for another
And that one calls for its own twin brother,
While the last lone piece looks so bereft
That it's always gone by the time I've left.
Lime pie. Oh, my!
How I crave that lime pie.

—Don Blanding (1941)

SEASCAPE

*T*his celestial seascape, with white herons got up as angels,
flying as high as they want and as far as they want sidewise
in tiers and tiers of immaculate reflections;
the whole region, from the highest heron
down to the weightless mangrove island
with bright green leaves edged neatly with bird-droppings
like illumination in silver,
and down to the suggestively Gothic arches of the mangrove roots
and the beautiful pea-green back-pasture
where occasionally a fish jumps, like a wild-flower
in an ornamental spray of spray;
this cartoon by Raphael for a tapestry for a Pope:
it does look like heaven.
But a skeletal lighthouse standing there
in black and white clerical dress,
who lives on his nerves, thinks he knows better.
He thinks that hell rages below his iron feet,
that that is why the shallow water is so warm,
and he knows that heaven is not like this.
Heaven is not like flying or swimming,
but has something to do with blackness and a strong glare
and when it gets dark he will remember something
strongly worded to say on the subject.

—Elizabeth Bishop (1946)

As with Emerson and Stevens, once again the New Englander's ambivalence about Florida's tropical charms arises as Elizabeth Bishop's heavenly **metaphors** give way to the lighthouse's Puritannical sensibility.

Reflecting on Florida's Hispanic origins, Alfonso Camín, a Cuban poet who visited the state in the 1950s, invokes the memories and spirit of the original Spanish explorers.

• **Menéndez de Avilés**, founder of St. Augustine. Chief Carlos of the Calusas offered his sister as wife to Menéndez. he demurred, Carlos insisted, and the girl was baptized Antonia.

*W*ith Balseiro at the wheel, Land of Florida
Greetings, greetings, greetings,
Menéndez de Avilés. Full sail
To the gentleman of the hurricane wind!
What ever happened to Doña Antonia? Tell me of her,
Oh, flame of heated passion,
Hair flowing in the wind,
Unloved lover,
She stood sobbing, her body trembling,
Her voice rising above the pounding waves,
Breasts, high towers on a firm body,
But you, looking for Spanish towers,
Did not embark on her galleon?
Had I been second in command, my friend,
She would not have escaped me,
Though later I might have swung
From a high mast.
     Speed on, Speed on,
       A woman, the sky, and the palms escapes me.
Jasmine, blue sky and sounding sea,
See that woman with the golden hair,
With thighs of flowering desire,
Laughter on her lips, and soft warm breasts.
Give to Avilés the cross and somber decorum,
I prefer the fountains
Of eternal youth, whether a stream or a torrent,
The sun, the sea, the clear blue sky,
And the siren and the woman swimming.
     Speed on, speed on
       A woman, the sky, and the palms escape me.
Better than with Menéndez de Avilés, I'll go
With Ponce de León, who loved the bronzed sirens,
The feathered ring-doves.
Intoxicated with their perfume,
Instead of returning maidens untouched
He would undress them under the stars.
And even today, with foam of orange blossoms,

The waves of the seas sing a nuptial song
In the name of him who offered his ships
To eyes as big as the morning star and to love.
       Speed on, speed on.
       A woman, the sky, and the palms escape me.
Miami, Shore of foam. Fountains. Canals.
No longer the Indian, his paddle and his canoe,
Now, sirens of flesh and blood
With arms for oars and a kiss on the lips,
And a nakedness, a nakedness that has
The shine and glow of marble.
Into my memories the Spanish influence comes,
And since all is confined to my illusion,
When I see a copy of the Giralda
My mind switches and the real Giralda appears
With a cluster of fold, California carnations,
Simulating flames.
Gold of peaches gilded with honey,
Gold in her faithful hands as in the branches.
       Speed on, speed on,
       A woman, the sky and the palms escape me.
On Biscayne Avenue
Tall helmeted palms,
       Speed on, speed on,
       A woman, the sky and the palms escape me.
On Biscayne Avenue
Tall helmeted palms,
Green hair and slender shape.
Palms and palms and more palms,
Marching past in a throng.
"What are you doing there Antillian palms?"
And they reply gracefully, "We are
Models for North American women,
They borrow their eyes from the sea and the sky
And from us our shape and height,
Blond from the sun and short of hair;
We give them their neck, voice and waist
And in exchange for this grace,
They give us the open spaces,
The air and our roots, they give us all."

In the canals are the ancient sails
Beneath them are the doves, and above, the stars.
Speed on, speed on,
A woman, the sky and the palms escape me.

—Alfonso Camín (1956)

PERO LO SOLO

BUT THE SOLE THING

After fleeing his native Spain during the Spanish Civil War, Juan Ramón Jiménez, recipient of the Nobel Prize for literature in 1956, lived in Coral Gables for three years. Reminding him of his native Moguer in southwest Spain, the city's landscape and culture inspired both *Los romances de Coral Gables* (1957) and *Espacio* (1958).

*L*a palma acaricia al pino
con este aire de agua;
en aquel, el pino, el pinó
acariciaba a la palma.

Y la noche azul y verde
es noche verde y morada,
la luna casi me enseña
en su espejo la esperanza.

Pero lo solo está aqui
pero la fe no se cambia
pero lo que estaba fuera,
ahora està solo en el alma.

*T*he palm caresses the pine
with this air of water
in that one, the pine, the pine
caressed the palm.

And the blue and green night
is a green and purple night,
the moon almost shows me
hope in its mirror.

But the sole thing is here
but faith does not change
but what was outside
now is only within the soul.

—Juan Ramón Jiménez (1957)

Translated by Kimberly E. Holtzer

OPPOSITION

*W*ildness of nature is in Florida,
Where senses open to the enveloping heat,
Where no Puritan lives, persons respond to excess,
The lust of the idea of Paradise.
Where Itchetucknee springs from limestone depths
Changeless through clear centuries,
As we float tubing down the enchanting stream.

Tameness of nature holds back the North,
Desolations of the past eroding the present,
The long, heavy shadow of the Puritans
Teaches the severe. They thought life could be better,
Prayed to God not to do anything wrong,
Held back their passion, aimed to kill,
Burned as witches free life-loving girls.

—Richard Eberhart (1981)

The Poet Laureate of New Hampshire and a recipient of the Pulitzer Prize and the National Book Award, Richard Eberhart offers two meditations on the Ichetucknee Springs, a favorite tubing haunt for generations of University of Florida students. Like Wallace Stevens in his "Farewell to Florida," Eberhart contrasts the richness of life in Florida with restrictions on life in the North. Unlike Stevens, however, he revels in such excesses of nature and finds in the state's springs a source of life, insight, and creativity.

ICHETUCKNEE

*I*t is the continuous welling up from the earth
We must remember. Dawn comes, and the waters
Spring fresh, clear, vital from the earth.
Night comes, they well unabated from the dark.
Strange, is it not, that the temperature
Is always the same. The clarity is without change.
As the water blooms upward to become a petaled river
Each grain of sand below is visible as in air.

Over the oval, the mouth, the maw, the source,
We cannot see down into the cavernous mystery
Into primitive limestone releasing the clear water.
We are impelled outward from the warm, strong center.

Our bodies delight in the flow of original life.

Freely in the stream of exhilarating non history
We can walk, swim, float in the clearest shallows.
Upon us the welling up of the source,
Around us the gift of the river, the way we must go.

Our bodies delight in the flow of original life.

—Richard Eberhart (1981)

LOOKING FOR GOD—ARCADIA

I have set flames of hell
in a village of fire ants
drying their venom
with liberal poison.

Amid tiny birds I have carelessly fed
bluejays and grackles
with a swing bell of suet and seeds.

Quail shake down the Sabbath
thankful for short stubble and silence.

Knowing the prayers of its leaves
I answered the citrus grove with food and water.

On the prairie the tightening rawhide
of a dead cow draws my eyes
to the wings and crawl of scavengers.
I point a finger at the glorying sunset
and cry Wait! Wait!

My camera records a full moon
juggled by multiple exposure
into a double-two domino.

—William Mundell (1984)

The Poet Laureate of Vermont, William Mundell has also explored what living in Florida demands. Mundell's attempt to find and record the divine in the midst of living and dying nature becomes both a quest and a game.

AT TEN THOUSAND ISLANDS

*D*iscarded pen shells
write a wavering sentence
along gulf sand
marking the shore
with iridescent ink.
The tide punctuates the lines
with capitals of coral,
commas of sea grape.

In these octaves Mundell describes the mysterious Ten Thousand Islands off the southern Gulf Coast. Pirates and other picaresque characters have historically found refuge in their inaccessible mangrove forests.

Black mangroves wade into the surf
on legs of salt-impervious roots
widening a jungle island that clings
to the limestone pinnacle of rock
of this shallow sea.
Anhingas dive,
ospreys hide,
herons pose.

The lone pelican
soars free and far.
The sea is his, the sky is his.
He knows the ways of the people
along the beach,
yet none of them can know
into which dark corner
of the sunset he goes.

—William Mundell (1989)

Tuesday: Four Hundred Miles

Yesterday at the motel desk in Ocala
    I could not remember my zip. Today
I can speak Etruscan. It came back.

It won't be called. It comes. And sometimes
my oath to Caesar, which need not be binding
in Ocala, but break it on the causeway

past Marathon Key and the sea is impassable:
you will be taken back, nailed upside down
to the cross, and be made to remember

sacred Marcia, who stole from her parents
to run from honor with you. She died
of bad air from the marshes, but first knew

all the words to all the songs
she took with her. I can't even remember
the tunes, till they start uncalled.

It comes and goes and I stay wary.
I have grown a beard but keep moving
and avoid most public places. Old comrades

can see through hair, and it is death
to be recognized. I did not call
my life to these environs, nor Marcia

to that fevered bed. It came.
Between Ostia and the Keys. In the new car
whose license number I can never remember.

      —John Ciardi (1989)

Known for his translation of Dante's *Divine Comedy,* John Ciardi finds the long drive from Ocala to the Keys an opportunity for memories, beginning with his Etruscan and Roman ancestors and focusing eventually on the vagaries of memory. The poem's form offers a modern variation on the **terza rima** used by Dante.

PAINE'S PRAIRIE

Few people have marked
Florida as powerfully as
Stetson Kennedy, editor of
the Federal Writers' Project
Florida: A Guide and author
of *Palmetto Country*. During
the 1930s he wrote this
finely detailed description
of what is now known as
Paynes Prairie State
Preserve, 18,000 acres
of freshwater marsh,
hammocks, pine flatwoods,
swamps, and ponds near
Micanopy.

I stand on the rim of the nut-brown bowl
that is Paine's Prairie:
listen as the cat-squirrel chatters and scolds
the sinking sun.

Clouds in the West
stretched, gauze-like
on the fingers of the wind,
dissolve into soft brown rust
and disappear.

The oaks weep crystalline tears
that drip from mossy beards
into white sand.

A marsh hawk screams,
swooping after the marsh hare that runs
trembling under a log.

Flapping white herons
rise in a long line from the ponds . . .
it is their wings that sing the finale
to the prairie's evening song.

—Stetson Kennedy

IN FLORIDA

May Swenson's poems, with
their rich sense of how the
world of nature echoes
human behavior, offer
valuable parallels to the
work of other poets. The
vivid, playful imagery and
development of "In Florida"
contrasts effectively with
Elizabeth Bishop's somewhat
bleaker vision in "Florida."
And her "Last Night at Long
Pine" reflects a very different
farewell to Florida from
Wallace Stevens's.

*C*ertain nasturtiums of that color, the gecko's neck
of urgent orange, a bubble he inflates until transparent,
then flattens, lets collapse. His intermittent goiter
swells, withdraws, pulls tight, and orange pimples
prick along his length. He's humping up and down,
announcing for a mate. She's not in sight.
Somnolent, gray as a dead twig he's been until today, stuck
on a plank of the porch. Or pale, hanging from splayed
toes on the hot stucco wall. Startling his fat cravat
that bloats and shrinks, his belly of suede sheen, apricot.

Florida screams with colors, soft blooms, sharp juices, fruits.
Day-Glo insects jitter across the eye. A zebra butterfly
in strong sun trails an aura silver and black, like migraine.
Orchid, called Bull Hoof, flares by the fence, and Divi-Divi's
curled pods, feathery foliage effervesces out of a hollow.
Ylang-Ylang, the perfume tree, spreads cadmium-scented plumes.
Hydrangea, Mimosa, Guava, Loquat, Spanish Lime, Poinciana
to follow. Extravagant blushes of bushes, blossom-dressed
trees are a crowd in the yard. Slim palm trunks arch up and
curve like tall sway-necked flamingos.

Fruit of the Queen Palm peeled to the pit discloses miniature
monkey faces. Graceful, straight, the smooth pole of the Date
nests its fruit in clusters of ten thousand flowerets. This
the palm of which Mohammed said to the Arabs, "Honor her,
for she is your Mother." And Pawpaw and Possumwood grow
near Mango's cerise hairy flowers formed at each branch tip.
Giant leaves of the leaning Plantain, whose slatted canopies
make shade for the stiff bunched fruit called "fingers,"
each bunch finally to expand to a whole plump hand.

Two nights ago, under the porch that pokes a little way into
this tame jungle, six kittens slid out of the white cat, Polar.
Scarcely larger than mice, they're fixed to her teats,
where she lies spread for them like an odalisque. Five are
white as she, except for variant sooty noses, ears or tails.
The sixth, runt of the litter, the only male and pitch black,
has been nudged aside. He sucks on a sibling's ear mistaken
for a spigot. To behold the tableau, get on your knees,
put an eye to the widest crack between the boards, where Polar
in the half-dark with her brood patiently endures.

A moment more, and she shakes herself loose from her blind
wriggling kits, crawls out from under to stand and stretch,
gardenia-white in dawn light on the porch, expecting
breakfast. Not far from a kitten herself, with her asking
purr, pink nose and slit green eyes, she crouches, laps her
milk, tugged teats hanging, heavy berries, in her belly's fur.

    —May Swenson (1987)

Last Night At Long Pine

*U*p and walking, 3:30 A.M., under the Southern Cross.
My horsehide jacket squeaks. It's dark on the path.
Is someone behind me? No, it's my shadow.

Bullfrogs whickering, splash of a night-diving duck.
My cigarette's ember to sticks of a fire
winks in the sleeping camp.

A far train bawls at a crossing. Mournful phantom
animal: "Of metal, when shall I mate?"

We strike at sunup, begin the struggle toward cold
incarnation in the North. From soft nights too soon
exiled under smaller, sharper, scantier stars.

—May Swenson (1978)

Ybor City

Ybor City, founded in 1886 as a company town by Spanish cigar makers, prospered and became the hub of Tampa's Latin culture until the change in American smoking habits and the misguided urban renewal that cut the area in half with an interstate. Duane Locke, a professor at the University of Tampa for many years, suggests the past glories of the cigar factories, mutual-aid societies, and social clubs lying behind the present realities.

*T*he antique lights
still there,
but
the checker boards
have buried
their scarves and berets.
The bread
by the coffee cup
grown stale.
It has become stone
and cannot break
into crumbs.
The sparrows peck
and break their bills.
The lost sweater
on the sidewalk
mumbled, "Change.
Everything changes."
We pick up

our bicycles
and from the closed shop
depart.

—Duane Locke (1979)

A WOMAN COMBING

*W*hy should I wish to tell you who I am?
Words: if you look closely the gull is ugly.
A scavenger and a bully, he loves crudely,
And he is, yes, restless, his eye always
On advantage. So, too, the pelican, but I
Can watch them skim the waves in formation
For hours and never think what swims beneath,
Nor of the basic monotonous rhythms of the waves.
The gulls cry out of your mouth when the comb crackles.
And that is impatience and pain; you go to it then,
Laugh across the room as determined as the ocean.
Finally, the long glide and a kind of mistiness
Above it all, a motionless in motion,
And no one has spoken, no, not a word.

—William E. Taylor (1976)

How do poets express in words experiences that seem to lie beyond language? William Taylor, a longtime professor at Stetson University, reflects on the limitations and possibilities of both words and relationships in this unusual and effective love poem.

KALUSA COUNTRY

A slight wind has licked the marshes' pelt
rousing the mild fury of cat-tails;
reeds empty of sound, mastered by the silence
sway in a dance, preparing preludes
the throats of birds will choir
in their wild hour.

Among the walking mangroves that thrust knees
through water dark as tea
and bitterer, an ibis stands

Poets often use form as well as sound to communicate a mood. As Fanny Ventadour's stanzas gently shrink in length, she prepares us for the **elegiac** mood of the spirit of the extinct Kalusa (Calusa) Indians.

mocked by his moire reflection,
gaudy spiders trapeze between the trees.

And by that mound of lime-white shells
picked clean in some prehistoric dawn,
softly in the tip-toe glade at night
Kalusa comes to mourn.

—Fanny Ventadour

CAUSEWAY
(Captiva, Florida)

Now that the causeway spans the channel
The venerable ferry is up for sale.
Mainland traffic edges out, bringing
Timetables, souvenirs, a new breed of trader.
The islanders go indoors, harboring their secrets,

But the birds line the causeway railing
To get a better view. Perched midway
Between tradition and progress, they enjoy
A little of both weathers, the dark
Ancestral green and the bright chromium.

—Allan Block (1972)

Many historians claim that Captiva received its name from the 1528 capture and captivity of Juan Ortiz, who escaped the island only after the daughter of a Calusa chief helped him flee to a friendlier tribe. Later, the island was reputed to have been the holding ground for the female captives of the pirate José Gaspar. In these quintets, Allan Block, in a rather more whimsical vein than Duane Locke, marks the passage of time.

A Winter Ode to the Old Men of Lummus Park, Miami, Florida

*R*isen from rented rooms, old ghosts
Come back to haunt our parks by day,
They creep up Fifth Street through the crowd,
Unseeing and almost unseen,
Halting before the shops for breath,
Still proud, pretending to admire
The fat hens dressed and hung for flies
There, or perhaps the lone, dead fern
Dressing the window of a small
Hotel. Winter has blown them south—
How many? Twelve in Lummus Park
I count now, shivering where they stand,
A little thicket of thin trees,
And more on benches turning with
The sun, wan heliotropes, all day.

O you who wear against the breast
The torturous flannel undervest
Winter and summer, yet are cold,
Poor cracked thermometers stuck now
At zero everlastingly,
Old men, bent like your walking sticks
As with the pressure of some hand,
Surely we must have thought you strong
To lean on you so hard, so long!

—Donald Justice (1960)

Selecting details from his childhood in Miami, Donald Justice traces the way our memories shape our understanding. These poems, which balance his present with his past, reflect the precise description and autobiographical insights that have earned him wide admiration and a Pulitzer Prize.

- **heliotrope**—a shrub or herb with small, fragrant purple flowers.

MEMORY OF A PORCH
Miami, 1942

*W*hat I remember
Is how the wind chime
Commenced to stir
As she spoke of her childhood,

As though the simple
Death of a pet cat,
Buried with flowers,

Had brought to the porch
A rumor of storms
Dying out over
Some dark Atlantic.

At least I heard
The thing begin—
A thin, skeletal music—

And in the deep silence
Below all memory
The sighing of ferns
Half asleep in their boxes.

—Donald Justice (1981)

MONDAY MORNING

James Merrill, winner of the
Pulitzer Prize and National
Book Award, owned a
house in Key West. Here
he juxtaposes his encoun-
ters with a parrot and a
local barber in an amused
commentary on daily life.

*H*ot sun on Duval Street.
Bicycling very slowly
I see, by all that's holy,
An acute blur of fleet

Parrot-green plumage coast
Onto the bus-stop bench:
Less bird, after all, than mensch
"Free as a bird"—its ghost

Face cocked. Now Daddy Kaiser
Of Angelo's Cut 'n Comb
Waddles forth, spry gnome
Waving his atomizer,

Diamonding with spray
One instant hedonist!
Pure whim? Fair-weather tryst?
Already a block away,

I keep risking collision
(In each year's crazier traffic)
To fix that unseraphic
Duo within my vision.

—James Merrill (1988)

FROM GARBAGE

*G*arbage has to be the poem of our time because
  garbage is spiritual, believable enough

to get our attention, getting in the way, piling
up, stinking, turning brooks brownish and

creamy white: what else deflects us from the
errors of our illusionary ways, not a temptation

to trashlessness, that is too far off, and,
anyway, unimaginable, unrealistic . . . .

                down by I-95 in

Florida where flatland's ocean- and gulf-flat,
mounds of disposal rise (for if you dug

something up to make room for something to put
in, what about the something dug up, as with graves:)

the garbage trucks crawl as if in obeisance,
as if up ziggurats toward the high places gulls

and garbage keep alive, offerings to the gods
of garbage, of retribution, of realistic

Part of the poet's mission is to find symbols and images that force us to reexamine what we often take for granted. National Book Award winner A. R. Ammons offers the rich mixture of the garbage dump next to I-95 in south Florida, popularly known as Mount Trashmore, as a **symbol** of the ways we recycle and recreate our pasts.

expectation, the deities of unpleasant
necessities: refined, young earthworms,

drowned up in macadam pools by spring rains, moisten
out white in a day or so and, round spots,

look like sputum or creamy-rich, broken-up cold
clams: if this is not the best poem of the

century, can it be about the worst poem of the
century: it comes, at least, toward the end,

so a long tracing of bad stuff can swell
under its measure: but there on the heights

a small smoke wafts the sacrificial bounty
day and night to layer the sky brown, shut us

in as into a lidded kettle, the everlasting
flame these acres-deep of tendance keep: a

free offering of a crippled plastic chair:
a played-out sport outfit: a hill-myna

print stained with jelly: how to write this
poem, should it be short, a small popping of

duplexes, or long, hunting wide, coming home
late, losing the trail and recovering it:

should it act itself out, illustrations,
examples, colors, clothes or intensify

reductively into statement, bones any corpus
would do to surround, or should it be nothing

at all unless it finds itself:

—A. R. Ammons (1993)

ESTERO ISLAND BEACH CLUB

Professor of English and Poet-in-Residence at Cornell College in Iowa from 1954-94, Dana
uses his familiarity with Midwestern farmers to humanize indulgent retirees at an exclusive
resort.

By day, they lie
beside the heated,
turquoise pools,
tanning to the look
of imported leather;
at evening, gathering
beachside on the terrace
to celebrate a sun
going down gold off
Sanibel and Captiva.
Businessmen, retired
farmers and their wives,
bearing a eucharist
of chips and dip;
nachos smothered
in Wisconsin cheddar;
olives of California
cardboard packed
in water. Booze
for the blood of Christ.
They talk mostly
of money, reckoned
in hundred thousands;
of acres of land;
plats, accesses;
strings of hot-dog
stands; the old
joke about the guy
who puts a twenty
in the collection plate
and takes out change.
Back in Illinois,
the farmhouse is modern.

No longer the flaking
shit-kicker cold
enough in winter
away from the wood-
burning stove to stop
your breath; in summer,
muggy as a sponge,
and smelling sickly
sweet of peonied
wallpapers, milk,
and manure. Behind
the barn, the White
Diamond silo tilts
in the air like
something Italian;
the colors of early
spring are Tuscan—
umber and ochre
under a breath of slip.
Hours later, passing
two vagrant kids
sleeping on a stolen
blanket, I'll still
hear them, these
voices raw-tongued
and democratic,
speaking without apology;
and the moon will rise
silvery over a talc
and powdered sugar
beach, and the Gulf
breeze strike softly
across the bright
praise of waters.

—Robert Dana (1991)

THE SHELL

*M*ust have come from another ocean.
The Florida shells are teeth
where this was smooth enough that an animal
had been carved there. The real
animal was gone
and here was this profile of a horse
as if someone taking the animal out
had felt bad
and brought it back larger.

We listened for the sea
in it, but the real sea kept drowning it out.
We hadn't seen a shell on this beach for years.
If an Indian had come by
it would have been no less strange—
and we would give him the shell
and he would give us the beach
and we would think
for a while we owned it.

—Judith Berke (1988)

How can small objects force us into new perspectives? Miami poet Judith Berke finds that an unusual shell can change a familiar beach.

VIZCAYA

the Deering estate

*Y*ou almost hate to walk in these gardens,
   they're so pure, so French in that way—abstract—
but we do, stopping to take pictures
as though we were tourists at Versailles,
or the Villa d'Este. Facing towards us
is the house, made of the bones, or is it the skin,
of how many Venetian palazzos.
And here is Mr. Deering, so dapper—
1910, he can afford
a little culture now, so he starts importing
gondolas, and peacocks, and statues
of peacocks. Stone faces of huge bearded

Berke explores the history and the mysteries of the Italian Renaissance-style villa of industrialist James Deering. Completed in 1920 after seven years of construction at a cost of $15 million, the estate is now a museum.

explorers, gazing out over Biscayne Bay
thinking, What went wrong?
This isn't the fountain, in fact
I'm tired, and it's hot, and where am I
anyway? . . . They say Mr. Deering liked to dress
as an explorer. Sat in the corners watching,
being shy. The guests
in their splendid Greek and Arabian
costumes. The house dressed
as an Italian, when all along
the bones were made of limestone, and key-
stone right out of south Florida.
Someone stops to take our picture—
my friend's and mine. Trying not to bother
the broad-leaved arrowheads, and the African
violets . . . Under here
are the runaway slaves, and the Indians.
On their sides, listening.
White now. Almost completely white.

—Judith Berke (1989)

LITTORAL

Once on a Sunday I took my sons where the sea
Had thrown up sandbars and tidepools far out
From dry beach until the moist, wave-stripped
Littoral had bared a nereid skin of sand
I scanned with skint eyes for the scampering
Beneath it of mollusks and crustaceans
And for whatever mortared with salt spittle
The primordial architecture of minute, chimnied
Castles out of broken shells, sand, and seaweed.

We saw fish answering our motions
Skipping on top of the water, chunks of palm
Trunk like huge pine cones, sand dollars in
Tidepools reaching seaward, sea the motionless
Inconceivable eye of ageless saturation
Of life and mineral in warm shallows and on

From the *Odyssey* to "Dover Beach," western poets have found in the sea a symbol of continuity and connection as well as an image of the imagination and mystery. Van Brock's outing with his sons on a coast, more soiled by man than either Homer or Matthew Arnold had experienced, becomes a voyage to the shore of insight.

- **littoral** coastal region, pertaining to the shore

- **nereid** sea nymph

The half-guessed ocean floor's terrain.
The rush of wave pulls back the shells with
Blackened tin can tops, pop or beer—among
Oil-tar painted rocks, chewed pilings
And huge stones thrown up against the sea's
Thrust, now worn and barnacled. We looked:
The nereid gone, seaweed scattered like hair.

Whatever general answers I have given them,
Denied or been unable to deny, I have
Shown them where the beach drops suddenly
To dark water with waves folding and folding
Themselves on sand like thick wrinkled skin
Dissoving on contact with land—a being
More amorphous and strange than any in it
And connecting all the extremes in the sun's eye.

—Van K. Brock (1965)

DRIVING AT DAWN

A dead rabbit by the roadside,
Sunlight turning his ears to rose petals.

A new electric fence,
Its five barbed wires tight
As a steel-stringed banjo.

The feet of a fat dove
On a high black line
Throbbing to the hum
Of a thousand waterfalls.

A flock of egrets in a field of cows.

Three Great Blue Herons like hunchbacked
        pelicans in a watering pond.

The red leaves of a bush
Burning inside me.

A swamp holding its breath.

—Van K. Brock (1965)

The influence of the past on the present in both his **imagistic** "Driving at Dawn" and his meditative "The Land of Old Fields" reflects the way we search for meaning in nature. Both poems begin with **images** of death and end with anticipation, and both suggest the drive to connect and understand.

THE LAND OF THE OLD FIELDS

After the latest mass murders
police scan infrared maps
for "hot spots" radiated
by decaying bodies;
they lug geiger counters
through abandoned fields listening
to the idiotstuttering, where
arrowheads lie on the ground
near bricks made by slaves,
and the names of slaveholders
who hunted Indians for bounty
are still hallowed in schoolbooks
shining with blood.

Large cats know in their paws
where they are by the felt
currents of underground rivers.
The earth has voice prints
I cannot hear even when I lie
near my father's house
with my best ear to the ground.

Snakes, cold-blooded,
spend their waking lives regulating
body temperatures. Deaf,
they hang their tongues in the night
to measure the slightest concussions
of air flowing into their mouths;
their scales decipher sound.
At night they are drawn like blood
to the best conductors:
large rocks that remember the
noon sun, new grave slabs.

Fossils and tooled stones litter
Apalachee.
"Tallahassee"—from Seminole—
the land of the old fields;
"Seminole"—from Creek—
they who went to a new place;

from
> "cimarron"—American Spanish—
> wild, runaway;

from
> "maroon"—French—
> runaway slave;

"A'palachi"—from Choctaw—
the people on the other side.
Old settlements, abandoned villages,
fathers known and unknown, scrambled
evidence, lost tongues.

Dark cat, I stealthily reenter
the country of my origin.
It does not give itself easily.
It hides its fawns. The rainbow
snake sinks its subtle spectrum
in swamps. The scarlet snake and coral
hide their red and yellow bands.
I eat its mushroom visions,
looking for passages in it never unlocked.
It will not learn my name.
My feet feel their way
by a braille my brain cannot read.
I listen, my whole body a tongue.

—Van K. Brock (1979)

THE MAGIC KINGDOM

Florida residents often regard the state's most popular attraction with a rather ironic, even sardonic, viewpoint.

*W*hy do so many fat people go to Disneyworld,
haunches lapping over the little seats
in the Grand Prix or Mr Toad's Wild Ride?
Does one feel weightless there, reality displaced
so you soon begin sniffing plastic roses
and they really smell like roses but better?

• E coupon—Disney World originally provided visitors with coupons lettered A through E for its rides. E coupons provided access to the most elaborate rides.

20,000 Leagues Under the Sea ("E" coupon)
we stare out our portholes at fake fish on wires,
the flat surface 6 inches above. Our kids ask,
Are the bubbles real?   Who knows?

The Master's dead: behold his Haunted House
at the top of Liberty Square (the orange map);
as Mickey said, he had a mind like a steel
mouse—and the smile of reason
that warmed the clean columns of Monticello
fades into the flat grin
of a mechanical Cheshire cat. Pink
pilgrims shoulder in the squares
cuddling the comic relics of infancy. In Fantasy-
land Mike Fink performs
an unnatural act on Dumbo the Unresisting
or is the heat getting me?

And yet
to stand in the middle of that circular movie
(admission free)
and see the crowd lean far to the left
feeling they're taking a curve
was (shall we say)
educational.

       —Peter Meinke (1977)

THE CLOUD, FLORIDA 1985

*A*bove mimosa and the flowering palm,
above the lights that narrow to a V,
beyond the streaming headlights, past the lake,
beyond the skyline biting at the sky,
below the lonely star pegged near a cloud
like a penny nail holding the whole thing up,
this cloud, solid as iron, chunky as coal,
squats like a Buddha on the pale horizon.
Clouds are Florida's mountains, palpable
as stone with snowy tufts, or dizzying
stadiums of sound and light. They
satisfy the heart by filling emptiness
with shape—but this one I have seen before. . . .

Born and raised in Brooklyn, Meinke sees in a storm cloud a passage into both the past and the future.

Underneath the lantern. My hands tighten
on the wheel. Not like a Buddha now but still
triangular, slabs of dust and gas layered
like steps, a boy could run right up or tumble
down. . . .
                    Slowly, the coalescing clouds
sharpen like snapshots in the darkening sky,
lit from below by the departed sun;
and I know the shape: the side view of
our house in Flatbush, even the right color—
slate blue-gray. *It is burning, burning!*
and I stop the car to watch as the light flares
one last time and the shape blurs and fades
into the broken air, racing always
farther away from Brooklyn, toward the last
borough where all their voices will sleep.

—Peter Meinke (1985)

DAWN AT THE SEASHORE

*A*t 6:07 the first beams slant
through the oak's rigging, its leaves
opening like hands and the saltshot
world gets ready to sail again.
Across our pathway, strung with pearls,
the pirate webs suspend, silken bridges
in the swollen air, constructions delicate,
dangerous, and foolhardy because
at 7:10, still half-drowned in sleep,
we step out to learn the news, wallowing
through web and shadow like whales through seaweed,
brushing these miracles from our eyes and arms—
each day reapeated, like a hit play
on the destuction of Atlantis. We could
go back and walk around the house,
or slither like boarders below the webs,
the paper instead of a dagger in our teeth.
We don't, of course: these are just spiders

In an elegant **conceit**, Peter Meinke, Director of the Writing Workshop at Eckerd College in St. Petersburg 1966-93, compares a spider's plunder to that of a pirate and seeks to attain the spider's concentration and directness.

we're talking about, air-breathing arachnids
trying to catch their dinner.

                              And yet

teach me to plunder each day
like the modest spider,
spinning out of itself in quiet
concentration against the odds,
something practical and lovely to the eye,
making no bones about what he's doing it for,
in fear of neither gods nor Davy Jones.

—Peter Meinke (1987)

MOON FLIGHT

Launch

*H*e will become excited
Within certain limits.
Then the elements will fume.

And with technicians numbering seconds
Like lovers
In some long drawn ponderous good-bye,
He will enter a silent heavy hesitance,
And then the timelessness of travel.

Some will turn away, others
Will follow him out of mind,
And a few will think, another

Emissary against dragons.

The Sea of Frigidity

Light, clumsy breath
Coming upon demand,
He will stand upon the history
Of a million, upturned, night-torn eyes.

From founding the Alaska Flying Poets to earning the nickname the "electronic poet" for his fascination with technology and computers, Edmund Skellings has long explored the edges of experience, geography, and art. Envisioning the moon flights a decade before Neil Armstrong first stepped on the moon, Florida's third Poet Laureate connects the exploration of the moon to both the romance of chivalry and the commonplaces of everyday experiences. "In Florida" suggests the ways land has a way of locking into our consciousness. And his satiric play on games and stereotypes in the ironically titled "Organization of American States" challenges traditional assumptions in a culture undergoing a radical transformation.

He will pick up a pebble of the moon.
It will be like the end of any love,
And he will stand,
Encratered, desolate,
Upon the stiffened shores of meteors,
The sharp horizon abruptly Near, and a clouded future
Pendant in his sky.

Terminal

The thunder on the moon is silent.
It is no less there. Ask
Any of the moon's pedestrians.
He will smile the smile of

No one *you* know.
And then his lids will rise
Like the doors on storm cellars
And you will see emerge
The ancient look of the survivor,
Pupils wide with aftermath,
The mind's streets filled with leaves and litter,
Black homes,
And a snapped blue sparking.

—Edmund Skellings (1963)

IN FLORIDA

A boy in a field nearby whistles his dog
And the dog comes fetching a stick
Too wide for his mouth, and the boy
Lifts him off his feet and swings
That dog around in circles containing
No let go.

I lived in the woods of Alaska long
Enough to know the cold that comes
To the trees at night, that can
Freeze a stream solid like a giant
Icicle laid on the ground. Knew
The cold enough to feel it
Seep through wool and fur and
Chill the body's hair. There was
One word the skin spoke then and
It is still here under the flood
Of sun. That dog knows well the
Word through his canine teeth
To his rigid tail.
Those two syllables are one word
Still. *Hang on.*

— Edmund Skellings (1978)

Organization of American States

The Mason-Dixon Line has moved
Down to divide Panama with a canal.
The deputies of two hemispheres
Gather under the moon over Miami.

Si, say the potential rebels,
Smiling beneath black mustaches.
They have oily skins and export raw
Materials. When they ask about
The Yankee dollah, we tell'm.

They carry the same look in the eye
As their father Indians who drifted
Down from Mongolia across the tundra,
Spearing bison en route.

Under the great Southern Cross
They have kept better time
Than any civilization.
They know how to wait, and watch

The North Americano Big Board.
When a crack appears here and there,
They mutter behind their hands.

Peasants are like dandelions.
They seed. And will not stay
Off the lawns.

—Edmund Skellings (1978)

INPRESSION: ORANGE COUNTY FLORIDA SPRING

*A*bout half way in April
the alarming tabebuia petals
come out: empty
save for occasional gusts
of gold, the tree comes
on in a ballet of
devastation: grey
hair netted   moss
tentacles grip
the juiciest nodes, bare
arms   jangle
a few buttery rings: the
startled eye rushes
in to awkwardness and to
dazzle. What can a woman
wood all these years
do: break out
in spectral yellow, brief
as a breath, then
fall
golden tigertailed pool
ring around
                        to liberation
the tree

—Jean West (1976)

With the selective detail of an impressionist painter like Edouard Manet or a novelist like Virginia Woolf, Jean West paints her impression of the tabebuia, a tropical American shrub blossoming in April. The professor of creative writing at Rollins College offers her homage to an earlier poet with a reflection on Elizabeth Bishop's "Florida."

"THE STATE WITH THE PRETTIEST NAME"

For Elizabeth Bishop

$\mathcal{W}$e live fifty miles from the water, dead center
in this peninsula on a piece of the shadowed
green land you mention. Hurricanes
wear themselves out (usually)
over those who live at the edges. And the sea
takes back anything it might have lost
to our imaginations. Most recently,
Andrew went down like a
great International Harvester machine
and separated the wheat from the chaff
leaving both not very neatly
redistributed. Not even the mangrove roots
were severe enough looking to anchor
the River of Grass. Moot
question whether the cattle
pollute its tributaries. They were here
grazing and lowing uncontroversially (white
herons tiptoeing beside them—such
unlikely companions it's amusing)
when John Cabot sailed down the coast and discovered
Florida. He was the King's map maker. There was
another map maker, too; French. But the Spanish
disposed of the French sailors in the "service
of the Lord our God" and all
that is left are the elegant map maker's drawings
of Indians. He found their costumes
wonderful and inventive
for savages. You

took a good look at
woods in the sunset, at the savages'
toenails; you found their habits
"pretty to watch." The digging
for gold goes on, for the first
Spanish fort, for the first
carrier of syphilis; you'd enjoy
the latest clues that are etched in bones

in an old Italian olive grove; you'd
enjoy that the Indians (apparently)
already were immune
through a look-alike
bacteria. Disease always
belongs to the enemy. You might ask
which is enemy? Which savage
will rise up through macadam and
fantasy to meet the green
gaze of the panther, the sparrow, the
princess
resting in her skirt of shells
and legend.

—Jean West (1994)

FROM SHELL MOUNDS

I. Turn of the Century

*T*rees have melted to circles
in shell; no roots, no
Caloosa chanting
                    their voices
shrunk to a drum
and the drum head gone to rags in the shell-heap,
no frame of bone where calcium traces its pattern:
an absence of music
                        in this slow and settled clock of shells
popping down each others' backs
as night air thickens.
            Mangroves settle the moonlight, turn
sawgrass down around their roots,
and raise the tide. Obelisks of branches
squash the water. Oaks grow taller: buoyed
giant seeds. They are rising
permanent as the dead whose voices ring
the thick oak trunks.
New moonlight pulls them, simple
in a calendar of stone.

Archaeologists have divided
the many shell mounds
found throughout the state
into four different kinds:
ceremonial, foundation,
refuse, and burial. Until
laws began protecting
the mounds, collectors
plundered bones and
artifacts and builders
used the shells as
construction material.
Mac Miller, professor
at New College in Sarasota,
editor of *New Collage
Magazine,* and proprietor
of the Ruskin House Bed
and Breakfast, contrasts the
natural life rhythms of the
indigenous peoples with
the modern age's clumsy
technology.

II. Road-Building. Boom-Time

Square 1920's trucks
back into everything; who said
a convict ever learns? Flat bush
rolls underwheel around the slough,
then jams reverse, as trucks
hump backwards, tailgates shove back
into hills.

III. Prehistory

The dead cracked abalone
                                 open in their mounds;
backwash of hot exhaust on oyster shell
steams like feast-days
                            when women gathered
their brown circles over fire
gleaming on their knees.
Short hot shells steam
                             open on the coal
steam spatters. Dusky fish thrashed
open in a never-drying pile
beside the fire.
No one would hold hands
if they could eat; they sat together breaking
shell on common ground.

      —A. McA. Miller (1983)

TRANSCRIPT

*H*ow old I felt that day—
that's what I was. '01. '03.
What's figures got to do with me?
You write so fast, like
chicken-tracks! 'Born and bred
in Eatonville?' Now that's a lie!
I hated Harris and his cutie talk:
Tar-Baby wasn't sticky, 'cause

How would Zora Neale
Hurston have answered her
critics had she been allowed
a final word? In this **dramatic
monologue**, Hurston touches
upon many of the themes
and controversies of her
work and specifically
parallels her legal problems
with those of her
contemporary, Marjorie
Kinnan Rawlings. The
language of the poem

recreates the variety of the styles the writer herself employed, including forms of dialect and satiric, derogatory humor.

• **Harris** Joel Chandler Harris, author of the Uncle Remus stories

he's black. But the 'briar patch'?
That was fine. I grew up everywhere
I moved. The slash-pine camps, Atlanta,
Harlem, floating easy anywhere. Sure,
I had a houseboat till it sank.
You got that down? Don't
frown, 'cause that's a lie.
No story's got the whole round truth,
so I tole lots. That Marjorie, she tried.
She lied about them deers and things,
like Harris. But Cross Creek was the whole
round little world, like Eatonville, and then
that honkie woman sued her ass! White folks
can sue. Real people got to go to jail
to see a lawyer. Write this down:
I'd sooner stick a dirty finger
in my mouth. We both got off,
that Marjorie and me. That's more or less
got off. Now write this down: Jews lied
about King Herod. He never hurt
them babies none. And white folks lied
about me too. Let someone do you wrong
it never stops. Remember that, young lady.
Lord, you write it all out—don't you?
No matter now. You got your book
still open. Jesus got his too,
and he don't sue. It's open flat
like this Eau Gallie land lays flat
and then the ocean eats it. Herod
didn't eat no babies. That's what I tell
the Doctor. He be comin' every three,
four days and bring me food. 'Round him,
I talk real white. Oh, I can speak as lovely
as the Harlem niggerati! That's a mean
Italian joke, you hear? Doctor's even
read my stories some, and Shakespeare too.
I tole him, "I am dying, Egypt, dying,"
and he laughed and quoted me, "I wish you
all joy of the worm." Oh, that man!
If I was younger, now, I'd bed him down.
You write that too, 'cause it's the truth.
I ain' no Uncle Remus and his talkin'

bears. I ain' no fluffed-up Harlem nigger
cluckin' like a broody hen. You spell it right,
I'm an-thro-pol-o-gist. I wrote it down.
I tole so many lies, the truth come out.

      —A. McA. Miller (1992)

BEAUTIFUL SWIMMER

*A*t anchor.
Egmont and Mullet Keys   squeeze the rush of Tampa Bay
out   like the dark of space sliding past . . .
until I pierce its void   bicep deep,
then stars leak from my fingers   spinning mare's tails of light—
a sudden comet streaks toward my play,
reminds me how soft my flesh.
I touch the tide   instead   with eyes:
Callinectes Sapidus: Beautiful Swimmer,   Blue crab.
I am safe   assured by names
and paprika-hued feasts of young Chesapeake summers.
Like God   I cannot resist joy.
My arm sparks the rushing ebb once more:
galaxies spring from my palm.
In the beginning was Word   they say.
Our brains dazzled the quiet of mystery
with names   like phosphorescence
wonder quickly fades. . . .
Another glowing   a larger streak   arcs toward me.
I try   but fail   to grasp my hand
with my mind—   life must eat . . .
words are not enough,   God knows.

      —Bruce Aufhammer (1990)

As poetry has become a visual as well as aural medium, poets have begun exploring the effects of space on the page. Bruce Aufhammer, chair of English at Seminole Community College, recreates both the stream of thoughts and pools of silence that work through his mind while swimming in Tampa Bay.

Carol Gillespie

*I'*m travelling through Myakka, through the ranches,
and the dust and the heat and the sagging clumps
of humped-back brahmas are starting to get me,
so I pull off at some windowless, cement-block bar,
but no one's there except the bartender,
and a young girl on a stage in the corner,
singing country-western, blues.
                                        Her name's
Carol she says, she's a music major at FSU,
in Tallahassee, making some extra money
for herself, for her little baby girl Cheryl,
and I know this sounds like I'm making it up,
but when I tell her my name, she looks at me like
my hair's on fire, says she's read my poems,
Well, some of them. Not bad, she says, especially
the one with the small boy, and I'm wondering
whether she's putting me on or she's crazy,
and then she tells me she even wrote a
song on it, that she'd seen it in a magazine
from out West, where she wishes she were now,
instead of here, at Lamar's, and I laugh,
tell her at least she's getting paid,
and not just in copies, and she gives me
this quick, surprised look like
Well, well what do we have here?
so I do a quick tack, say to her,
Why don't we stay in touch,
send each other some stuff
from time to time, but of course
neither of us does, and then four years later
I get a call from her, she's in town she says,
playing at the Hyatt, she'd like to see me,
her little boy Randy is with her,
he's six now, Remember Randy?
and I tell her, Yes,
but all the time I'm thinking,
What little boy? It was a girl,
but the next thing I know I'm at the Hyatt
and she's on stage in this black silk dress

Justin Spring, founder of the performance group Sarasota Poets, champions the poetry of ordinary speech and experience. In this poem of chance encounters, he explores the vagaries of memory and the joy of the moment in a near **stream-of-consciousness** narration.

that keeps crinkling like anthracite,
and when she sees me, she winks, nods down
to her left, and I see him
sitting next to the bandstand,
the little boy, or whatever he is,
and he's looking up at her and
laughing and clapping and he has this
little, checkered sports-coat on and a
black bow tie and these tiny black shoes,
Like a ventriloquist's dummy,
I keep saying to myself,
and then she says to the boy,
Randy, this is Justin, you remember
Justin don't you, the man mommy met
at Lamar's who wrote the poem about the boy
that mommy wrote the song about?
and he's just sitting there, beaming,
looking up at us like he's in heaven
or church or somewhere only he can imagine,
and then she tells me she's sorry
she never wrote or anything
but life has been hectic,
but when I look at the boy who keeps changing like
I'll bet it has, she doesn't miss a beat,
she's right on to me, telling me her song
about the little boy is the best one
on her album, Everyone says so,
even Randy, and all the time
Can you believe this?
and then I feel someone
push the boat away from the dock
and I'm drifting around
in circles, looking at her,
thinking, God how I love this woman.

      —Justin Spring (1990)

THE UNFINISHED SUSPENSION BRIDGE:
TAMPA BAY, MORNING FOG

*T*he bay is so white, peaceable. Everything
is lost in light. Even the normally
boisterous steel-workers are perched on cables,
walk-ways, hoops
                      like angels,
gazing at the flowering light,
thinking what they'll tell their wives,
later, over beers. When the jukebox slows.
Eternity. I saw it. Really.
                    Even
the homosexual foreman
far below them on the caisson dock
is lost in thought.
                    Occasionally,
out of habit, or maybe for the hell of it,
he'll look up at the hazy bridge
as though he could see it. He knows
the boys are goofing off. He doesn't care.
He loves the fog, the way the light
disguises things.

                    He's five or six,
standing in a neighbor's yard.
Yellow boots, yellow coat.
He loves it here.
No school. No rules.
The morning is so soft, so white
he can barely see the house he left.
For the first time in his life
he is happy.
                    He smiles,
seeing himself again.
A yellow finch. Strutting about.
Aglow inside.

            —Justin Spring (1989)

the space behind the clock

one
15 year old afternoon
    while watching amputated frog legs
twitch
convulsively
    in mother's hot skillet
      I wondered . . .

it is cold
    in the early morning starlight of the everglades
and the weatherbee .470 express
  wears heavily
    upon my shoulder
as the guide urges
  caution
for this is the mating season
  and they become angry
if interrupted
  from their passion
but I move on
  scornfully
being filled with youthful arrogance
  when
    suddenly
the ground
      shakes
  bushes explode
and before us
  trembling
squats an enraged giant bull frog
who
  with brass knuckles gleaming
hurls himself toward me
  in mighty two hundred and fifty pound
bounds
  while i
coolly lighting up a marlboro
  spat defiance
from the hip

Imagination has invariably served as a source of escape from the humdrum and a defense against the uncomfortable. In the title poem of a collection of works by Florida inmates, the author, who borrowed his pseudonym from the famous comic-strip artist, recreates the vivid fantasy and often brutal nonchalance of a teenager escaping from his mother's kitchen to a highly imaginative hunt.

as the inevitable jaws
sought me

the cold bites sharply
and while the scavengers circle hungrily
 i begin to
 twitch
convulsively
  to the sound of wild applause

—r. crumb (1976)

LEAVING RAIFORD

In leaving Florida's
forbidding state prison,
perhaps best known as the
home of "Old Sparky," the
state's electric chair, the
poet recognizes the
physical, emotional, and
psychological hold Raiford
still has on him.

That morning I walked out
the main gate.
I had not meant to turn back
to see the Rock with those
paint-chipped bars
and the paled faces behind them
trying to squeeze their eyes
into four inch squares of sun.

Yet I turned and looked again
as if that gray monster
could not give up
what it had owned for six years,
roaring its whistle,
clanging its bars until I was deaf
with the knuckles of my fists.

(1976)

WINTER CONDO

*N*ight has covered the beach, a black
    Lotion, chasing home the tanners,
The sun dried to their skins like paint.
    From three poles small nets of light drop
Onto the sand settling around
    A wooden bench where two lovers sit,
The salt air moving across their faces
    Like desire. Along the rims of light
Vacant umbrella chairs are laid out
    Like gutted fish, the days catch,
And barely visible the white edges of waves
    Wrinkling in where this afternoon
Tourists stood and applauded the sunset.
    In the penthouse the rich old widow reigns
Robotic at bridge and gossip and complaints
    And as always amid the chatter someone
Spills a drink. In 201, the TV
    Washing them in palsied light,
The newly retired couple from Vincennes
    Bravely lounge on strange rattan
And tell themselves, again, they will
    Not worry about the hardware store
They left in the hands of their only son.
    Two floors up a pallid woman
From Quebec sees Montreal in the small
    Window above her sink as she
Washes dishes and sings in French. . . .

    This is St. Petersburg where people
Live like dials measuring the sun
    And tonight along the moonless shore
To the end of Pass-a-Grille a thousand
    Lighted rooms struggle to keep good cheer
As the eclipsed Gulf collapses, a black hole,
    And the oracular surf chants all night long:
We have all come here from some place else
    Our lives at our backs.

—Jack Crocker (1995)

Each winter seasonal snow-birds migrate to Florida's beaches to join the permanent residents, many of whom are themselves Northern refugees. A college dean and resident of St. Petersburg Beach, Jack Crocker describes the customs and culture of his migrant neighbors.

THOSE ANCIENT FLORIDIANS

Sonny Cockrell, a professional archaeologist specializing in underwater archaeology and Early Man studies, paints a rich portrait of the peninsula's earliest inhabitants.

*T*hose ancient Floridians sat pondering the deep, florescing
                                                          sunset,
And, once the orb, suddenly red-swollen, had sunk into the
Western sea,
Returned to the present necessity.

One month dead now, their brother lies decomposing on the rack,
The now-diminishing flies only partially blackening the rigid,
Straining,
Corse.
The surrounding pines, wind-swept, crested by tear-eyed
                                                          vultures,
Harbingers of the dark kingdom,
Stare erectly down at the mourners below.

Reverently, reflectively, the People watch the Old Woman gather
The scattered bones, some still linked by dried brown skin,
And wrap them in the reed-woven shroud.

While they pray individually, and chant collectively,
The Old Woman gathers all the molding parts, and walks slowly,
                                                          stoically
Toward the funereal mound,
Earthen bier,
Soon to be capped by the annual addition of the dead.

The bones laid (some full-length, newly dead, and others,
                                                          bundle-bound,
transported from prior graves), the women bring baskets
Of white sand to cover the resting place.
To the side, quietly sitting, the mourners now chant,
                                                          murmurmering,

Indistinctly, each remembering a deceased as a fellow being
One last time, and then gaze resolutely, necessarily
Forward.

—Wilburn A. Cockrell (1978)

A FLORIDA CHILDHOOD

The brick-red Spanish rooftiles overlapped in patterns
reminiscent of a snake's scales and the rainspouts held
emaciated fingers to the soaking eaves. The windows
flickered eyelids with oblique
pupils of lamplight muffled beyond the glass.
Some houses were grandees. Others wore
palm-fringes at their throats like swaddled
muftis whose senescent eyes
fluoresced like aggies. At the banyan's thunderous
foot we gambled on mumblety-peg. I saw
spiders blazing coldly like faroff stars
while the pink dewdrops wobbled on their webs.
An ancient scorpion dwelt behind the broom.
Its warm brown eyes gazed in two rows from the tip
of its head like the curtained windows of a ship.
Its immobility made me dream of voyages.
And the blue-muscled skinks along the pebbles
sported tuxedo-twills down their deceptive backs.
There I pierced a grasshopper with a sharpened match
and once, in a solution hole
of the hammock, I bellied deep into the moist
limestone crevices of a decaying reef. The earth
smelled fresh as a new-worn shoe. I could have
dozed forever in that unmarked place. The soft
desperate moths at nightfall sealed our house
and the thresholds were spelled. Only the brass
hours chimed from the London clock, and the moon
grappled in its white branches at the windowsill.

—Eric Ormsby (1992)

Director of Libraries at
McGill University in Toronto,
poet Eric Ormsby was
raised in Florida. His
remembrances of his
childhood, framed with
houses but filled with
nature, contrast with the
more urban recollections
of Donald Justice.

Burning the Field for Spring
LaCrosse, Fl

Yet another Northern transplant, a French Canadian, struggles with the nonparadisiacal aspects of making Florida home.

*D*og fennel and partridge pea crackle and char.
Shovel in hand he watches, big French Canadian,
as the flame creeps towards the square
he plowed around his trailer, the home
he can leave any time. For a moment,
he really thought he could burn it all.
The live-in coffin that cooks in summer
and chills in winter, the addition he built
but never got into because it leaked.
Burn off the lost job at the pipe plant,
melt the stolen tubes of pvc that fence
his land. But when the first low flame
slips the break, he beats it down.
Long after it's out, he slaps his shovel
Whack whack whack on the blackened grass.

—Lola Haskins (1984)

Being Saved in Daytona Beach

A poet who can reveal the mystery and irony in the everyday, Enid Shomer moves easily from urban to natural jungles. Whether juxtaposing the sacred and profane in Daytona Beach or imagining reincarnation as kudzu, the south's ubiquitous vine, her poems are both deeply personal and richly comic.

*O*n the oceanside wall of the pool
at the Nomad Motel
a florid orange script asks me
to *Praise the Lord* while the slats
of a bus stop bench on the strip
proclaim that only He can heal
this land. An arrow points
to the Drive-In Church.

The nearly nude bathers
must not have heard the news:
on that final day corpses
will rise up from their graves
to be judged, each indiscretion
weighed as they pose
on the Staircase to Heaven.

From my beachside balcony
the moon seems stuck
to the surf, a slot machine
spilling its silver luck
down an endless chute of waves.
You beside me, love, in the vinyl chaise,
your sex rising from its dark pulpit
like a sermon.

　　　—Enid Shomer (1987)

WALKING IN KUDZU

June now: the vacant lot
　　draped with kudzu, kudzu
slung between the trees
like abandoned sheets,
a place of kudzu
raising minarets
against the sky. Once I

slough-slogged in the Everglades
the thick black soup
of decay, and sank
into that richness
up to my waist. Here,
depth-perception blurred,
everything solid suspect,

I wade into the vines,
into the deep green hollows.
What dishevelment! Walls
crumbling as they rise,
broken limbs trapped
in the weave, kudzu
pouring itself over the tin-

roofed shack and junked
appliances. If it's true
we come back to another
life, I'd choose this one—this
headlong rush, this stammer
of green, this slow
stampede towards light.

—Enid Shomer (1987)

FLIGHT 318 TO ORLANDO

Shadowed by the clouds I fly above
those common Florida lakes below
mark their deep agate circles
into the distant swamps
like great mastodon footprints
treading their ancient journey
through the Panhandle
Each step an urge forward

My flight carries me back
to my hometown for the last rites
that we the living offer
my grandmother   my grandfather
born a year and a week apart
died a year and a week apart

Lake Eola and 48 lakes below shine
near the St. Johns bulbing hyacinth
the cold sand-bubbling spring rivers
the groves of orange blossoms
the purple and raspberry crepe myrtles
the oak trees hung with scarves of moss

I weep until the wheels set down
then step through the mottled heat
to drive to my grandmother's grave
to place my grandfather by her side

In order to make a poem breathe, the poet must find a way to create some kind of rhythm. Nable slows down the movement in this **elegy** for her grandmother by emphasizing single-syllable words and creating pauses, not with punctuation but with line breaks and white spaces.

I see him dressed in J.C. Penney workclothes
a hammer in one hand at his side
I see her dressed in her housedress and hairnet
a long spoon held like a scepter across her breast

Each smiles like a doll asleep in a shoe box

Their city and their time have passed
and I do not recognize the straight cut roads
though I know these shopping centers
and neon beef palaces in other places

Here their stiff squares smirk and crouch
to stifle the low breath of the swamp
to cover its mounds and memory with asphalt

Soon even this cemetery will be real estate
the tombstones and bones crushed and erected upon
just like my granpa's mother's Scottish-laid garden
with 60 years of hummingbirds migrating South
through purple althea, guava, and gardenia   gone
bulldozed under   paved and boxed over with buildings

So I end my flight back to this burial ground
to pour water from a Dixie cup into the dark
squared cavity that holds my granma and granpa
and I wish it were a limestone cave
to cradle their naked flesh through time

A cave from which we mourners emerge
being glad for the shadows and clouds
the cooling shroud of the great oaks
that give us our quiet assuming breath

          —Eugenie Nable (1989)

CUBAN REFUGEES ON KEY BISCAYNE

Memory and imagination have traditionally proven comforting refuges from repetition and boredom. Barbara Winder's portrait of these old men napping suggests how powerfully the search for a fountain of youth continues to shape the image of Florida.

*B*reathless when the breeze deserts them
old men

in aluminum chairs
face the sea.

Their hands
flutter in sleep

their mouths fall open
they are great, tired beaks.

They breathe,
they breathe!

their sons have invested wisely.

Over the tangle of magenta and purple
voice of birds

in staccato.
Mama is calling.

Imperious, final,
she is a tambourine

gathering her girls, black-eyed
wrens whose ears are pierced
for tiny crucifixes.

Great hotels where old men gambled and kept whores
are schools.

Gulls circle Veradero
with cries.

—Barbara Winder (1977)

THE HEMINGWAY HOUSE IN KEY WEST

If he wrote it, he could get rid of it.
Fathers and Sons, *Ernest Hemingway*

*M*y father left me a book of Hemingway's stories
& I understood he meant this as an explanation
& one year later I drove to Idaho to see Hemingway's grave
& phoned his house as if to beg permission for a grief
that held me like a second spine & I saw the room upstairs
where he killed himself & that night I slept dreamless
in a field until the sun's blank stare singed
the loss into my eyes.

Twenty years later I visit Hemingway's house in Key West.
"You look like you want to hear the real dope on Papa,"
the guide says, pointing to the kitchen table raised
to fit Hemingway's height during late-night eating binges.
Like the good wedding guest buttonholed by obsession,
I listen: insomnia, black dreams, his fear of death
without honor—"His father killed himself too,"
the guide sings by rote as we head toward the back cottage
where Hemingway wrote each morning, "depressed, hung over,
he never missed a morning. . . ."

I stare at this cottage as if into the pit
his insomniac hunger only deepened.
This was where his despair was hammered
into an alchemy of language that still echoes
in my own insomniac ears. Yes, the sons of failed fathers
have much to undo, but language doesn't soften the pain
that blackens the heart's Torah & absolution
isn't what I'm after.

There is something dark in my nature.

One night I woke to see my father staring
out of my bedroom window. "Papa," I cried
as he turned to show me the fire fading
in his eyes like a pilot light. Our shadows
locked like clock hands as he whispered,
"I am bankrupt . . . there's something I must tell you . . ."
but he said nothing & the next morning I found his body

For many poets, writing about intensely personal experiences becomes a way of understanding both the experiences and themselves. In this powerful **elegy** for his father, Philip Schultz searches for answers and comfort in the work and world of Ernest Hemingway, who shot himself in 1961.

• **Torah** the Hebrew word for law, used to describe the first five books of the Bible.

in a bed soaked with urine & his eyes staring at the ceiling
as if asking a last question the silence would never answer.

All my life I have wondered what he meant to tell me.

—Philip Schultz (1984)

FOSSILS

*D*own in the glen
where Bill Adkisson
found the trilobite in 1958,
at the source of a primal river
in the mile of his house,
you could hear U.S. 45—Illinois—
even above the hush of waving corn,
the tassels flirting with the bees,
you could hear the tires on concrete,
the farmers winding out their Farmalls
as they crossed the road,
the travelers passing through
in heavily chromed Fairlanes and Electras.
Bill's dad ran the local airstrip,
and you could hear spray planes
banking out over the fields
and swinging in to land—
you could hear it all
from that quiet glen, curled
at the whim of the river into the quiet middle
of a half-mile section
of steaming half-grown corn we called "The End"—
we'd spend the afternoon there,
making plans.

He found it
among the rocks
that collected on the bank
when the water was higher—
it was encased in stone,
a perfect specimen.

Although the word fossil
originally meant any rock,
mineral, or other object dug
out of the earth, it has come
to mean the impression or
trace of animals or plants
preserved in the earth's
crust. Phil Deaver's
meditation in a Florida
cemetery connects his
memories of an old friend,
his awareness of the
physical traces we have
built upon our earth, and his
questions about our future.

- **trilobite** an extinct marine
  arthropod

You have to wonder how that place sounded
the day the trilobite died—
since then we've had
a glacier and a hell of an earthquake.
Maybe even the whisper of that old river
came later.

Now I'm in a cemetery, some noon, 1986,
age 40 and looking for quiet,
and across the street north
is a clinic where shrinks work,
serviced by a busy three-lane street;
and to the east beyond palms and cypress
drones Interstate 4, backbone of Florida.
The sound from that crazy road
is amplified crossing the manmade lake.

These sounds aren't like the lazy hack-hacking
of distant tractors borrowing the highway
to scramble from field to field—
they're the sounds of men and women who live alone
murmuring to themselves in traffic,
rushing in small cars between day-care
and their jobs.

And above I don't hear the drone of
the ghost of
John Stoop's Waco
lazily setting in just above the wires
and dropping onto the grass strip
so he can catch lunch with Skeezics at the hangar
but instead 737's high, aligned
on Runway Outer Four, International Airport—
sounds of steady commerce,
the management class, pure paper,
like a storm,
building,
building, and

Bill
didn't plan
to get half killed in Thailand
and again later to nearly lose a leg

in a motorcycle wreck in Texas,
and I didn't plan to work in that glass building
I come to this sad place to seek shelter from.

The woman buried here last week
had many friends
whose flowers wilt on her grave today.
The man next to her
doesn't share her name—
she's buried
forever in the ground, closer to him
than she might have been willing to stand
while waiting for stamps at the post office—
who knows,
in the clatter and crunch of things now,
whose dead profile staring up we'll rot beside,
whose blood will mix with ours
when the tap root of the post oak
pries open our shells
and a chance tilt of the land
allows the water through?

—Philip F. Deaver (1995)

POETRY WORKSHOP
for Paula

*T*hey'd straggle in one at a time,
sometimes giving a quick nod,
not speaking nor smiling,
embarrassed at finding themselves
sitting there,
calling each other poets.

A seventy-year-old doctor from Brooklyn
operated on a poem in
open class,
while he told us how

Highly respected poet and
editor Mario Petaccia recalls
the agonies and ironies of
sharing poetry during a
graduate class at Florida
State University.

he had to stuff similes
in his shoes in 1929.

An ex-actor juggled his poems
in mid-air with glossy black & white
pictures of celebrities
and every time
he caught a poem in one hand,
he changed hats with the other.

There was a dark-haired artist's
model from Miami who pulled words
out of her mouth like a marvelous
hat trick, but a guest poet came
one night and killed her poem as
it rolled off her tongue, and it
had to be buried the next day.

Two weeks later, a ballet dancer
pirouetting in meters
hung a poem by its rhyme and it
was pronounced dead at the end of
the class. An exile from West Palm
Beach who only spoke in metaphors
performed the last rites.

Within six months, there was a
cemetery between the Williams
building and Dodd Hall with poem
titles on the markers. A man
from the Sierra Club planted
flowers between the graves.

Soon I could see death as
it passed across their faces.
A forty-year-old teacher
aborted a sestina in front
of the blackboard. A twenty-nine-
year-old cab driver with a Bachelor
of Arts took an overdose of words.

A lifeguard gave him artificial
respiration. Images bled from

his nose and mouth. Syllables
dripped from his eyes. Colors
ran from his pores, covering
his body in rainbows, and poems
formed on his heart.

—Mario Petaccia (1986)

CIVILIZATION POEM

*P*ompeii was gone
within a few hours
on an August afternoon.
Elder Pliny rowed across the bay,
died ferrying hysterical survivors
on a blackening day with no moon.

But men build the houses
and tear them down.

Just a backward run
from Biscayne Bay
five palms are whistling
on the leveled waterfront.
Crossing the white bridge,
I see the old Spanish mansion is gone.

Maybe Mafia danced there
with pretty stars gunning down,
the bay dragged for victims
after widows called
that breakfast was getting cold.
Or, running from the crash,
some 1920's tycoon
smashed the portico floor
in an expensive leap.

A history lesson too late,
the house burning wood,

The loss of an old Spanish
mansion reminds the poet of
the burial of the Roman city
of Pompeii by the eruption
of Mt. Vesuvius in 79 A.D.
The **refrain** of the **couplets**,
however, suggests that
civilizations rise and fall by
the efforts of men, not the
accidents of nature.

• **Elder Pliny** (a.d. 23-79) a
Roman naturalist who
perished when he went to
investigate Vesuvius' s
eruption.

our teacher said an old matron,
former Latin scholar,
lived for years hiding there.

The men build the houses
and tear them down.

—Yvonne Sapia (1983)

SOUTH BEACH: PROTEUS, S-SHAPED IN THE SAND

Over clear water sun burns soundlessly;
sun-soaked children play in Miami sand.
He plays dead and they believe him to be.

A retired old man listening to voices in the sea
offers nothing to young girls seeking a tan.
Over clear water sun burns soundlessly.

His groggy subconscious wearily
rises like slow water over a dam.
Playing dead and believing himself to be,

he dreams of round stones and broken pottery
of sea life, of one legged cranes stand-
ing over clear water. The sun burns soundlessly,

as shameless cries of Cubans heavy
the afternoon heat and crowds expand.
But he plays dead and believes himself to be

listening to the sirens, to the history
of wave, to the system of sorrow spread like a fan
over clear water. But sun burns soundlessly,
though he plays dead and they believe him to be.

—Yvonne Sapia (1983)

The auditory repetition created by Sapia's adoption of the **villanelle** form and her use of **alliteration** suggest the sound of waves on the shore that whisper their secrets to an old man.

- **Proteus** the Greek god of the seashore, a shape-shifter

- **sirens** mythological nymphs who lured sailors to their deaths with their seductive songs

NORTH FLORIDA PASTORAL

*F*ramed by the window
    she smiles in;

she holds out to me
a basket

of fresh strawberries.
She asks for

sugar and thick cream.
In two bowls

we divide summer
between us,

taste the red berries
sweetly burst-

ing in our red mouths.
Flies buzz our

eyes and ears, longing
for sharing.

Lost in vibrant sun,
I dizzy

with the heat and place
her cooled hand

to my warming breast,
as wild birds

call down the evening
through the pines.

    —Yvonne Sapia (1983)

In these **syllabic couplets**, the poet alternates between five-syllable lines and three-syllable lines, creating a rhythm that suggests invitation and hesitation.

EBB TIDE
(Route 92)

The road spills into you
as if world peeled
its skin back, yielding
a lush green heart;

mangroves prevail,
frothed up from baywater;
leaves, branches tangle,
chaos of bristling lace—

and under water's glaze
flat muck packed with
fists of old roots
pushing.

—Cynthia Cahn (1982)

Cynthia Cahn feels the pulse
of Florida in the natural
landscape rather than in
the stories historians tell.

MOCK-UP

The Museum of Florida History
presents for your education
war under glass:
thumb-sized white soldiers
dig dirt, hack wood, stack
weapons, pore over plans
for a fort against Indians
presumably bivouacked in
shadows beyond the shiny case.
It's a Lilliput gone frontier—
twigs all over the place,
scrubby grass-stuff, deep
brown polyester resin river flanked
by rubber yuccas. When
you press the big red button

The museum's "war under
glass" display, although true
to the facts, cannot recreate
the true horror of history.

spotlights come on, a voice
tells details. For further knowledge
you can go to the gift shop, buy
books with names, dates, theories
on What Really Happened.
Better yet: go to sleep and
dream yourself plunged in thunder,
gunsmoke grating throat, nose
choked on spilled organs,
filth. When you wrench awake
sweat-drenched and screaming
you'll know your history.

—Cynthia Cahn (1982)

CARSWELL READS IN ST. PETERSBURG

The life of an itinerant poet leads Donald Caswell into strange venues, unfamiliar beds, and even new identities.

*A*rriving anonymously, I bought
a six pack of beer behind
a barefoot girl in cut off
shorts, who was purchasing
a bottle of cheap Sangria,
a Playgirl Magazine, and six
pieces of Double Bubble Gum.

On every poster I found my name
had been copied from a recent
magazine which had spelled it
wrong, crediting a non-existent
Carswell with a poem this Caswell
wrote, and linking me by my wrong
name with the Tallahassee Carswell
that Nixon picked and Congress
nixed.
         The bay breeze blew
my papers around; the sun burned
me like a fever sore; I sweated
beer and seawater; and read
my Caswell poems. Then,

my one good eye fixed like an anchor
on the Sunshine State Skyway Bridge,
which spanned Tampa Bay apparently
unattached to land on either side,
I read the Carswell poem.

It seemed a voice from someone
else's past. Its every line
cried out: this is not me, this
is not me. The crowd applauded
Carswell and his poem, but Caswell
had to pay the restaurant bill.

Sometimes the slightest shove
can turn a boat around. Momentum
makes the difference. My own
momentum is a sleeping ghost
that never wakes. The night
after I read in St. Petersburg
I slept curled like a hobo
on a stranger's couch, dreaming
all the memories I have constructed
only to deny, the lives I run from
even as I build. If the number
of new leaves turned over in a life
is the measure of a man, I
will soon be a saint. I dreamt
I finally understood my fate:
and slept late.
      When I awoke, free
of the past I'd carried like
an old suitcase so long, I
shaved carefully, and changed
my name. The check came.
To Caswell.

      —Donald Caswell (1977)

FLORIDA SANDSPUR

An Indiana native who now teaches at Manatee Community College in Bradenton, Carole Cole uses a gardening **metaphor**, similar to that of Mundell's in "Looking for God: Arcadia," to learn an unfamiliar landscape.

"*W*ell," she said to me
"if you can't tell
society garlic from sandspur,
why are you in the yard
with shovel and hoe?"

But I need to know
how to make this odd
earth yield, this sand
alien to hands stained
by Indiana loam.

> Once, squatting in
> my backyard garden, not
> thirty miles from
> my grandparents' farm
> I pulled a dandelion
> and muttered in
> my mother's voice,
> "that come up easily."

Here in this arid land
not even weeds sink deep
roots among the fire ants
and crab grass.

But every day, armed
with fertilizer and
seed, I kneel in
the freshly turned bed;
my hands move in the slow
motion of gardenias about
to open, petal by
graceful petal.

My hands want to learn
to coax azalea from
their beds of fallen oak
leaves, to part
fragile petals

of hibiscus,
coax them all

to blossom
in the heavy-scented
air.

       —Carole Cole (1995)

CROW IN FLORIDA
(For Ted Hughes and Jim Brooks)

*W*inter took the northland—
freezing bugs under rocks, in tree barks.
Trapping worms under frozen soil.
Crow, belly empty and beak chipped
by the stone earth, flew toward Florida.
God saw Crow's departure, and snickered.

Crow landed in December Florida,
gorged on crawling things.
The more he ate, the more there were.
Crow could not keep pace. God chuckled.
Insects of every kind
swarmed over Crow's body.
Snakes and birds followed,
girdling and dive-bombing
Crow's bug-ridden flesh.
Each creature shrieked at each torn part
of Crow, "We never sleep, we never die!"
Soon there was nothing. God
held his sides and roared.

On the hot sand lies one
undevoured brain lobe
screaming for snow.
From the skies a blizzard
crashes, burying every living thing.

With an **extended conceit,** Stephen Corey, poet and associate editor of *The Georgia Review,* savagely satirizes poets on tour, when they feed upon and, in turn, are fed upon by their admirers. Ted Hughes, England's Poet Laureate, published a collection of poems titled *Crow* in 1970.

Through the white crust bursts Crow,
belly bloated with food and cold.
God keeps still. Crow sets a course
for the equator.

—Stephen Corey (1979)

THOUGHTS WHILE GAZING AT A CYPRESS FENCE

*Y*ou are taking pictures
        of cypress knees
about three miles from the campsite.
We are standing on the catwalk
it is dusk
and I am careful not to touch you
as you focus
the camera.

In the orange grove
an old woman in tennis shoes and a yellow rain hat
cautiously extends an apple core
to a fidgeting deer
her hand quivers against the light drizzle
the ears of the deer
as serious
        as your eyes.

An old man crouches
by a pair of mating yellow/red grasshoppers
the smaller one on top
the larger
grasping the knotted oak trunk.

An armadillo trudges
through the brush
silver between the trees
unconcerned with the clicking of your camera
oblivious
to your frown.

What sort of encounters can be captured with a snapshot? Suzanne Keyworth contrasts the effect of the photographic image with that captured in memory.

I hide a smile in the midst of all this
yet you are so serious
wiping your hands on the coarse of your jeans
adjusting the camera
just so.

By dark the mosquitoes drive us
back into the tent
and to hot coffee
the lantern slightly tilted
on its perch near the center
pole
the shadows so comfortable
against the damp hum outside
that we put the cards away
and fall on each other
like lenten wolves.

By dawn
there are no more pictures
to be had

so we pull up the stakes
one
  by
    one
watching
as the tent collapses
into a flat green film
that blankets the pungent smell of pine needles
on the forest floor.

We pack the Ford
unhurried
gathering what is left
of our life
together
into the trunk
then ride against the yellow lines
that ink us
home

the pots clinking softly from the back seat
your eyes
chattled to the road ahead
mine
the road behind.

—Suzanne Keyworth (1984)

THE PRINCESS AND THE PEPPERTREE

Using fairytale **conventions**,
the poet examines the
protocol of a modern
marriage.

• **peppertree** the Brazilian
pepper whose berries are
reputed to intoxicate
robins

*O*ne grey morning in Florida a princess awoke
to the cramp of too many peas in her bed,
a loud knock at the door, the clutter of robins
on the back lawn. She recognized the sign.
Time to tidy up the living room.
(Whenever robins indulge in the intoxicating berries
of the peppertree, the mother-in-law won't like herself
in the mirror.)
                    She'll get dressed and drive
across three counties, rise up out of the traffic,
flap into the living room, screech and point
until her son zips his pants and pours the coffee.
She'll take him home to repair the roof.

When he leaves, the robins will get so drunk
the princess spends the afternoon collecting feathers
off the lawn, sewing a pillow so rich in the color
of wild birds that when he comes home again,
he'll sleep for a hundred years, and nothing
so simple as a kiss to awaken him.

He'll visit the bad lands, the castle towers,
unlocking every door as he goes. If he cries out
from his nettled sleep, the princess apologizes
to the guests, passes the delicious cakes.
This goes on for years.

Until the morning she awakes to the sound of robins
disappearing in the migrating winds,
to his yawn and stretch in the bedroom.

She'll rise and take the scissors
to her hair, nothing broken
except the spell.

— Suzanne Keyworth (1995)

SUNDAY AT THE LONE CABBAGE FISH CAMP

The shirtless band grinds country
from a fiddle and electric guitars,
but luckily music can't matter
when air boats thunder up the St. John's.
Outside on the screened-in porch
babies sleep in infant seats
on planks above the river;
their folks pitch horseshoes out back.
An enormous woman in fire-engine pants
whales at a boy with a fishing pole,
threatens to tell his mama.
None of us saw what he did,
but nobody's betting on the kid.
Old men talk trucks by the bar;
the women in the shade observe
the halter-top who sidles in,
orders another beer.
The rattlesnake skin on the wall
is bigger around than her arm.
She ignores it and gently tugs
black shorts down on her thigh.
Her lips pull at the beer.
Every man eyes her, shifting his legs.

— Bridget Balthrop Morton (1989)

With a fine eye for detail, Bridget Balthrop Morton paints memorable scenes of average Floridians at work and play far off the tourist track. Lone Cabbage along the St. Johns River on Route 520 in Cocoa is a classic Florida fish camp.

MIDWAY

The three-fingered carny man is bored:
bored with the toddlers, their eyes glittery
with cotton candy and new-found power
driving fast circles in rusted-out cars;
bored with the boys and the girls, their hands
in one another's jeans, rocking the ferris wheel.
He takes tickets in his flattened palm,
twitches one thumb and the cars jerk.
He never looks into a face.
Not that the carny man is dreaming -
but what he'd like is a soft, clean shirt,
a friendly woman to take it off,
who's glad he's here and glad he's leaving.
Tomorrow they'll strike and head for Kissimmee,
Palatka two days after.
It's Saturday, his paycheck's gone,
along with a fifth of Jack Daniel's black.
Between his thumb and his index finger
he pinches the Camel from behind his ear,
snaps his pinky in one calloused hand
and flicks my ticket in a cardboard box.
Gray smoke blends with a lowering sky.
Behind him I watch the merry-go-round
spin its ridiculous tune.
The most we can hope for is rain.

—Bridget Balthrop Morton (1995)

For decades after John Ringling selected Sarasota as the winter home for his Ringling Brothers and Barnum & Bailey Circus, the state developed a rich culture of active and retired circus and carnival workers as depicted in "Midway."

SCAVENGERS AT THE PALM BEACH COUNTY LANDFILL

Since a dozer buried a man from Belle Glade
even the poorest must be licensed to scavenge this landfill,
and they come in boots and red vests
fearing neither poverty nor the dozer's grave.

We back the trailer to the mouth of the pit,
dump the crippled chairs, the fractured table,
the pine frames warped around faded watercolors,
and watch the sanitation drivers resting under cabbage palms,
the dozer blades already stripping up land
to cover the tracks of the scavengers.

Like harvesters
they are moving toward us with canvas bags,
picking through our crop for aluminum and copper,
certain always that something fruitful has been discarded.

A dozer groans behind a wave of sand
and they scatter toward the edges of the pit.
Egrets fall around them like a shower of white leaves
as they wait in the palm shade,
dreaming of dumpsters,
hoping for the redemption of all things cast aside.

   —David Bottoms (1980)

Like A. R. Ammons, David Bottoms finds in our garbage dumps a rich mine of material about human life and behavior as scavenging through a landfill becomes a quest for knowledge and the past as well as a search for usable objects.

IN FLORIDA

When the phase is no moon,
beside the dark there is silence;
no crickets, birds, dogs—
even the leaden tropic breeze
barely stirs a leaf to rustle.
It is already summer in May.

A member of the faculty of Broward Community College, Barbra Nightingale finds Ponce de León's Fountain of Youth in the languid change of Florida's seasons.

With each dry fall of a coconut
another season passes.
We become confused about annuals,
biannuals, perennials—
flowers bloom over and over,
for regenerative heat
a true barometer of summer.

Because we have only two seasons,
we advance more slowly.
The secret of Ponce de León
lies locked not in water
but in time passing gently
like the gardenia which blooms
only once, then yellows and fades.

—Barbra Nightingale (1993)

St. Armand's Key, January 1992

*C*old, like in this subtropic, palm-footed place
it's not supposed to be, yet cold on the fingers
and face, with a light wind and the water
briskly whipped, riding brightly toward the shore.
Feathered seabirds sit in military lines,
all dressed alike, their black caps pointing
west on the white sand, and beyond them
rows of abandoned prams, their blue awnings
stretched against the sun. So quiet here,
so far away from home, so seemingly on the edge
of time—like sometimes, with the wind
blowing and the cold turning the cheeks red,
I need, having the freedom just to breathe
and to be.

—Joann Gardner (1993)

In this carefully detailed portrait of a very non-Floridian day on the beach of Sarasota's St. Armand's Key, Joann Gardner finds an unexpected **epiphany**.

THE LAST RESORT

$\mathcal{I}$t all ended at the Last Resort,
a shabby biker bar off Route One,
south of Daytona. She sat on a ripped
bar stool, sucking on cigarettes,
swilling the usual cheap American
beer, while above her hung trophies
of earlier revels: her bra among
the others stapled to the ceiling.
Two men beside her listened as she wove
the inevitable story of loss: Tyra Moore,
her brown-haired lover gone North,
turning away from her in confusion
and fear. Whatever they had together;
whatever it took to stay alive:
coming home after with cases of beer,
howling over football games, Elvis
records, the same old scratchy magic
until dawn. This life made possible,
as the TV tells us, by a long list
of anonymous donors—bikers, drifters,
laborers—up and down the highway,
turning tricks from sixteen-dollar-
a-night motels. "This is my whole life,"
she murmured, holding between her fingers
a tarnished metal key. Behind some lock
somewhere, the booty, razor blades
and football cards, treasures she had
taken from the now dead men. Outside
under starlight she raised her arm and
pointed, offering directions to her friends.
Then flashed silver a handcuff in the moonlight,
dropping its bright jaw around her wrist.
One of the men, then, pushed her—sudden,
like justice—hustling her tired body
to the ground.

—Joann Gardner (1993)

One of Florida's most dramatic investigations, the search for the serial killer of seven men ended with the capture of Aileen Wuornos.

In his orange-drenched
dream, Rick Campbell,
Director of the Anhinga
Press, paints a more
romantic picture of the
life of Florida pioneers
than Keyworth's
"Grandmother Pauline."
Both works, however,
reflect the power
of love.

*H*ippies with money
were buying subdivided orange groves
out along the Loxahatchee River.
I wanted one, imagined sleeping
in a small white frame house
with a wrap-around screened porch.
In the night, oranges would glow
like shallow stars.

We walk
the old orchards and watch nighthawks
feed on fat mosquitoes. Moonlight
shows us kites and osprey
and glints in raccoon eyes.
All the air smells of oranges.
Cupboards and pantry full of juice.
Bowls of shining globes on every table,
blossoms floating like hyacinths
in blown-glass pools.

Even the alligators
floating the slow black river
dream of oranges. When
winter's sinking sun fills
the sky with pastel light,
green, rose, violet layered
one upon another, nothing
is left but the near horizon
of cabbage palms, and, of course,
rounded orange trees.

On cold nights
when the air could kill we light
the smudge pots left in the sheds.
Smoke drifts into our bedroom
through joints, cracks in sills,
jalousies that won't roll tight.
In our dreams the world is a hazy
picnic of orange-glazed chicken,
leeks with orange ginger sauce, orange
ambrosia, orange flan, blood-orange tea.

On the Seaboard tracks,
distant trains lull us to sleep.
Out in the black night
under almost Southern stars, our grove
snuggles and we curl, spooned
under quilts. In our house without heat
we could find the way, like pioneers,
like settlers homesteading acres of love.

—Rick Campbell (1993)

THE BREATHERS, ST MARKS LIGHTHOUSE

$\mathcal{J}$ stand at the point of the oyster bar
where the water darkens and deepens,
begins to turn for the Gulf. This morning
I am early. Light is new and I think
of Mexico. Somewhere south

past clouds that ride the horizon
the Yucatan jabs into the sea.
The tide's almost slack, turning
like a man remembering his keys.

Pelicans splash like stones; snakebirds
on pilings hang their wings out to dry. Crabs
scuttle the brown shell bottom. All the fish
I do not want are alive and hungry today. Every cast
brings pinfish, needlefish, baby cat.

Dolphins tail over turtle grass beds,
roll and hump through the flats.
Water so shallow it will not cover
their broad, gray-green backs.

All four turn toward me, swim
just a few feet off the bar.
I am almost close enough to read
their minds, to put my thoughts
in their great deep eyes.

An early morning fishing
expedition connects the
poet both to the renewal
of nature and to the past.

• snakebirds Anhingas

As they surface I hear them blow
and it wounds like the gasp of a runner
opening his lungs to the rich air.
I listen to them, the breathers.

Where the map says Apalachee Bay,
where Narvaez sailed west in his patchwork
ships, our eyes meet; we breathe the same
air. Today, together, we are so old,
the world begins again.

—Rick Campbell (1993)

Pánfilo de Narváez, the Spanish conquistador who landed near Tampa Bay in 1528, marched his men to the site of St. Marks, south of Tallahassee, where they built rafts to return to their ships. Scattered by a storm, nearly all of the company, including de Narváez, died.

BODY ART POSES RISK OF INFECTION

(Headline: Daytona Beach News Journal, *March 1990)*

*T*attoos and pierced body
parts have more
in common than being
part of the hard core
biker's lifestyle:
both use the needle. This worries
local health professionals.

It was unanimous among skin
artists and Bike Week
revelers—the risk is
minimal, outweighed by
the joy body
embellishments can bring to those
who get them for the right
reasons. Shana Patch
visiting us from Chicago
has a cleanly shaven
head and gold hoops
in her ear. This biker
whose rolled-up sleeves
reveals a likeness of her pet
pit bull said Go

Alison Kolodinski's poems present sharply contrasting styles. The direct journalistic language and flat tone of "Body Art" underline her description of the rituals of Bike Week at Daytona Beach, an annual pilgrimage for thousands of motorcycle enthusiasts.

to someone who's been
around, who sterilizes right
there. Wondo Loski, owner
of Ahhh Southern Refried
Tattoo Parlour, agrees.

Body piercing has sensual
advantages once
the soreness disappears.
Professionals in Orlando
specialize in the total
ear, nose,
and all points south. Mostly
they do older married couples
where the wife has had children,
has nursed and lost
sensitivity (piercing increases
sensitivity, not
the other way around.)

But the threat of infection hasn't stopped
Kay Coker whose upper body
is covered with a collage
of significant events.
When something merits remembering,
Coker adds on. Her advice:

so you get drunk one night,
get a Tweety Bird or something . . .
that's foolish. Have a good
reason for taking a needle
and shoving it
into your skin.

—Alison Kolodinsky (1992)

New Year's Eve Sestina
Daytona Beach, Florida

In her **sestina** for the new year, Kolodinsky uses a very traditional form and heightened language to describe the equally distinctive rituals of the Space Coast's New Year's Eve, ceremonies that link the space age with the inevitable cycles of nature and love on the same beach.

In these long, noble minutes before the new year,
I roll down my window, wait for the light
to say *go*. Surf pounds the shapeless fringe of earth
along A1A as I check my watch,
think of friends who, loaded for love
who are toasting each other and themselves, for time

to ring out all that was squandered once more, time
to ring in whatever makes sense before the year
that begins this quivering decade lets love
descend on Times Square. Suddenly a light
from a secret launch appears up ahead. I watch
one more golden bullet pull away from the earth.

Usually they let us know before earth
has a patriotic quake. There's always been time
enough to phone the neighbors and still watch
Houston finish the countdown. Year after year
I've run outside to witness the white light—
that second sun for all those who truly love

their country, or adventure, and who love
to imagine a second chance after earth.
I'd shield my eyes from that violent light,
take my place among tourists who don't have time
to park decently on the front lawn. This year
I even clapped for those who couldn't watch

those so sure it would blow up again. I watched
the replay just to feel good twice—an uneasy love—
while I reflected on another resurrected year
and received the rumbling earth.
But tonight it's different somehow. This time
I feel alone, abandoned by this light

secretly orbiting around me. Some may be fooled by light
so cleverly disguised among the stars they watch.
Drunks under the boardwalk have lost track of time
while dizzy adolescents making back-seat love

on the World's Most Famous Beach don't know their earth
has come full circle for them, another year.

The light disappears, but high tide and true love
make it hard to watch the stars or feel the earth
trembling this time, ringing in this New Year.

—Alison Kolodinsky (1995)

El Capitolio

*B*orn on the 20th of May, the Republic is a Taurus.
Except for the diamond embedded in the floor
beneath the cupola, "from where all distances
in Cuba are measured," the capitol is a copy
of the one in Washington, at least
from the pictures, except "it is smaller,"
looks like a toy, and its powerful
are all married men in *guayaberas* and cigars
who have young mulatas on the side.

The generation of my parents—
the generation of Fidel,
the generation that grew lame from dancing rumbas,
and hoarse from shouting *Paredón* in 59
and ran to Miami and thinks it's in Cuba—
recite the details of this building with accented ecstasy.
"The Parthenon of the Republic had French chandeliers."
The movie projectors in my eyes drown
them in a blur of cigar smoke.
Their amethyst tears quiver from the nubile,
high-decibel chatter of rubbery senators.
The dome's air layers into a giant
agate of mists numbing in the features
of the bronze and alabaster fathers of the nation.

In my studio in Miami I uncork genies
of smoke from my mouth. They thicken
into saturnine halos around my books and maps.
Above one shelf dust has folded

Born in Cuba, Ricardo Pau-
Llosa emigrated to the
United States with his family
when he was five. The
children of immigrants learn
of their birthplace through
the memories and
reminiscences of parents
and grandparents, but the
nostalgia of the older
generations cannot totally
satisfy the hunger of the
child.

- **guayaberas** short-
  sleeved, embroidered
  cotton shirts traditionally
  worn by Cuban men

- **paredón** the wall against
  which a firing squad
  executes its prisoners

an abandoned spider's web into a lock
of grey hair. From it a moth twirls
from its jaws like a sequined acrobat
so that its coned wings smear into a dome.
It dances like a petal in a fountain's revolutions
and ponders the rim's baroque plunge, a panic
so breathless with mercuries
you can't measure anything from its skeins
that bend like memory and shift like smoke,
unannounced, out my window.
The Spanish word for chandelier is *araña*, spider.
No angels come from the memories of others,
even if their losses are assigned to you.

—Ricardo Pau-Llosa (1991)

FRUTAS

*G*rowing up in Miami any tropical fruit I ate
could only be a bad copy of the Real Fruit of Cuba.
Exile meant having to consume false food,
and knowing it in advance. With joy
my parents and grandmother would encounter
Florida-grown *mameyes* and *caimitos* at the market.
At home they would take them out of the American bag
and describe the taste that I and my older sister
would, in a few seconds, be privileged to experience
for the first time. We all sat around the table
to welcome into our lives this football-shaped,
brown fruit with the salmon-colored flesh
encircling an ebony seed. "*Mamey*"
my grandmother would say with a confirming nod,
as if repatriating a lost and ruined name.
Then she bent over the plate,
slipped a large slice of *mamey* into her mouth,
then straightened in her chair and, eyes shut,
lost herself in comparison and memory.
I waited for her face to return with a judgement.
"No, not even the shadow of the ones back home."

- mameyes and caimitos—
  fruits native to Cuba

She kept eating, more calmly,
and I began tasting the sweet and creamy pulp
trying to raise the volume of its flavor
so that it might become a Cuban *mamey*. "The good
Cuban *mameyes* didn't have *primaveras*," she said
after the second large gulp, knocking her spoon
against a lump in the fruit and winking.
So at once I erased the lumps in my mental mamey.
I asked her how the word for "spring"
came to signify "lump" in a *mamey*. She shrugged.
"Next time you'll want to know how we lost a country."

—Ricardo Pau-Llosa (1991)

VIEW OF MIAMI

*L*ike a dolphin the causeway arcs
between almost lands.
On the root-weaved shore,
Miami's nervous quartz
parodies the future.
From the bridge's crown
I gaze upon a passing yacht.
Dozing on deck,
two naked girls shine
like dropped coins.
Their breasts like peaches
roll in the salsa of waves
as the boat leaves
a milky V on the bay.

Clouds crumple the last
cliches of a pink sunset.
The light changes.
The gulls are more vulture than dove.
The sky counterfeits the sea
with mirror and mist.
The skyline shifts
like seaweed at tide's rim.

An unusual vantage point gives the poet a different perspective on his city that shifts as the sun sets.

Languages all around us chew
into idiocy. Lumps of manatee turn
on the bay's slow edge like drugged fish.
Trees turn to leather after a minute's rain.
Already the yacht girls embrace in their ocean.
Already the shrimp are flocking to lights
hung over the sides of dinghies.

—Ricardo Pau-Llosa (1992)

FLYING CLOUD MOTEL

*T*he way the sun comes up on
Sunday mornings. Clothesline
full of blue shirts. He says

you are what you are
till you catch yourself
falling. She won't read

the letters. Envelopes
with blue borders she keeps
in a drawer. The word *Mis*s

curling around itself and
beside it her own name is
a stranger, a young girl

in a wool coat. Down on
Nebraska Avenue, wind full
of the earth. 6 a.m. and

Tampa's streets are empty.
Sad, like the first layer of
skin, like holding up a mirror

to the sky. She says *Joseph*
Joseph Joseph. Shirts
flapping in the air.

—Silvia Curbelo (1987)

SNAPSHOT, KEY WEST

*I*n that sidewalk café
she is the only woman
when she tilts the straw hat just so,
the sudden half smile
that sends you scrambling
for the camera in a kind of ecstasy
while the other side of the lens
holds the day out of context, up close,

how the feeling frightens you a little
as you move three steps back
to take in the whole story,
the new Florida morning
stupid with sunlight and trees,
the other tourists, slightly out of focus,
irrelevant in their summer clothes

when she tilts her hat like that,
her face suspended in the vague space
between loveliness and need,
the way the angled light divides her
from the world and nothing crosses
that thin subjective line,
not love or lust or even luck
waiting beyond this moment
when you point the camera
and whisper *Smile*. And she does.

—Silvia Curbelo (1993)

PASCO 41

*O*ff the road, a place they call Spring Lake.
The lake dried up years ago. No one here
remembers more than a story passed down
like water. This is how names outlive
the things named. I know I've said this
again and again. It's important to say things

Although language
inevitably defines and limits,
in these two poems Dionisio
Martínez shows us that it is
imperative to speak the
truth, to tell stories, and to
ask questions in order to
guard against the oblivion
that complacency can bring.

till they hurt. The people of Spring Lake
know the stories so well that they speak
of them as memories, swear they saw the lake
becoming what it is today.

Something is always threatening one story
or another. Someone is always asking questions.
There have been questions since the lake dried up.
Each question has been answered with a legend.
Someone will say all the water was swallowed
by the moon. The moon gathering water
for the next drought. The moon is popular
with those who have nothing to say and those
who have nothing.

—Dionisio D. Martínez (1989)

COMPLACENCY

*L*ast winter I picked four oranges each
night from the tree outside the kitchen door.
Each morning I squeezed the oranges,
poured the juice into our clear glasses,
rested my elbows on the clear
surface of the glass table, looked
through the table at you, half naked, half
asleep.

This year I watch the disease crawl
up the branches. The oranges
turn black on the tree. They fall and rot
outside the kitchen door.
The tree suffers from the same
complacency that killed us once or twice,
that kills us even as we walk
away from our only common vision—our
grief—and the sobs behind the voice that
finally whispers what it meant to
say in the first place.

I used to think I cried out of love, or

that a tear was love making itself palpable.

The way I explained it to myself, love

was dangerous, too much love was lethal, and

I was either dying or learning to live forever.

—Dionisio D. Martínez (1993)

DIRECTIONS FOR DRIVING THE TAMIAMI TRAIL

After you've done it,
if anyone asks,
say the sky there
unfolds itself like a riddle
and part of it is a godly blue
and part of it is puckered with clouds
of summer thunder

Tell them
beneath the bell of the sky
the Miccosukee still honor the Everglades,
the flowing womb
spreads out like an altar
the cypress lift their humble knees
the sabal palms stand reverent as priests

Say
the gators and moccasins own the swamps
but when sunset blooms like a sacred fruit,
all gold and wine,
the great-winged waterbirds soar like deities
then mosquitos and bullfrogs
rule the night

After this,
if you're really pressed,
explain what happened years ago,
that the life-waters were drained like a pox,
put in a straight-jacket of canals
now poisons thread the pulse of the land

When the Tamiami Trail (now part of U.S. 41) linking Miami and Tampa was built in 1928, it included the longest dike built outside the Netherlands and was hailed as an architectural marvel. Since then it has become a symbol of how we distance ourselves from our environment. Gianna Russo's poem offers a spiritual road map for narrowing that distance.

Tell anyone who wants to know
under the brilliant hibiscus sky
the final panthers lie bloody
by the roads

Then,
use the closing of your choice:
that over the ancient river of grass
the healing prayers of the Seminole
still hover
or
that like the woodstork
and the great blue heron
they have lifted their wings
and gone.

—Gianna Russo (1993)

CHILD'S MORNING IN SAINT AUGUSTINE

*C*ame tinkling in on Sunday bells
early through the open window,
ringing like the voice of delight,
like the peals of my best friend's laugh
through the windowpanes and over me,
fresh from my visit of dreams,
for I was the child-guest
in this gold locomotive city
with my nine years wrapped around me,
a safe and clean simplicity,
my one night spun like a fairy-tale
between the fountain of youth and fort,
and then this one morning flashing,
brightly falling through the window
as I woke to myself in a borrowed bed
and understood I was separate,
wise, and warm as the singular night
of my visit in Saint Augustine,
and this is the way it happened,
in a hailstorm of whiteness
and certain angels of the sun

—Gianna Russo (1995)

The Man Who Went Straight at the Fork in the Road

*I*t was suicide
He couldn't decide which way to go so
he closed his eyes and hit the gas

Next thing he knew he was chained to a mirror
searching for a place unflawed
with bathing beauties and alligators
Pink flamingos mastering balance
A picture perfect place
like on a postcard
Not some brat who got into her mother's rat fur
and fake jewelry and loves herself to death
Feeling an infinite fool
he waits for a sign, a signal, a wink, a blink, a nod
Maybe even an act of God
But it never quite happens
He should've pulled off to the side somewhere
to figure things out
to roast some love letters
He should've conned himself into putting on the brakes
pulling the plug on the whole thing
like Lady Liberty in the harbor falling apart
or a big fat mama spread-eagle on the beach
sucking in whatever washes up
(the slutty version of freedom)
It's all just surface now
Nothing but glitter when the good-humor man is dead
It's all just for show
The ignorant acting like it knows something

Still chained to the mirror
the man who went straight at the fork in the road
wages war on himself, draws his sword,
and tries to poke holes in his imagination

There are times when he wishes he could turn around
and go back home
Home to that place unflawed
with bathing beauties and alligators

In contrast to Robert Frost's persona who chooses "the road less travelled," Miami native Howard Camner's traveler refuses to choose, closes his eyes, and gets stuck in the mirror image of his imaginary perfect past.

Pink flamingos mastering balance
A picture perfect place
like on a postcard
But it's too late
That place is long gone
He doesn't know his home now
And the worst part is
it doesn't know itself

—Howard Camner (1993)

NEAR PIGEON KEY

*where pigeons migrate to Florida
from Cuba each spring.*

On Pigeon Key, between
Marathon and Big Pine Key,
Carolina Hospital's capacity
for sympathy with the
migrating flock suggests a
deeper sense of cultural loss
and hope.

Seventy year old Cuban Royal Palms
share the coastline
with cabbage palms and slash pines.
Dead now from a freeze,
some stand bald
without their majestic feathers.
As I stare up at them,
I see ducklings pile out
of the holes and drop
thirty feet onto a tapestry of grass and needles.
The hollow stumps have become their homes
and I am filled with an unexplainable relief.

—Carolina Hospital (1991)

IN SEARCH OF STEVENS AND HIS DISCIPLES

She who sang the sea to life
now watches you sit by the shore
calmly listening to her sounds.
She is the maker and reminds you
of dreams of sea lions,
phosphorescent springs,
and whirlpools.
Her silhouette whispers love.
She approaches you,
tries to lure you into the
waters.
But you have fled,
to look for order in the skies.

—Carolina Hospital (1995)

Wallace Stevens' influence on poetry in south Florida helps shape both his disciples and those who, like Hospital, would challenge him.

MIAMI BEACH

Old people still bathe there,
gather the winter warmth
between soft folds of their
flannel skins.

Beckoning, the long, white
fingernails of the waves
scrape the sands and bodies.
Bodies called
to rest. Effortless floating
like occasional seaweed,
every year some wash up
along shore.

—Marisella Veiga (1995)

While Barbara Winder entered the dreams of her retirees, Marisella Veiga's evocative description of Miami Beach's elderly residents focuses on external detail as her humans merge with the sea.

It's A Cold, Cold Day On Satellite Beach And

Sylvia Maltzman uses **shaped verse** to visualize as well as memorialize the explosion of the space shuttle *Challenger* on January 28, 1986.

it's falling
it's falling
like a white silk handkerchief
a plume
three minutes seventeen seconds high
three miles down
it's falling
it's falling
like a diamond burnt and cracked
hacked
from the rock of a hurtling star
it's falling
it's falling
the screams stretch long and white
an aviator's scarf with
the plumes of a mangled ostrich
it's falling
it's falling
like a pale plastic womb
aborting
grief rushes in
through the cracks in the bulkhead
it's falling
it's falling
the fickle white tombstone of smokey spider silk
up above whisks away on the wind
the hot salt tears of the sea engulf
them
a violated grave
it's falling
it fell
Hush Hush
says the cold current
to the last gasp in the darkness
You're Home

—Sylvia Maltzman (1991)

NEPTUNE

"And the sea gave up the dead which were in it . . .
and they were judged every man according
to their works."

(Revelation 20:13)

*T*he river, clotted with tar
of freighters bound for tropical
sunsets, circles the city down pine
avenues, splintered as the lens honey-
mooning tourists capture our peninsula;
coast guard cutters lower their flags
under the arms of the mac arthur cause-
way, stuck upright like the fists
of the admiral's statue below the gilded
dome of the freedom tower, burrowing
through clouds suspended against the blue
like puffs from a crack pipe;
quay side bars offer cuba libre,
the revolution's song of tomorrow that begs
for daily bread; horizons blotted by skysc-
rapers: miami beach loses itself in a flash
of pastel neon, eighth street, heading south,
remakes herself into calle ocho
each street crackles with dialects
variegated as the garish crotons
lining the boulevard with billboards
of seminole bingo, lottery fever:
a trail of broken promises through
the everglades; yet only these are allowed
to enter dead counties of america; dog
tagged, names manacled to their arms,
bright as bangles from benin, tucked
tightly in freighters, ringed with rust,
along the gold coast's meridian
secure in their hold, oranges, cocoa,
coffee, baseballs; the seeded remains
of empire's gold sinks between jeremie
and port-au-prince; for the gulf weighted
down with so many prayers, whispered
over the sea's sermon, cannot contain

Jamaican-born Geoffrey
Philp reminds us that Florida
shares the history and
culture of Africa and the
Caribbean—the cruise ships
taking tourists from Miami to
the islands share a kinship
with contemporary freighters
bringing in coffee and cocoa
and the earlier slave ships
of the Middle Passage. As
the poem develops, Philp
draws the reader from the
privilege of cruise liners
and the comforts of familiar
language into an increas-
ingly diverse world of
cultures and dialects. Part
of the pleasure in the
macaronic verse of this work
resides in working through
the different languages and
allusions of this journey to
the mythical kingdom of
Atlantis.

our faith: the poinsettia's rage december's sun
startles into petals of blood as the capitol
calcifies into stone, into coral;
our hope: the tremor of bois caiman swallows
the statue of the indian outside the palace;
our charity: fathers, mothers, sisters, comrades;
kernels strewn across golfe de gonave;
husks we count as beads on the neck-
lace of erzulie doba, mere stones in the palm
of papa legba, married to our island
in the kingdom of atlantis.

—Geoffrey Philp (1994)

UNA CARTA PARA ANDREW

*B*arrelling down the Turnpike
with you bundled in your child's seat,
we overtake U-Haul trailered cars,
trunks padlocked with furniture, clothes,
photographs, Bibles with full family trees:
a flash of gray hair in the rear view,
like your grandmothers' Merty or Ana;
before them, Kathryn and Victoria,
and the irretrievable African and Indian X's
who claimed a stake in transient America,
hoping their names would survive translation
across longitudes more familiar
than this highway's map, undecipherable
as the lines across your palm,
with the marked towns of Apopka, Davie,
St. Augustine, places I must teach you never
to enter, for their flaming crosses
bar entrance to destinations pointing north
that the illuminated signs cannot guide
and the Turnpike offers no exit.

—Geoffrey Philp (1994)

Philp's letter to his son Andrew explores the difficulties of preserving heritage and culture in a world challenging assimilation. His trip on the turnpike through Florida becomes an **allegorical** journey on a road with no safe exits.

WHY MY GRANDMOTHER FEEDS THE CROWS

*M*aybe it's because she dated five men at once
      as a young woman living on her daddy's farm
      in Greensboro; maybe because her daddy was a
Yellow-skinned tung oil man who dreamed of tangerines
      and Crystal River packing crates while sitting in
      shade, fingering the brim of his straw hat, seeing green.
Red is her favorite color although her favorite shirt
      has been washed so many times it's whitening in spots,
Telling a story all its own about a woman who got
      just enough and
Learned to use
Every bit of it and then some, wearing life till it
      thinned out, denim thinning into silk.

Maybe it's because sometimes she calls me my mother's name,
      having worn her memories so thin she sees me right
      through them.
I'll never know what she sees but I know she loves to
      feed me corn bread and pot
Liquor and can't stand to see me walk away but always
      lets me go, knowing
Life has to be worn, and like a stiff starched shirt, the
      more we brush up against it the
Softer it wears, till it's threadbare, a leaf eaten to
      a web, nothing wasted.

—Lu Vickers (1990)

In this **acrostic** which spells out her grandmother's name, Myrtle Mills, Lu Vickers, who teaches English at Tallahassee Community College, gives us a portrait of an ordinary, yet remarkable, woman.

PLACIDA

Admiration for expertise and knowledge has traditionally evoked strong poetic response. Richard Brobst's sharply etched portrait of a practical expert in the small fishing village on Charlotte Harbor also becomes a study of alternative modes of language.

There is no scholarly language
of pretense
in the fish house:
only an educated guess
now and then coming
from the salt whiskered man
in the corner
wiping blood and scales from his hands.
He knows the tide
by the smell of oysters
and by which direction the egrets
circle to land.
When he commands,
"pompano are running,"
or "reds in the flats at dusk,"
the wisest among us
do not bother with why.
But here the spoken word is scarce.
He works the jagged edges
off of days. 7, 14 in a row:
where one ends,
where the next begins,
matters little.
What matters is the current of the moon
measured out in childish notches
from his pick
upon the ice room wall.
A calendar without numbers.
A primitive, accurate testimonial
of a man's life
among crates of broken fish.
The last time
we came in a pack
to buy "jacks"
at 2 a.m.
he had his lunch out
and was sharing a sandwich
with a raccoon.
And they shared the language of smell

and another sense
unknown
that comes only to those
who have mingled their blood
among scallops and rays.

When we left
with our half-frozen fish
sucking the ink off its newspaper wrap
he was leaning against the scales
in his rubber boots
in a cement pool of oily water.
He said nothing to us that night
as many other nights
when he spoke only with a nod
and knife.
That is how we learned
that he hid his greatest knowledge
in silence.
That is the language he spoke
with raccoons, pelicans, and mullet
the language of truth
with no margin for error.

—Richard Brobst (1986)

FROST IN MIAMI

A quarter-mile off
the steady two-lane
and down a spongy
leaf-soft path, you reach

the plot he wintered
in his 70's,
a fairytale copse
lush with tendrilled shade,

While staying in Key West during the winter of 1934-35, Robert Frost spoke at the University of Miami's Winter Institute of Literature. He returned to the Institute the following winter and rented a cottage at 3670 Avocado Avenue in Coconut Grove. During his first visit, he observed, "It is what is beyond that makes poetry—what is unsaid. . . . Its unsaid part is its best part."

two acres of choice
real estate he penned
"Pencil Pines," and twin,
tiny cottages,

much-weathered pink frame
and affixed with small
brass plates labeled *East*
and *West*. He quartered

in the half called *East*,
where some morning sun
might trickle past thick
forest-pulp. *West*, then,

was for guests, and though
you would be hard-pressed
to tell from outside
the difference (inside,

far fewer bookshelves
brace *West's* small fireplace),
to liken these like-
unminded hemi-

spheres to the mind's own,
said to be the homes
of "thought" and "feeling,"
is to suggest how

some men choose to live
in one, visiting
at times the other—
although Frost himself

would have fast dispelled
any notion aimed
at simplifying
the mind of a man.

He might have instead
found his analogue
in the dense tangle
growing overhead,

and choking the laced
gazebo spanning
the buildings, whose snarls
confirm suspicions

that the passageway—
and each dark cottage—
has been maintained clear
and free of clutter

only too rarely
since his departure.

   —Peter Schmitt (1989)

BLISS MOBILE VILLAGE

We got a nice little unit with our name on a sign.
We got grass, a bit, and two pine trees.
We got Florida sunshine,
what more could you ask?

We got Highway 19 right outside the door,
McDonald's, Burger King, everything,
a brand new multiplex moviehouse,
though we don't go much.

We got three malls, all the chain stores,
and they're always running sales.
And there's always the beach,
if you go for that.

We got our monthly checks and a good Jap car,
soaps in the morning; at night, the VCR;
Bingo, shuffleboard, and time.
Mister, we ain't got winter.

   —Philip Asaph (1995)

Philip Asaph's two sardonic
views of contemporary
Florida life reveal the
dangers and limits lurking
behind the smugness of
suburban complacency.

*B*ack, into the mouth
of the monster, you go,
leaving us in our fragile houses
considering the precipice
beyond our front doors;
leaving us again,
this January morning
in Starke, Florida,
jerking and burning
in the electric chair;
the cave, for a time,
closing around you.

You leave us as children
afraid to step outside.
Our neighborhoods
suddenly compose a maze
where every store-front glares,
carnivorous,
and every slowing car
stalks the sidewalk.
So we must think,
so you have taught us.

We see the knife in the wave
of the crossing guard;
and the nod of the bus driver
conceals an urge,
a need, like a lion's,
to rip open a throat.
We know you at last,
the boogie man with the human grin.

We will listen for your voice
in the bright babble of toddlers.

—Philip Asaph (1995)

FLORIDA PRELUDE

*N*ot unlike those Indians
who first saw a white man
and dreamed nightmares of ochre skies,
of big wind
and built
huge piles of oyster shells,
we too sometimes see ourselves
riding off cliffs.

In this South,
it is all so much armor
that makes it difficult to walk,
and survival a possibility.
We mime that large reptile
this land is known for—
we say to ourselves,
"Wait a million years;
things will improve"—
and learn patience.

Or we mime that fish
this land is known for,
that worries the tourists
at the oceanside,
and we display our appetites
our own furies—
and learn hate.

We live our own sad myths down here.
We hear the wind blowing
down here.

—W. C. Morton (1989)

What can we learn from the creatures that precede us? W. C. Morton's melancholic observation that we and our myths both resemble and fall short of the aboriginal Indians, gators, and sharks clearly suggests the need for some reexamination of values.

THE KNIFE THROWER

Gibsonton, across
Hillsborough Bay from
MacDill Air Force Base in
Tampa, has become a
popular community of active
and retired carnival
performers.

*B*ack to Gibsonton to visit the knife thrower.
Alcoholic ventriloquist Scottie MacNeil
threw knives with precision at Miss Jeannie,
and the drunker he grew, the more precise he threw,
missing her thin middle by inches,
drawing the carnival crowd watching with caution,
this delicate surgery believing
he would simply inch the giant blade of the knife
inside her small frame.

Pete the sword swallower,
throat greasy from fried chicken,
mouthed long sharp metal further
than any eye could follow.
He married the Stone Lady born with excess calcium,
stiff joints, and child-like arms.
And they toured together, double billed as
The Most Unusual Couple in the World:
Sword Swallower and Stone Lady.

Gibsonton, a carnie town
where giant rides rest
on front lawns in between tours,
frozen metal Loop to Loop rides,
mythical mechanical spiders protecting
36" men and 700 pound women.
Row after row of empty vendor stalls,
neon-dead, asleep in hibernation.

The knife thrower throws practice throws
in the off season which land dangerously
close to a silhouetted frame,
a blackened target in the shape of a woman,
tiny slice marks in cardboard.

—Janet Heller (1993)

ON LIVING ON

I have learned that nothing understands
the stiff palmetto better
than the dry grass beside it.
So I ask this desert landscape,
the scrub palm and Australian pine,
flowering weed and stiff winter-brown
wild grass to give me
their special powers of speaking,
their way of translating
the tropical heat.
More and more I understand
how growth will take
whatever form it must
to survive.

   —Richard Smyth (1989)

How do poets find patterns and language for their visions? In these two poems, Richard Smyth discovers in ordinary surroundings the form and voice of poetry.

SAINT AUGUSTINE

Outside at night
the streetlamps could be stars
or angels descending from heaven—
beams in the shape of burning crosses.
I have come this far to see them,
and their reflection in the water,
how they twist like diamonds through trees.
Travelling for hours is worth it
when your vision is restored,
when you can see once again in words.
I realize for the last time that a poem
is a way of speaking in the world,
a way of raising one's voice, like
these crickets and frogs and katydids,
to make, with the others, the only noise I know how.

   —Richard Smyth (1989)

A Florida

Bestiary

BIG OLE ALLIGATOR

Big ole alligator looks like a log
    Lyin in the swamp
But he can growl and bark like a dog,
And he can chew and eat a whole hog,
And he can look and see in a fog—
    When he gits good and mad!

Big ole alligator sleeps all day
    Lyin in the swamp.
But he can open his eyes at night,
And he can kick and he can fight,
And he can switch his tail all right—
    When he gits good and mad!

Big ole alligator he got dead
    Lyin in the swamp.
He got skinned, his hide was shed—
He got a bullet through his head,
I got alligator shoes of red . . .
    Bet he's good and mad!

—Lois Lenski (1971)

ALLIGATOR

A hundred years your sluggish length has known
The squeeze of ooze, the stab of August heat,
The rain of poinciana petals blown
Across the blue on soundless crimson feet;
But you are young tonight. The pointed moon
Has pricked you with a turbulent desire,
Your mighty tail is stirring like a spoon,
Your eyes are moving marbles of sapphire.

And one will come across the silver slime
To share with you this ecstasy of will,
To link the moment with eternal time,
And let the gods of destiny fulfill
In her rough hide that cycle which prepares
For each tomorrow alligator heirs.

—Vivian Yeiser Laramore Rader (1931)

ALLIGATORS IN THE SUN

S tretched in the sun along the grassy bank,
Like primal beasts the alligators lie,
With prehistoric shape and moveless eye,
As though they dozed in jungles damp and rank,
In jungles of the Eocene, when dank
The Planet steamed beneath a brazen sky;
Before the race of dinosaurs went by
And tropic life beneath the glaciers sank.

Primeval monsters in the river sun,
What visions you invoke, what dreams of dread
Of early earth when time had first begun
In the hot dawn before the glacial night—
When rivers knew no herons' airy flight
But pterodactyls sweeping over-head!

—Agnes Kendrick Gray (1932)

Meeting at Alligator Lake

*W*hat terrified faces open:
resigned to a knowing,

water lilies raise and lower
painful heads, jabbing with

white eyes that stare. Creased petals stir
on unseen stems, bending,

almost breaking before questions.
Windy sighs part them and

they hush for an answer; for an
answer they turn to shore

and closely study the quiet
power of kudzu vines

(we too in their grip). Trying to
create a connection,

what elegiac crows hawking
from pines bristling the sky

bring messages of death to the
white flowers within us.

—Yvonne Sapia (1983)

Watching Gators at Ray Boone's Reptile Farm

*W*hile we stand behind the concrete railing
and yellow cockatoos cry through mosquito heat,
the gators never move,
but look like floating logs almost ready to sink,
wait as though long patience had taught them something
about humans,
an old voice crying up from the swamps of our brain.

Once that cry called a small boy
over the railing and the logs came alive.
A black man in Bush hat salvaged the legs.
On the bottom of the pool
Ray Boone found a shrunken white hand clutching a stone.

Our hands clutch concrete as we lean against the railing
as though leaning might bring us closer
to the voice crying now through our common memory,
the answer to all the animal inside us.

—David Bottoms (1980)

CORAL SNAKE
(American Cobra)

Out of this ghoulish swamp,
Over this smoke-grey grass,
I saw, as dusk came down,
Two coral cobras pass.

Lustrous as Chinese silks
Their brilliant colors glowed;
Fluent as molten streams
Of jewels their bodies flowed.

He who stoops to watch
Narcotic cobra eyes,
The jungle's opiate,
Falls asleep and dies.

I could not look away,
Death's drug was in my heart;
Their beauty burned my brain,
I watched the grasses part.

Then, with a jungle cry,
My body, like a knife
Self-sprung, instinctively
Ran backward into life.

* * * *

The furrows of this grass
Conceal eternal sleep—
Within this sacred swamp
Two coral cobras creep.

—Marlise Johnston (1932)

RATTLER

*Y*estidy
    I got me a live rattler
and I ain't got snake-bit yet.
No-sir-ree!
I was out a-ramblin in the scrub
and I come to a little branch
and my hound-dog
           bayed a rattlesnake . . .

I smelled him first
and in a minute I seed him
I caught him
           with a long rope loop
like a lasso
on the end of a bamboo pole.
I swung my pole
and looped the loop
           right over his head,
pulled it up
and dropped him in my sack!

Yes-sir-ree!
Got him in a cage now.
Gonna make him a pet.
           Gentle him. Feed him.
Gonna feed him live rabbits.
That's what he eats
           when he runs loose.

He et one up

        slick as a whistle

Gonna ketch me

        a live alligator next.

Yes-sir-ree!

        —Lois Lenski (1971)

THE COPPERHEAD

A dwarfed limb
or a fist-thick vine, he lay stretched
across a dead oak fallen into the water.
I saw him when I cast my lure
toward a cluster of stumps near the half fallen trunk,
then pulled the boat to the edge of the limbs.
One ripple ran up his back like the tail
of a wake,
and he lay still again, dark and patterned,
large on years of frogs and rats.

I worked the lure around the brush,
oak and poplar stumps rising out of the water
like the ruins of an old pier,
and watched his spade head shift on the dry bark.
But no bass struck
so I laid the rod across the floor of the boat,
sat for a long time watching the shadows
make him a part of the tree,
and wanted more than once to drift into shaded water,
pull myself down a fallen branch toward the trunk
where he lay quiet and dangerous and unafraid,
all spine and nerve.

        —David Bottoms (1980)

BALLAD OF THE GREEN TURTLE

*W*here the green turtle comes in the dark of the moon
    To this lonely spit of sand
And crawls from the waters—amongst the quiet dunes
    And buries her eggs in the sand

The hatchlings are bound to the call of the sea
    According to nature's plan
They scurry thru danger and into the waves
    A cycle older than man

    First chorus:
And the sough in the wind
    Tells the song of Conch Island
How sharp the Spaniard Steel slashed and crimson'd her land
    And left bones to whiten—bleach in the sunlight
But the green turtle still lays her eggs in the sand

Near four-hundred years of the cross and the sword gone
    With the galleons of Spain
Foot prints from Jack-Boots of black spanish leather
    Erased by the wind and the rain

Conch-Island lies peaceful serene in the moon-shine
    Varmints are drawn here to play
They frolic and spoon to the music of night-birds
    Lost in the spell of their way

    Second chorus:
And the sough in the wind
    Tells the song of Conch Island
A song of destruction that ravage'd her land
    And man leaves no memory in finned, furred or feather'd
But the green turtle still lays her eggs in the sand

    —Will McLean (1980)

LOGGERHEAD, JUNO BEACH

*O*ld enough to sense the confusion
of the sacred and the profane,
I'm sprawled in the Juno Beach sand
as the moon pools its light on the surf.
and June pulls us all to the shore. We
have come from a bar on US 1, a waystation
where migratory tourists greet
the locals. This night we trekked
to a stretch of sand where bodies
and blankets tangle in a dance, mate
in a ritual our singular need fills
with passion. I was there staking
some kind of territory, pulling
at the tight jeans of a woman
who had journeyed long from Akron
to find this beach, this stranger.
Less sense of purpose than geese,
we fumbled at buttons, snaps and zippers
endured sand fleas feasting on our soft flesh
because something that no one explains
called us to explore
the shores of our bodies.

In the roar of surf and skin
I almost didn't hear behind me
the grunting, like an old woman
lugging family laundry.
I turned and saw the loggerhead, slugging
through the hightide wrack of weeds,
bogging down in sugar sand.
She too was called by June,
by the moon, maybe by the lack
of cops and city lights.

She entered our world from the ocean
we thought backdrop, dwarfed
our curious passion, brought me up
short, so to speak. I sat
on our blanket, rapt, as she dug

and grunted each egg into the sand.
I wanted to see everything like a biologist,
an anthropologist of the heart.

She went slowly back to the sea, less dramatic
than her coming ashore, less awkward
than our parting. With forgotten names,
we climbed the dunes and she dropped me off
at a 7-11, where the light of neon beer signs
glanced off the hoods of cars. We went on,
down dark roads home, somewhere.

—Rick Campbell (1994)

SEA TURTLES

I. *The Mother*

*I*t is cold and dry
here on this strange sand.
I am tired from the long swim,
but it is my time;
my egg sacks are full.
I must dig quickly
in this harsh gravel bed.

Once, these beaches were soft,
the white sand a cradle.
It was safe and often
I hovered in the shallows
dreaming of their birth.

Now I am no longer certain.
The wide-empty spaces are gone,
stacked and trampled by stone,
the babies crushed beneath.
Still, I go on digging deeper,
drop them one by one,
cover them gently,
my flippers moving quietly
under the moonless night.

II. *The Hatchling*

*U*nder a sandal moon
I answer the call—
instinctive home of sea.

I move, stretch, nose
through ping-pong shell of egg,
crack a hole, emerge
flipper first, rest,

kick; I am free.
Wet head gathers sand,
a mask across my face,
eyes blink grit. I
circle around. Where
is the sea? I hear it
in my skin.

In the loud surf
my cold blood rings.
I lose control, tumble
head over end, am thrown,
carried out, back again,
again, flippers

spin wild. Deeper now,
I have it right: smooth
clean swim to coral rock
to hide, grow 300 times

larger than now, then
find my way back
to cry my young
into warm dry sand.

—Barbra Nightingale (1993)

LIZARDS

*P*atio-squatters
water-seekers and
heirs to insect-rights

sun themselves on
MY
furniture

copulate on
MY
concrete

come and go as they please
through the crevice
under my screen door

they cock their jutting
arrow-shaped heads
in my direction
calculating me coldly

as though I were the heat
or the landlord finally arrived
for the rent

I never thought my patio
resplendant with colored leaves   ferns
and hanging ivy

would become a reptillian ghetto

ashamed before my friends
I confess
I have become a slumlord

> —Sylvia Maltzman (1995)

To a Buzzard Swinging in Silence

I never knew how fair a thing
Was freedom till I saw you swing
Ragged, exultant, black and high,
Against a hollow windy sky.
You that with such a horrid gait
Lumber and flop with red raw pate;
I did not learn how beauty grew
From ugliness until you flew,
With soaring somber steady beat
Of wings rough-edged to grip the fleet,
Far coursing horses of the sky—
To ride, to ride them gloriously.
Oh, brother buzzard, you whose sin
On earth is to be shackled in
To horror, teach me how to go
Like you to beauty, sure and slow;
Like you to slip from carrion ties,
And lift and lift to high clean skies,
Where winds and sun and silence ride,
Like you, oh buzzard, glorified.

—Marjory Stoneman Douglas (1932)

THE MOCKING BIRD

Superb and sole, upon a pluméd spray
That o'er the general leafage boldly grew,
He summ'd the woods in song; or typic drew
The watch of hungry hawks, the lone dismay
Of languid doves when long their lovers stray,
And all birds' passion-plays that sprinkle dew
At morn in brake or bosky avenue.
Whate'er bird did or dreamed, this bird could say.
Then down he shot, bounced airily along
The sward, twitched in a grasshopper, made song
Midflight, perched, prinked, and to his art again.
Sweet Science, this large riddle read me plain:
How may the death of that dull insect be
The life of yon trim Shakspere on the tree?

—Sidney Lanier (1877)

THE MOCKINGBIRD

Enraged by a red crest,
A cardinal, his own rival,
Battered our sliding doors
Until he broke himself
Of illusion, striving.

The yellow-throated warbler
Also shattered his glass eye.

But the mockingbird who lately
Mated and nested in our sylvestrus
Now in the first chill of autumn
Woos with daily diligence
The unlikely bird
Locked in our bedroom window.

I draw and undraw the drape.
Turn the light on and off.
Still he sees his gray
Recessive self.
Chak Chak Chak
Again he flies to the glass
And beats his wings against it.

Only my approach from within
Sends him to a near branch
Where he perches and offers
His cubist musical crest
To the form that for
A moment dissolved in me.

—Van K. Brock (1965)

TAMPA ROBINS

*T*he robin laughed in the orange-tree:
"Ho, windy North, a fig for thee:
While breast are red and wings are bold
And green trees wave us globes of gold,
    Time's scythe shall reap but bliss for me
    —Sunlight, song, and the orange tree.

Burn, golden globes in leafy sky,
My orange planets: crimson I
Will shine and shoot among the spheres
(Blithe meteor that no mortal fears)
    And thread the heavenly orange-tree
    With orbits bright of minstrelsy.

If that I hate wild winter's spite—
The gibbet trees, the world in white,
The sky but gray wind over a grave—
Why should I ache, the season's slave?
    I'll sing from the top of the orange-tree
    Gramercy, winter's tyranny.

I'll south with the sun, and keep my clime;
My wing is king of the summer-time;
My breast to the sun his torch shall hold;
And I'll call down through the green and gold
> *Time, take thy scythe, reap bliss for me,*
> *Bestir thee under the orange-tree.*

—Sidney Lanier (1877)

ONE HUNDRED ROBINS

*W*e had been freezing in separate wings
when the robins came, puffed up and proud,
ridiculous as senators, round bellies
bobbing the branches, acorns rattling the roof
like proclamations. Drunk on holly berries
they purpled our porch and picnic table,
filibustering through the unraked leaves,
chasing the sparrows like pages down the aisle.
I thought I saw one smile.
You thought you heard one burp.
The sky swelled with its loosening rain,
making amendments.

—Peter Meinke (1987)

CAT BIRDS

*S*ome birds sing a melody,
  Others screech and yell;
Cardinals sing heavenly,
  Cat birds sing like—well,
Not like larks and robins gay,
  Each a charming sprite:
Cat birds, modest bits of gray,
  Sing like dynamite!

—Elizabeth MacEvitt (1931)

WHIPPOORWILL

*A*s breaks the crystal bowl
Attuned to a singer's note,
So breaks my heart.

"Whip . . . poor . . . will, whip . . . poor . . . will . . ."
Clear is the roll
Of the cadenced song that seems to float
Upon the dusk—to start
Where the moon drips gold
Through the Everglades.

"Whip . . . poor . . . will, whip . . . poor . . . will . . ."
As breaks the crystal bowl
Attuned to a singer's note,
So breaks my heart . . .

Afar
Under a star,
Flying . . . dying . . .
"Whip . . . poor . . . will, whip . . . poor . . . will . . ."

—Ruby Pearl Patterson (1935)

PELICAN

*T*he pelican's a homely fowl.
It's not as comely as the owl.
The owl is not a pretty bird.
The pelican is quite absurd.
It has an unattractive skin,
A baggy pouch in place of chin.
Its manners are grotesque and rude.
It's very sloppy with its food....
A dozen fishes at a gulp.
Its body is a shapeless pulp
With much-too-much or not enough
To make a bird you'd want to stuff.

Its toes turn in, its feet are flat.
Its neck is thin, its figure fat.
It has a mean and jaundiced eye.
It isn't graceful flying by.
It bulges where it ought to curve.
I think it has a lot of nerve
To look so pompous, pleased and smug
With such an unimpressive mug.
And yet I shouldn't carp nor scold . . .
Perhaps it has a heart of gold.

—Don Blanding (1941)

To a Pelican

Means the sea but fish to you,
Queer-shaped fellow from the blue?
Is its plaintive song of need
Lost to you in just one greed?

Eyes to find and pouch to hold,
Has the sea no secret gold
Save its fish? O foolish bird!
Had I half your skill or third,

I should bolt me on and on.
Out to where the vivid dawn
Stands triumphant and alone,
I should know why oceans moan;

Why the curly corals grow
Cradled in green undertow,
Why the sea and sky caress
With such candid eagerness.

But instead you stand and stare
At my shoes, my dress, my hair . . .
Can it be that from your view
I'm a wee bit foolish too?

—Vivian Yeiser Laramore Rader (1926)

FLAMINGO

Tall uncertain crimson
That pales behind a wall,
When you stood in Eden
By a blue waterfall,
And Eve looked upon you
Through the mist of her hair,
She must have thought you lovely
  Beyond compare.

She must have called to Adam
In high white words:
Look, my lord and lover,
The king of birds!
And Adam being summoned
From his cave-retreat,
Must have answered sagely:
  The sun on feet!

No doubt they fed you fishes
And pale green ferns,
And brought you jeweled water
In earth-brown urns;
And when you spread your crimson
And soared from sight,
I'm almost sure that Eden
  Was wrapped in night.

   —Vivian Yeiser Laramore Rader (1932)

FLAMINGOS

*I*f there should never be another dawn;
    If gray skies held the world beneath a pall
And no more sunsets flared with colors drawn
    From vats of fire beyond the sky's blue wall,
The memories of such glories would remain
    To haunt our hearts and sad remembering eyes
So long as wild flamingos fly again
    And spread great wings of flame against the skies.

—Don Blanding (1941)

FLAMINGOS

*D*ays ago I saw you in a photograph.
You, eating out of my aunt's hand,
she, laughing, as you tickled her palm
while she sat outdoors at a table.

I see you now,
on this paper, behind this glass,
and wonder which stem in
Emmanuel's heart you have sprung from.

You have come to the north
this winter, to a land as foreign
to you as the color in
the body of these skies,
a land where it is difficult
to take the farmers' eyes
away from the white in their fields.

Flamingos,
you urge me to pull my kite
from the closet and fly it,
a palm against the grey,
a womb against the clouds,

already my ankles are in water!

—Marisella Veiga (1986)

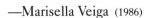

*S*tuffed pink stocking, the neck,
toe of pointed black, the angled beak,
thick heel with round eye in it upside down, the pate,

swivels, dabbles, skims the soup of pond all day
for small meat. That split polished toe is mouth
of the wading flamingo

whose stilts, the rosy knee joints, bend
the wrong way. When planted
on one straight stem, a big fluffy flower

is body a pink leg, wrung, lifts up over,
lays an awkward shoe to sleep on top of,
between flocculent elbows, the soft peony wings.

—May Swenson (1978)

SEA GULL, SINGER ISLAND

Jamuary 1, 1973—the day Roberto Clemente died

*W*inter gulls searched the beach for food.
We tossed them bread soaked in New Year's vodka.
They stumbled like tourists in soft sand.
Wings dragging the ground,
one wobbled to the water and bobbed
until a wave tossed him to shore.
He stood confused, as if the world
suddenly slanted, lurched and flew
low to the ground, uncertain.
Two quick plunges, then he lifted
into the air, flew in loose circles, fell,
banked out of his line, recovered
and flew again like balsa glider
launched from a rooftop.

He floated toward the Islander hotel,
high enough to clear it and sail
over the lake where the winter wind
could keep him aloft, until his head cleared
and the drift boats came back
with scraps for dinner.
I saw him there safe, but
above the north wall he slid
down the bright sky in a long arc
and crashed into the seventh floor.
I wanted to be looking up from an air show
crowd, sure he would pull out, tip his wings
and leave us cheering, hearts in our hands.

—Rick Campbell (1993)

ANHINGA

*W*hat is this bird whose trackless days are spent
Between the air and water? Anchored in
A mangrove tree it might be some great leaf
Of rusty black and brown, blown out of time
Before man walked the earth. And then it moves. . . .
It raises white-flecked wings, unfolding them
To catch the sun. It twists its snake-like neck,
While spade-shaped head and pointed beak thrust up,
And silence of the leaning reeds is shattered
By its discordant cry. With fanning wings
It rises far above the brackish bay,
Then plummets, breaking water smooth as glass
Into concentric circles, which widen first
Before they dissipate. The bird, now out
Of sight, swims underneath the surface, under
The mossy algae, under water lilies
That bear the weight of alligators; it swims
Beneath the coots, bobbing like painted decoys
In clusters. Finally, a hundred feet
From where it dived, it reappears. And then
It takes to air again, a craft that seems

Too heavy for this medium. It flies
Once more into the mangrove tree, unmindful
Of snowy egret near its resting-place
Or purple gallinule below. Again
It is a giant leaf of black and brown
Blown out of time. And I, who stand within
This wilderness, uncharted and untouched
By man, am one with it, and feel that I
Was here before, when all the world was young.

—Harriet Gray Blackwell (1970)

SNIPE HUNTING AT ELLIOT KEY
For Fred Searcy

Tap-tap-tap swish
tap-tap-tap swish

This is the mythic call
in Florida
to the small, furry bird
living among shadows
frightened by light
yet lured from the dense bush
by the rhythmic sound:

Tap-tap-tap swish
tap-tap-tap swish

It is said he can be caught
running blindly into paper bags,
shy groundling who loves to be touched;
who wouldn't risk mosquitoes, snakes,
the dark moonless night
for the chance to discover?
This is the story told 'round
campfires at dusk
to faces eagerly lit.
Here, like this: hold two sticks
just so; the woods are waiting.

—Barbra Nightingale (1993)

Noted In The *New York Times*

Lake Buena Vista, Florida, June 16, 1987

*D*eath claimed the last pure dusky seaside sparrow
today, whose coastal range was narrow,
as narrow as its two-part buzzy song.
From hummocks lost to Cape Canaveral
this mouselike skulker in the matted grass,
a six-inch bird, plain brown, once thousands strong,
sang *toodle-raeeee azhee*, ending on a trill
before the air gave way to rocket blasts.

It laid its dull white eggs (brown specked) in small
neat cups of grass on plots of pickleweed,
bulrushes, or salt hay. It dined
on caterpillars, beetles, ticks, the seeds
of sedges. Unremarkable
the life it led with others of its kind.

Tomorrow we can put it on a stamp,
a first-day cover with Key Largo rat,
Schaus swallowtail, Florida swamp
crocodile, and fading cotton mouse.
How simply symbols replace habitat!
The tower frames at Aerospace
quiver in the flush of another shot
where, once indigenous, the dusky sparrow
soared trilling twenty feet above its burrow.

—Maxine Kumin (1989)

THE IVORY-BILLED WOODPECKER

*It lived on a restricted diet of wood-boring larvae that
infest dead and dying trees of certain age and this required
large tracts of mature forest for living space.*

The ivory-bill scans the swamps.
His large beak stabs the air.
The interstate's red incision,
Stretching from the Ochlocknee to
The Wacissa, from the Aucilla
To the Chipola, slowly turns black.
In the widening circle of his flight,
The line like the lid of an eye
Lengthens as it narrows
And closes on him. Okefenokee,
Big Cypress—
                        "pait, pait-pait"
(Audubon said),
He circles burial mounds unearthed
Beneath a chief's floor.
For thousands of miles believers
Look for the last surviving
Ivory-bill, tracing rumored sightings
(the Singer Wilderness,
The Big Thicket), sifting
Piles of chips sheered in huge
Swipes by his airhammer beak.

The unfinished interstate sinks
In the vanishing swamp and the swirl
Of the sun's heat. He dips
Toward illusion, the slime
Of green water (there are three,
Four of them, pileated, not ivory-
Bills; smaller, charred beak in
Each flaming head. Nor is it water.)
A green front-end loader
Starts with a loud chirr to clear
Topsoil, tree, and more at a time.
From a tree nearby, the birds look
Out of alternate sides of their

Heads and fly away,
The distorted landscape
In their half-round eyes,
Ignited trees rising.

—Van K. Brock (1965)

CHICKEN IN A FLORIDA CITY

There is a chicken outside
the Krispy Kreme doughnut store.
5 a.m. tends to be the same
along the suburban avenues
of this medium-sized city,
but this dawn features a chicken.
He paces the sidewalk surrounding the store.
The workmen keep quiet
as they get their coffee,
but when the young children
begin to arrive with parents at 7,
they hop and shout, "There's a chicken out there!
Why is there a chicken out there?"
The Egyptian woman behind the counter
leans to see, but can only shrug.
This is not her country.
The parents grimace,
press down on their children's shoulders,
and order the usual.
On the way out nobody feeds the chicken.
Flour mills still grind in the Midwest,
cane-presses lift sweet winds over the Caribbean.
No customer plans to change his days.
Tomorrow they will come holding dollar bills
and the curious memory of a chicken.

—Stephen Corey (1984)

GRACKLE

*I*t's hard not to like the wise-
guy grin, the almost sarcastic chatter
of the boat-tailed grackle by the Everglades
Cafe. He has an acrid cackle,
a cacophony of slick and klaxon cries,
with tinsel whispers like a breathy flute.
His repertoire seems meant to flatter
us by mimicry and so exonerate
our grosser faults, our greeds,
our clumsy cunnings, our minute
duplicities.

        Watch how he hops elastically
from roofbeam down to a potato chip
and shrills and wheedles while his hard claws grip
whittled bench-rims and the slats of rails.
He strides like a chimney sweep,
char-coloured, and yet, see:
his cinder eyes are absolute.
Cunning of hunger makes his feathers bright
in smoky lapis, iris-indigo.

      —Eric Ormsby (1992)

O-PA

*W*ithin the late hours of the night,
He sits perched upon the cypress branch,
silhouetted by the moonlight.

Peering down upon the world below.
He looks through those mysterious eyes
of perhaps, someone you know!

He roams the night.
To some, a friend or a foe.
The stories and legends surround him
as every Native child will know.

He dances to the songs
of those who roam the night.
His laughter deep within the glades
can cause a deathly fright!

Though a superstitious character,
within him humor still abounds,
From the campfire to the grave,
or even to the ceremonial grounds.

And throughout the night, the noises
and sounds are all the same.
Then there are those who fear
the sounds will break from O-pa,
calling out their name.

The stories, legends will go on
though different in language and word.
And behind it all will be
the wit and character
of one noble feathered bird.

O-PA is the Creek word for "owl."

—Moses Jumper (1990)

hawk

no one
at state road
or land office
knows
that a hawk,
lowered wingtip
stiff & spread
like fingers
in tonic arch,
made a turn
in moored sky
above the houses,
swept low
across the grass,
cats frozen.

i heard
  the pounding
of his blood,
  the sound
of hammers
  bouncing
from trees,
  the weight
of the six inch
  slab
growing snake-like
  out of the east
swallowing whole acres;

felt resistance
crumble,
as his eyes,
that part
of him
that holds
the fire,
rode by
like sunsets
in the pine woods.

—Sam Harrison (1975)

UNDER THE VULTURE TREE

*W*e have all seen them circling pastures,
have looked up from the mouth of a barn, a pine clearing,
the fences of our own backyards, and have stood
amazed by the one slow wing beat, the endless dihedral drift.
But I had never seen so many so close, hundreds,
every limb of the dead oak feathered black,

and I cut the engine, let the river grab the jon boat
and pull it toward the tree.
The black leaves shined, the pink fruit blossomed
red, ugly as a human heart.
Then, as I passed under their dream, I saw for the first time
its soft countenance, the raw fleshy jowls
wrinkled and generous, like the faces of the very old
who have grown to empathize with everything.

And I drifted away from them, slow, on the pull of the river,
reluctant, looking back at their roost,
calling them what I'd never called them, what they are,
those dwarfed transfiguring angels,
who flock to the side of the poisoned fox, the mud turtle
crushed on the shoulder of the road,
who pray over the leaf-graves of the anonymous lost,
with mercy enough to consume us all and give us wings.

    —David Bottoms (1987)

LATE NIGHT IN EARLY AUGUST AT THE GANDY BRIDGE

Nightwater fish pass barely under the surface.
They are large. They are unnamed as far
as I know. Out here they move slowly,
carrying the dull glow of the new lights arched
above the road, all across the bridge.
We wait for the perfect catch:
saltwater trout on their way south just ahead
of the desperate yellowtail. We hear
the yellowtail breaking through
and diving back under. It's the sound
of abrupt whispers or scattered applause.
By now we know the odds. If not the perfect catch,
we've decided, then let it be the perfect story.
We speak a strange language
as we reel in the dying bait. We give it
back to the bay. It comes back to us. We speak
a strange language in the stillness above
the current. Then we move on, the odds
still against us like an early warning of pure wind.
We speak a strange language about returning,
about the shark that cut my line earlier tonight,
about the small moon
and how we got here at the wrong end of the tide.

—Dionisio D. Martínez (1989)

THE DANIA PIER

Someone has caught a hideous fish,
Spiny and speckled,
Dull brown and battleship grey,
Nothing anyone would stuff on a wall.

Never having seen anything like it,
And not caring either,
The lucky fisher has already rebaited.
Neighbors turn back to their own trickeries.

And the fish
Dries slowly on the wooden deck
Not even gasping.

It seems a day for negatives.
The sky brown and spiny.

—Edmund Skellings (1978)

DANIA FISHING PIER

It's no tourist spot this time of year,
and fewer fishermen come, preferring waters
to the north where dredging is still rumor.
In the baitshop at the base of the pier,
there are two snapshots: a boy poses
with snappers too large for him to handle,
and a night angler hefts his trophy snook,
both angler and fish red-eyed to the camera.
All other photos pale from the salt air.
Behind the counter, where bait tanks foam
with fresh oxygen and shrimp snap like fingers
against the surface, the night man wiggles
a tv antenna, searching for better reception.
"You fishing or just looking?" he asks.

I want to say I've been too far inland,
that tonight the air becomes my salt lick.
I've come without tackle to catch every scent,
to let offshore winds rush against my face.
Tonight, let the sibilant surge of waves
break against the shore, sift away the sand.

My weak vision paints impressionistic
fishermen lingering at the end of the pier,
their shadows grey against the black
of sky and sea. The charter boats light
the offshore with stars while a freighter
shimmers a small and distant constellation.
To the south, streetlight glare reveals
a bank of clouds, the first hint of horizon.
I pretend for myself an imagined horizon
and think of clouds pressing towards Bimini
where the light no longer penetrates darkness.

What I see clearly are these gulls and terns
pecking here and there for bits of bait,
the salted wood whiter under flourescent light,
dried fish scales everywhere, and always
the mechanical motion of waves towards shore.

—Stephen Reilly (1986)

TROLLING FOR BLUES

for John and Barbara

As with the dapper terns, or that sole cloud
Which like a slow-evolving embryo
Moils in the sky, we make of this keen fish
Whom fight and beauty have endeared to us
A mirror of our kind. Setting aside

His unreflectiveness, his flings in air,
The aberration of his flocking swerve
To spawning-grounds a hundred miles at sea,
How clearly, musing to the engine's thrum,
Do we conceive him as he waits below:

Blue in the water's blue, which is the shade
Of thought, and in that scintillating flux
Poised weightless, all attention, yet on edge
To lunge and seize with sure incisiveness,
He is a type of coolest intellect,

Or is so to the mind's blue eye until
He strikes and runs unseen beneath the rip,
Yanking imagination back and down
Past recognition to the unlit deep
Of the grass sponges, of chiasmodon,

Of the old darkness of Devonian dream,
Phase of a meditation not our own,
That long melee where selves were not, that life
Merciless, painless, sleepless, unaware,
From which, in time, unthinkably we rose.

—Richard Wilbur (1986)

BARNACLES

I

*O*n the sailboat's belly/hull
slimy green/ossifying
like the knife-growths/kidney
stones. Mouths

clenched like clam shells/hair
oozing seawater/fuzz
of algae/salty
licks on parched lips.

Sun burning/ninety
in the shade/white
dot in a turquoise
necklace/flashing—

careful—as if
the sun had conscience or
those bony mussels could see
me/pounding
the typewriter.

II

First a shaky bridge/logs
laid across rack and water
waiting for the step/stumble
of a rolling bone/a rock

sand shifting/or a log
itself/misplaced. Then
the turning/weight
too quick to see/falling

past the rocks/safe
but a submerged limb reached out
like the bony arm of a salt water
troll/sliced long lines

on my belly and chest.
Barnacles. Hairy
mouths sucking cloudy
water in and blowing it
out again/again/ignoring
me.

III

White dots well the eyes/breathing
short and shallow/current
tugging at my cuts/a rushing
foreign tide/I watched

my blood curl up like smoke
and disappear/water into
water/food for fish protozoans
barnacles eat/hugging

what had hurt me/pressing
cold wood to my face/wanting
the tree to bring me back/water
to wake me/I pulled

the old bridge down/freed
logs to float like boats
on the rising tide/sloshed
toward home through sucking

mud on a finger
of land that reaches
into the sea/coastline curved
like a comma.

—Donald Caswell (1977)

HORSESHOE CRAB

She is surprising in her lowliness.
She follows the immemorial furrows
along the tidal floor of the bay.
Her manufactured look disarms,
brown as molded plastic or poured bronze.
The silt-dulled sheen of her carapace
fits the hand, despite thorny protrusions
of chitin and that lacerating icepick
of tail.
            Underneath her frail rigidity,
sculpted like the death-mask of a queen,
her pale, segmented legs beckon and gleam.

—Eric Ormsby (1989)

HORSESHOE CRABS MATING AT
CARRABELLE BEACH

*T*hrough the shallow water,
warm as a bath,
they swam locked together
like elaborate buttons.
Large and sharp,
dinosaurs of love and necessity.

Nothing pretty in their mating
to move us to wonder
at the ways of the moon,
but they moved us to shore.

Creatures of whatever god,
these armored mines resist
tenderness, the sloppy thought
of romance and the sea.

I wanted trout,
not rutting crabs blindly knocking
against my shins. In the dirty water

I danced around each piggybacked couple
that swam in a line straight west,
driven like pioneers toward some end,
something we could mistake for love.

—Rick Campbell (1991)

GAR

All night the river house swayed
on stilts, and mosquitos navigated the slit screen to find me
asleep on the top bunk and salty with sweat.
From a dream of fish
their kisses stung me into the stifling heat
and the steam rising off the river,
and I rose dazed and found my clothes,
my line and my tackle.

A red sun bobbed into the rushes
and pricked the skin of the river, long needles of blood
stabbing the bank where a ribbon snake slipped
off a root and into the water, where a skink climbed
a brown stone, where my reel whined
at the river thrashing under the rush shadows, a rusty snout,
a saw blade from the old world, hacking
like a memory at the light.

—David Bottoms (1987)

SHARK HUNT

The old man sensed something big
Lurking in the canal.
"Shark," he muttered to
Skeptical neighbors.

To prove his point
He skewered a young pig
On a steel meat-hook
And hung it by a log chain
Under a huge, floating balloon.

Watchers saw the balloon dip
Once and then again before
It went skittering madly about the canal.
After many inept barrages

From pursuing rifles and shotguns
The creature was dead.

Towed to the marina
By the exultant yeomanry,
The ten-foot lemon shark weighed
Over eight hundred pounds.
The valiant safari
Posed for pictures and gave interviews.
The shark had nothing to say.

—Frederick Gilbert (1989)

FISHING FOR SHARKS

*O*ur landmark, the old Coast Guard
tower, wavered in front of us
like a blip on radar. The coast
road, sand-baked corduroy, shook

the car to its Phillips screws.
Momo's dad held it to forty-five
miles an hour, saying that you
skimmed the bumps at that speed.

He should have pushed it faster.
At the tower we unloaded the gear
and slogged over the dunes, the hot
sand curling the rubber sides

of our sneakers. We hiked over water
on the pier which ran straight out
into the Atlantic like a scratch
across a window. We spent all morning

sitting with our rods aloft—
antennae waiting for a signal
from Spain or whatever country
lay across from us, beyond

the spine of the ocean. We heard
from sharks—repeatedly. And by noon
we had stacked a couple of dozen
little sands behind us on the gray

boards. The sun never let us
forget our frailty: We printed our
burned skin with our fingers, testing
the exposure time. We knew we would

be only scraps of seaweed drying
to whispers if we stayed, so we left
at noon and headed inland for lunch
at the cafe by the river. The last

fish Momo's dad caught was a hammerhead.
We left them all on the pier,
a rick of firewood waiting for winter.

—Malcolm Glass (1978)

SHARKS, CALOOSAHATCHEE RIVER

*I*t is so quiet. It is 1957.
You can place the year
by the fins of the new cars
lined up in the parking lot of The Gulf Motel.
Even in the middle of the day
the rooms are dark, rooms
where lovers thump their beds
against the walls, where someone
goes to sleep forever with the radio playing.
You can't hear the river in those rooms
although the river never stops.
It goes on flowing gray to silver
down thorugh the glades and forests
where the people lived who named it
Caloosahatchee.

A boy opens a door and steps out
into the shock of sunlight, the flashing
chrome of bumpers and grills.
In the shadows between the cars
sparrows peck at the asphalt.
He watches as men line up on the dock
the bloody sharks they caught.
The fins gleam like the waxed fins
of the new cars. Their eyes don't close either.
After the snapshots and jokes
they heave the bodies back into the river
and stroll off to their separate rooms.

They say a dead shark
sinks so slowly its body
is dissolved by saltwater
before it reaches the bottom of the sea.
There in the Caloosahatchee, in the shadows
between the long bodies of sharks
the current pulls toward the Gulf.

Then it is Sunday. The boy's mother
still sleeping, he leaves the darkness
of the room with a quarter in his pocket
and walks a few hundred yards of sunlight
along the river to the Arcade Theater.
It's cool and dark, just a few kids waiting
for the matinee. The screen,
blank silver like the river. Dreaming
and quiet, he could be anyone. He is
the little brother of sharks, a boy
who slips into a car and guns the engine.

Tires burn, blue smoke shoots up, fins
slice the sunlight. Blank eyes and grill
grinning the car speeds across the parking lot
off the dock and into the river.
It sinks so fast, the river so shallow
you can hear the thud of rubber
on the bottom before white water calms
and it's gone.
The doors to the motel open
one by one, light streams in, people walk out

and gather as the boy steps dripping
from the river. No one speaks a word
but stares, as he does, at the water.
The only sound is the murmur of the river
as it moves toward the Gulf. They will listen
until they hear.

Or, more likely, the boy is knocked unconscious
and never steps from the river. The sheriff's
boats drag the bottom with nets and hooks.
Divers search for the body in the gray murk.
But he is gone, drifting with sharks, gone
in the silver glinting on the river.

—Greg Pape (1984)

TO FISH, TO REMEMBER

*D*addy is with me here on the pier
at Cedar Key. The fish strung by their gills,
the shower of water from the bait bucket
bring him back. Night fishing
from Biscayne Bridge. I'm six,
chewed by mosquitoes, sticky with cocoa butter.

Again and again his spinning reel unzips
the black water. He is never pleased,
except by a record haul.
We are the baggage he drags along,
my mother pretending interest
in chum, swivels and lures.

I don't want to fish. I want to comb
the Saran hair of my Toni doll,
cuddle her as if I know how it's done.
I am made to stand on the bridge quietly
so as not to scare them away
from the king of fish, the king

of the sport of kings, the king
of ulcers. He needed silence
when we ate, silence when we fished
and the anonymous roar of the track
where he gambled away two businesses.
For years I took his angry looks

for love. For years I avoided water.
Now I bait my hook as he taught me,
pleating the shrimp to conceal the barbs.
I try to forgive him with each fish
I catch, but every time it's myself
I see on the end of the line—
struggling silently
intimate with the hook.

—Enid Shomer (1987)

VETO

*T*here's a law of nature I'd like to veto . . .
It's the life and love of the (blank) mosquito.

—Don Blanding (1955)

ZING ZONG

*Z*ing! zing! zing!
The mosquito is on the wing,
     He's not the least spiteful,
          When he takes a biteful,
               But it isn't delightful,
The cute little thing.

Zing! zong! zeee!
A sly little fellow is he.
     When he sticks in his bill
          To suck in his fill,
               You can slap all you will,
But THERE he won't be!

Zing! zeee! zip!
He can really give you the slip,
     They say it's the she
          Makes no dif'rence to me,
               If they're blind or can see
When they sit down to sip.

Zing! zip! zwooo!
His neighbors come along too,
     You smoke 'em or spray 'em
          You think you can slay 'em
               You only delay 'em,
For a crop that is new!

Ding! Darn! Gee!
That's not the mosquito it's me!
    There are three thousand kinds,
        But they all have their minds,
            Set on punching on our rinds,
For their afternoon tea.

—W. Robert Wilson (1974)

Hibiscus on the Sleeping Shores

I say now, Fernando, that on that day
The mind roamed as a moth roams,
Among the blooms beyond the open sand;

And that whatever noise the motion of the waves
Made on the sea-weeds and the covered stones
Disturbed not even the most idle ear.

Then it was that that monstered moth
Which had lain folded against the blue
And the colored purple of the lazy sea,

And which had drowsed along the bony shores,
Shut to the blather that the water made,
Rose up besprent and sought the flaming red

Dabbled with yellow pollen—red as red
As the flag above the old café—
And roamed there all the stupid afternoon.

—Wallace Stevens (1923)

Walking Stick

*N*ot since a child, when, strung between
Two jacarandas in a rainbow striped
Hammock, one walked unwavering
The length of my arm, have I seen
The bladed mantis, angled now in sunlight

Like a knife in the porch railing.
It does not move, its forelegs crossed
And posed in air; the leanly muscled
Biceps of a bantam weight, daring
The crew-cut lawn, and I shuffle,

Dulled by the sun, through my limited
Catalogue of mantis lore to the entry
Where, after coupling, the female
Devours the male who dies without
A struggle, and, one must assume,

Happy. It is a ritual I would gladly
Acquiesce to (these, again, are thoughts
From a hammock) on a still, summer evening
With one so strong, so utterly consuming,
Joplin on the radio, my clothes folded in prayer.

—Sam Harrison (1989)

DRAGONFLIES

*A*ll morning I walked
through palmettoes
and cabbage palms
to arrive at the oak
hovering above the path.

A cloud of dragonflies
moves over the field.
Some dart away,
green, geometric shapes
fading into the reedy grass
along the shore.

One lags behind,
suspending himself
in the darker air
beneath this tree,
iridescent eyes seeing
each image repeated
a hundred times:

quail on the path,
a heron standing in the river,
a man sitting in the darkness.

and for a moment,
the time it takes an insect wing
to stroke it once through the sky,
everything stops:

the quail stand like stones,
the heron's uplifted leg
bends like a branch
above the unbroken water.

Clinging like the humid air
The remaining dragonfly
rides the hand that moves
in delicate lines across
this wide expanse of paper.

—Ray Wonder (1989)

FLY

On the red plastic chair—
dimpled like fat,
the opal of a fly
stares roundly at the world.

His eyes
split and sow
the earth
into themselves.
I eat a slice
of cold pizza which, too,
his diamond lens inhales
the way a promise fills
the belly of the poor.

His eyes equal the world
all of it in them, all of it
the same, be it shit or banquet,
he finds it all attractive metal,
with neither lust nor patience.
A cloud's ghost passes,
and he darts from it
as if his own
lightning
could purge his fear
of smaller speeds.
My hand but for the swatting
could be the cloud,
an angel, manna falling.

My eyes—
who see like and if—
would starve him
in harvest Egypt.
The squandering son
has grown his eyes
to hunger for all.
Where all is appetite
not even God can play vulture.

—Ricardo Pau-Llosa (1989)

ANTING

*W*hen I was 7, I peeked
through a curtain
and watched my mother
placing ants on her clothes
to crawl up her sleeves
and across her bare, painted feet.
I saw her put them down her blouse
and smile.

We had a tick slatboard fence
around our back yard
so neighbors couldn't watch
as my mother held out her arms
and preened like a sparrow.

As the years passed
I tried to ignore those
moving freckles, to pass them off
as little ink stains
or floating cinders
come to rest.
She never spoke to me about the ants
and I never asked.

For parties, Mother would shower
and dress in sheer decolletage
but I'd still imagine those little tunnelings
under that long silk screen
as they made their winding way
up the back of her neck
and into her beehive,
loaded with winter provisions.
I remember that drugged-sensual smile
with which she served the hors d'oeuvres.
She was always picking lint from her dress,
hitching up her slip, scratching a swollen ankle
with the tip of a high-heeled shoe.
Upstairs when she tucked me in
she would pat that bouffant to sleep
and rejoin her guests.

I'm in another city now.
I don't know if my mother
still dances with the ants,
but lately, I've observed
long lines of black workers
inching up my fingers like travelers
who know their way.
At first I was appalled
and flicked them off my skin
and out of my apartment.
But that touch to my fingertips
was tantalizing.
I wanted more.

It's a vice, I know,
but once a month, sometimes twice,
I drive out to an empty field,
bare my skin to the sun,
and spill little tracks of honey
down my arms and toes.
With a drop on each nipple
and behind my ears,
I let them have their way with me.

  —P. V. LeForge (1979)

COCKROACH

You are a bruise
  on that wall.

You are red tile
on the floor,

part of the air—
a smooth sheet

moving on
to another bed.

While a girl sleeps
your wings flutter

widening and shrinking
causing a wind.

A thread moves
across a calf;

hair trickles
across a face.

The girl turns
and you, lover,

twist with her
all legs and wing.

   —Marisella Veiga (1995)

The Mammals Of Florida

THE BAT

*U*nreal
As death, against
The velvet beauty of
The moon, a dark shape flies into
The night.

—Vivian Yeiser Laramore Rader (1976)

THOUGHTS ON SAVING THE MANATEE

*W*eighed down by its dense bones
the manatee swims so slowly
that algae have time to
colonize on its spine.
I know a woman who rode
one down the river gently
scraping with a clamshell
letting drift free a bushel
basket of diatoms and kelp.

At one time you could order
manatee steak in any
restaurant in Florida.
It was said to taste like veal.
My friend reported that hers
bubbled and squealed its pleasure
beneath her making it well
worth risking a five hundred
dollar fine for molesting
this cow-size endangered aquatic
mammal whose name derives from
the Carib word for breast.

And from the overlook
at Blue Spring, pendulous
disembodied breasts
are what I see dappling
the play of sunlight on
the lagoon. They swim up here
from the St. Johns River
—mostly cows and their calves—
to disport in the temperate water

and stay to choke on
our discards. They swallow
snarls of fishing line or
the plastic ribbons that tie
beer cans together.
Along with acorns sucked
from the river bottom
they also ingest large numbers
of metal pop tops that razor

their insides. Grazing
on water hyacinths, they're
sideswiped by boat propellers.
Many have bled with bright scars
they come to be known by
and yet, many deaths
are mysterious, if not willful.
Worldwide less than five
thousand manatees remain.

For a small sum you can adopt one
through the Audubons.
Already named Boomer or Jojo
tricked out with a radio collar
it will ascend tranquilized
to be weighed and measured on schedule
but experts agree that no matter
how tenderly tamed by philanthropy
survival is chancy.

Consider my plan.
It's quick and humane:
Let's revert to the Catch of the Day

and serve up the last few as steak marinara.
Let's stop pretending we need them
more than they need us.

—Maxine Kumin (1989)

The Manatee

We stole a sailboat and sailed out
beyond the sandbar where skiers wait

their turn, past skin divers,
past the rocks, past bayhouses

on phone pole stilts, to open
water where we saw a manatee

swimming lazily in the bright, clear sea
below the boat. It surfaced

just in front of us and blew a stream
of water to the sky. A mermaid,

graceful as a cow could ever be,
moving with short flicks

of its languorous tail, it led
us slowly out to sea. The sailboat seemed

to sail itself
toward some imaginary point that split

the horizon perfectly.
The sea cow didn't need a siren's song,

her easy glide was meant for following.
We might have sailed forever

but the manatee
unnerved us with a sideways turn

that brought the boat around so we
could see how far we were

from land. We started back and I wished for
the lumbering pace of the manatee

whose sluggish swim had us this
far out. But winds were right

for racing. The sailboat skidded like a stone
across the flat, wide bay.

We beached her south of Turkey Point
and hitchhiked home.

—Donald Caswell (1975)

THE DEATH OF THE PILOT WHALES

*E*very few years, down at the Florida keys,
where bones chew the water like mad dogs
and spit it bubbling out on yellow sand
the sea darkens, and we crane toward the skies,
toward the airplanes casting their shadows,
but there are no planes and those dark shadows
are not shadows, but mark the silent forms
of pilot whales charging the shore like wild
buffalo charging a train, driving toward
reef and sand till the foam sprays red
below the rainbow stretching from sea to land.

The fierceness of it all, unstoppable,
those broad flukes churning the water, that buried
brain and heart set inflexibly on their last
pulsing, the energy and beauty of all that
flesh turning away from its cold fathomless
world, like the negative of some huge
lemming following God knows whose orders
in a last ordered chaos of frantic obedience
stronger than love. With what joy and
trembling they hunch up the beach,

shred themselves on shoals, what sexual
shudders convulse them at that sweet moment
when they reach—at last!—what
they have burned to meet.

And we, who may be reminded of thoughts
we wish not to think, we tow them back to sea,
cut them open, and they sink.

—Peter Meinke (1981)

COWS WAKING IN A PASTURE

Black and white splotches
on a ground of dull green
space themselves
with the precise irregularity
of their own patterns.
They have carefully varied
their postures and positions
to their own needs.

One is raising her head
and opening her eyes.
One is stretched out
on her side, still asleep.
Another has been lying
on a hummock all night
and is trying awkwardly,
to raise herself,
hooves in the air.
One by one they will
mock her motions.

—Van K. Brock (1979)

Among The Cows

*A*dvised to breathe with the Holsteins
    as a form of meditation,
I open a window in my
    mind and let their vast humid breath,
sticky flanks, the mantric switching
    of their tails drift through. I lie down
with them while they crop the weedy
    mansions, my breasts muffled like the
snouts of foxes run to ground. I
    need to comfort the cows, the way
heart patients stroke cats and the grief
    of childhood is shed for dogs. I
offer them fans of grass under
    a sky whose grey may be the hide
of some huge browser with sun and
    moon for wayward eyes. It begins

to rain. How they sway, their heavy
    necks lift and strain. Then, like patches
of night glimpsed through a bank of clouds,
    they move toward four o'clock, the dark
fragrant stalls where dawn will break first
    as the curved pink rim of their lips.
I want to believe I could live
    this close to the earth, could move with
a languor so resolute it
    passes for will, my heart riding
low in my body, not this flag
    in my chest snapped by the lightest
breeze. Now my breath escapes with theirs
    like doused flames or a prayer made
visible: May our gender bear
    us gracefully through in these cumbrous frames.

—Enid Shomer (1992)

EE-CHO

*Y*ou have given me warmth
on cold winter nights.
My feet are indebted to you
for the protection you have given them.
My arrow shoots straight and true
from the strength you have given it.
My drum is loud and clear
from the sound you've given it.
You have led me to land
that is fresh with fruit and water.
You have taught me to be swift,
quiet, and cunning.
I've grown strong
from the food you've given me.
Your kindness to us has carried us
through many a day.
Yet, Ee-cho, we now send you away.

EE-CHO is the Creek word for "deer."

—Moses Jumper, Jr. (1990)

THE POLAR BEAR AT CRANDON PARK ZOO, MIAMI

Panting, immobile, his head lies flat
in fly-buzzing shade, his brown eyes
shut against the glare. Before him,
pelicans and flamingoes strut brown and pink,
peck shells. Small children suck fingers,
watch him roll. His nose glistens.
His stink, his feces that were meant
to sink in snow, draws generations
of flies. One boy holds his nose.
The bear rises, swings his hulk
around to see the growing crowd,
cool in dacron. Concrete burns his pads.
His small eyes burn like brown suns.
From the ocean a quarter-mile away
he smells the cool of salt, the thread
that holds him through the long lizard days.

—Barbara Winder (1978)

ARMADILLO ALLEY

*I*t is only two lanes
for the hour I drive from Oviedo
to Samsula on these summer nights,
through live oaks and scrub pine
interrupted by a single stop sign
and a blinking yellow light.

The "nine-banded armored pig"
burrows on either side of this
deserted strip and hunts by night
for palmetto bugs, puffballs,
fire ants, and eggs. Her identical
quadruplets, all male or all female,
lick up whatever their narrow
tongues can catch. One can find

baskets made from their shells, sold
in curio shops
or at roadside stands. The flesh
has a pork-like taste.

Their lack of hearing
and sight make driving at night
nerve-racking: when scared,
armadillos give a frightened leap
high into the air, squeal
on impact, inflict flat tires.

Like a teenager playing
mailbox baseball, my Dodge and I
annihilate any that jump
at the headlights. At dawn
Animal Control will clean up
in time for the new day.

                    —Alison Kolodinsky (1995)

STALKING THE FLORIDA PANTHER

Everglades National Park

*C*amped near fresh tracks, we wait.
Such blackness—the leafy horizon
closed shut like a fan.

The fire burns in whispers.
All night it has eaten itself
like a trapped animal

down to glowing red bones.
We lie on separate hummocks
in this river of grass,

the water moving
as stealthily as I imagine
the cat—its plush paws

dimpling the black muck
as it hunts. What I know:
that desire spreads like light

without doctrine. By morning
the sawgrass will shatter
the swamp to a million

glittering shards. Now,
moving for each other
in the darkness, our skin shines

like flares, I want to think
the cat is watching as our bodies
pull the wilderness in.

—Enid Shomer (1987)

A GLOSSARY OF LITERARY TERMS

Acrostic: A poem in which the initial letters spell out a name, word, or phrase (e.g., "Consummatum Est," "Why My Grandmother Feeds the Crows").

Allegory: A work of art in which **images** represent abstract ideas, moral qualities, or historical events and figures; an extended **metaphor.**

Alliteration: The repetition of consonant sounds.

Anachronism: Placing a person, object, idea, or event outside its correct historical time.

Anapest: A metrical foot of three syllables in which the heaviest stress or accent falls on the last syllable. Originally a Greek marching beat, in English it often creates a vigorous, upbeat rhythm (e.g., "Hernando de Soto," "The Clime of My Birth").

Assonance: The repetition of vowel sounds in stressed words; often used as an alternative to rhyme (e.g., right/mine).

Ballad: A simple narrative poem usually in **quatrains** with alternating lines of four and three feet, in which the second and fourth lines rhyme. Originally **folk songs,** ballads have attracted many writers who imitate the form's impersonal style and dramatic dialogue (e.g., "Fort Desoto," "My Cindy").

Beat Movement: An American countercultural literary movement of the late 1950s and early 60s characterized by spontaneous, loosely structured, highly personal work. Influenced by Buddhism, jazz, and the drug subculture, the group adopted its name as a play on both beaten and beatific (e.g., "Poem in the Form of a Snake").

Catalog: A list of persons, places, objects, or characteristics (e.g., "Chorus of Welcome," "Poem in the Form of a Snake").

Chant: A simple song in which several syllables are intoned, often associated with traditional rituals (e.g., "Florida Jungle").

Charm: A poem or spoken formula invoking magic powers; a spell (e.g., "The Mangroves Dance").

Chorus: *see* **Refrain.**

Conceit: An elaborate, ingenious **metaphor.** When such a metaphor is carried through an entire work, it becomes an **extended conceit.**

Convention: An established or traditional practice or custom; a literary device associated with a particular genre.

Couplet: Two-line stanzas.

Dionysian: A term used by the German philosopher Friedrich Nietzsche to describe the ecstatic, irrational, exuberant qualities associated with Dionysus, the Greek god of fertility, wine, and drama (e.g., "Sea Grapes"). These traits balanced the Apollonian qualities of reason, symmetry, logic, and balance.

Dramatic Monologue: A poem in which the author establishes a dramatic situation with a single speaker revealing his or her character to a silent but well-defined audience (e.g., "Christ in the Sun," "Transcript").

Elegy: A formal poem mourning the death of a particular person (e.g., "Grandmother Laura Pauline Wilder-Hancock," "The Hemingway House in Key West").

Ellipsis: Marks (. . .) which indicate the omission of a word or group of words (e.g., "Childhood").

Epic: A long narrative poem in an elevated style, with a central hero, which celebrates the history of a nation or race. **Elegiac epics** lament the defeat or dissolution of cultures (e.g., *Twasinta's Seminoles*).

Epiphany: A sudden moment of insight.

Fabliau: A realistic comic poem generally satirizing people's foibles. Normally written in eight-syllable couplets, the form flourished in medieval France (e.g., "Fabliau of Florida").

Folk Song: A song, usually of unknown authorship, associated with an entire community and passed on by oral tradition (e.g., "Jump Isabel," "Three Songs from the Turpentine Camps").

Foot: A group of syllables with varying stresses that constitutes the unit of rhythm in a line of poetry.

Heptameter: A line of verse with seven **feet** (e.g., "The Homespun Dress").

Heroic Couplet: A rhymed pair of iambic pentameter lines.

Hexameter: A line of verse with six **feet**.

Iamb: A metrical foot of two syllables, in which the second is more heavily accented than the first. The most common foot in English, it is often used to recreate normal speech patterns, especially in iambic pentameter.

Image: The portrayal of a sensory experience or of an object known through the senses. One of the most widely and loosely used terms in discussing literature, it originally meant a sculpture and often refers to a work's figurative language, especially its metaphors and similes. Imagery describes the collection or pattern of images within a work of art.

Macaronic Verse: Poetry which combines two or more languages (e.g., "Speaking Diversely," "Neptune").

Metaphor: A comparison implying that an image or phrase can be applied to an object or action to which it is not literally applicable (e.g., William E. Taylor's "June . . . is a fog of gnats").

The most common form of using language symbolically, metaphors generally attempt to draw attention to new comparisons in contrast to their unconscious use in standard conversation (e.g., table leg, government branch).

Meter: The pattern of rhythms that recur in lines of poetry. Most English poems use an **accentual-syllabic** meter in which each line has a fixed number of syllables and a fixed number of accents.

Neo-romantic: A 20th-century resurgence of Romanticism, the 19th-century literary movement which emphasized the beauties of nature, the value of imagination, and the validity of the emotions (e.g., "Seminole Sleep Song").

Octave/Octet: A poem or stanza of eight lines (e.g., "From the Flats").

Pentameter: A line of five **feet**.

Poetic Sequence: A series of poems connected by theme, character, or plot (e.g., Lola Haskins' *Castings* with sequences on Patsy, Julia O'Halloran, and Jane Marshall).

Quatrain: A stanza or poem of four lines.

Quintet: A stanza of five lines (e.g., "Causeway").

Refrain: A phrase, line, or group of lines repeated at regular or irregular intervals, generally at the end of stanzas, sometimes called a **chorus**.

Rhyme: The repetition of words or syllables that sound alike, especially at the end of lines of poetry. Internal rhyme involves two or more words rhyming at places other than the end of a line. Two variations on such true rhyme are near rhyme, half rhyme, or slant rhyme, in which the consonants match but not the vowels (e.g., ride/raid) and **assonance**.

Sestet: A stanza of six lines.

Sestina: A poem with six six-line stanzas, ending with a three-line *envoi* (i.e., concluding stanza). Each stanza of this medieval French form uses the same six last words (i.e., *talons*) arranged in fixed sequences (e.g., "Christ in the Sun," "New Year's Eve Sestina").

Shaped Verse: A poem written so that its printed form will reflect its subject (e.g., "It's a Cold Cold Day at Satellite Beach").

Simile: A comparison of two very different objects, actions, or feelings which uses "like" or "as" to qualify the parallel.

Sonnet: A traditional, highly formal poem with fourteen lines of **iambic pentameter** arranged in one of several set patterns of rhyming. A **Petrarchan** or **Italian sonnet** has an introductory **octave** of eight lines rhyming abbaabba and a concluding **sestet** of six lines rhyming cdecde, cdccdc, or cdedce (e.g., "Tampa"). A **Shakespearean** or **English sonnet** has three quatrains, usually rhyming abab cdcd efef, and a concluding rhyming couplet (e.g., the sonnets of George Dillon).

Spenserian Stanza: A stanza of nine iambic lines in which the first eight are **pentameters** and the ninth a **hexameter**, with a rhyme scheme of ababbcbcc. Created by Edmund Spenser for his epic *The Faerie Queene* (1589-96), its heavily interlocked, dignified form has become associated with serious, elevated poetry (e.g., *Twasinta's Seminoles*).

Stream of Consciousness: A literary technique that attempts to reflect the apparently random flow of thoughts, feelings and memories through a single person's mind. Its use reflects a belief that artists should reflect interior consciousness rather than narrate exterior action (e.g., "Carol Gillespie").

Syllabic Verse: Poetry in which the length of a line is determined by the number of syllables rather than by the meter (e.g., "Biscayne Bay," "North Florida Pastoral").

Symbol: A concrete object, scene, or action used to represent an idea, feeling, or state of mind.

Tercet: A stanza of three lines in which the lines generally rhyme with each other or adjacent lines.

Terza Rima: A set of three-line stanzas with an interlocking rhyme (i.e., aba bcb cdc). Invented by Dante for his *Divine Comedy* (c.1320), it is often adapted in various ways in English poetry (e.g., "Tuesday: Four Hundred Miles").

Villanelle: A poem with five **tercets** rhyming aba and a concluding **quatrain** rhyming abaa. Originating in France during the Renaissance, in this intricate form line 1 reappears as lines 5, 12, and 18, while line 3 reappears as lines 9, 15, and 19 (e.g., "South Beach: Proteus, S-Shaped in Sand").

ACKNOWLEDGMENTS

$\mathcal{W}$e would like to acknowledge our debt to all the writers and scholars who have preceded us in our endeavors, without whose loving efforts this book would not have been possible. And for their invaluable assistance and encouragement, we express our heartfelt appreciation and thanks to:

Ann Henderson, Ron Cooper, Joan Bragginton, Susan Lockwood, and their colleagues at the Florida Humanities Council for their public support and interest in the poetic voices of Florida;

Rollins College for its valuable financial support;

Walda Metcalf of the University Presses of Florida and Rick Campbell of Anhinga Press for their aid in attaining permissions;

Van Brock, founder of Anhinga Press, and Mac Miller, founder and editor of *New Collage*, for their decades of nurturing and publishing Florida writers;

Kimberley E. Holtzer for her assistance with Spanish translations.

Writers who helped to spread the word about our project and to discover the poetry and poets of Florida, especially Mike Temple, Justin Spring, Ricardo Pau-Llosa, Yvonne Sapia, Dionisio Martínez, Lola Haskins, Judith Berke, Stephen Corey, Enid Shomer, Peter Meinke, Suzanne Keyworth, X. J. Kennedy, Geoffrey Philp, and Stetson Kennedy;

The librarians of Florida who have become the repositories of our memories;

Karen Slater, Patricia Rockwood, and Carol Tornatore for their indefatigable technical support;

Ken Hawk and Frank Lohan for their visual interpretations;

June and David Cussen of Pineapple Press for their determination to advance awareness of Florida and its culture;

And our families: Douglas, Caitlin, and Benjamin Jones and Sue, Quinn, and Brendan O'Sullivan for their patience and encouragement.

PERMISSIONS

Jack Crocker, "Winter Condo" ©1995. Reprinted by permission of the author.

r. crumb, "the space behind the clock" from *The Space Behind the Clock* ©1975. Reprinted by permission of Anhinga Press.

Silvia Curbelo, "Flying Cloud Motel" from *Organica Quarterly* ©1987; "Snapshot, Key West" ©1995. Reprinted by permission of the author.

Robert Dana, "Estero Island Beach Club" from *What I Think I Know: New and Selected Poems* ©1991. Reprinted by permission of the author.

Rebeca Daniels, translation of "La Florida" from *Sensations Magazine* ©1991. Reprinted by permission of the author.

Philip Deaver, "Fossils" ©1995. Reprinted by permission of the author.

Frances Densmore, "Seminole Songs" from *Seminole Music* ©1956. Reprinted by permission of the Smithsonian Institution Press.

Marjory Stoneman Douglas, "To a Buzzard Swinging in Silence" from *Miami Muse* ©1932. Reprinted by permission of the author.

Joann Gardner, "The Last Resort" and "St. Armand's Key, January 1992" from *Back to Front* ©1993. Reprinted by permission of the author.

Frederick Gilbert, "Shark Hunt" from *North of Wakulla* ©1989. Reprinted by permission of the author.

Allen Ginsberg, "Poem in the Form of a Snake that Bites Its Tail" from *Cosmopolitan Greetings* ©1990. Reprinted by permission of HarperCollins Publishers, In©

Malcolm Glass, "Fishing for Sharks" from *Bone Love* ©1978; "The Dinky Line" from *The Dinky Line* ©1992. Reprinted by permission of the author.

Sam Harrison, "Hawk" from *The Space Behind the Clock* ©1975; "Walking Stick" from *North of Wakulla* ©1989. Reprinted by permission of Anhinga Press.

Lola Haskins, "Burning the Field for Spring" from *New Collage Magazine*" ©1983; "Jane Marshall," "Patsy," and "Teaching the Miccasukee: Later" from *Castings* ©1984. Reprinted by permission of the author.

Janet Heller, "The Knife Thrower" from *Back to Front* ©1993. Reprinted by permission of the author.

Carolina Hospital, "In Search of Stevens" ©1995; "Near Pigeon Key" from *Mid-American Review* ©1991. Reprinted by permission of the author.

Langston Hughes, "Florida Road Workers" from *The Panther and the Lash* ©1967. Reprinted by permission of Alfred A. Knopf, In©

Zora Neale Hurston, "Prayer" from *Jonah's Gourd Vine* ©1934, renewed 1962. Reprinted by permission of HarperCollins Publishers In©

Juan Ramón Jiménez, "Pero lo Solo" from *Romances de Coral Gables* ©1948. Reprinted by permission of Francisco H. Pinzon Jiménez.

William Johnson, "Timucuan Cadenza" from *New Collage* ©1984. Reprinted by permission of the author.

Moses Jumper, Jr. "EE-CHO," "Major Dade," "O-PA," and "We Are As One" from *Echoes in the Wind* ©1990. Reprinted by permission of the author.

Donald Justice, "Childhood" from *Selected Poems* ©1979. Reprinted by permission of the author. "Memory of a Porch" from *Night Light* ©1981; "A Winter Ode to the Old Men of Lummus Park" from *The Summer Anniversaries* ©1981. Reprinted by permission of Wesleyan University Press and the University Press of New England.

Stetson Kennedy, "Paine's Prairie" ©1995. Reprinted by permission of the author.

Stetson Kennedy, *Palmetto Country* ©1942, 1989 for the following folk songs: "Big Jim," "Chain Gang Theme Song," "Come All You Rounders," "My Cindy," and "Sponger Money." Reprinted by permission of Stetson Kennedy and the University Presses of Florida.

X.J. Kennedy, "Ponce de Leon" © 1995. An earlier version of this poem appeared in *New Collage* ©1984. Reprinted by permission of the author.

Suzanne Keyworth, "Grandmother Laura Pauline Wilder" ©1995; "Great Grandfather Dose

INDEX